The Galilean Wonderworker

The Galilean Wonderworker

Reassessing Jesus' Reputation for Healing and Exorcism

&

Ian G. Wallis

Foreword by James Crossley

x

CASCADE *Books* · Eugene, Oregon

Cascade Books
An Imprint of Wipf and Stock Publishers
199 W. 8th Ave., Suite 3
Eugene, OR 97401

www.wipfandstock.com

PAPERBACK ISBN: 978-1-5326-7592-8
HARDCOVER ISBN: 978-1-5326-7593-5
EBOOK ISBN: 978-1-5326-7594-2

Cataloging-in-Publication data:

Names: Wallis, Ian G., author.| Crossley, James, foreword.

Title: The Galilean wonderworker : reassessing Jesus' reputation for healing and exorcism / Ian G. Wallis ; James Crossley, foreword.

Description: Eugene, OR: Cascade Books, 2020. | Includes bibliographical references and indexes.

Identifiers: ISBN: 978-1-5326-7592-8 (paperback). | ISBN: 978-1-5326-7593-5 (hardcover). | ISBN: 978-1-5326-7594-2 (ebook).

Subjects: LCSH: Jesus Christ. | Bible.—Gospels—Criticism, interpretation, etc.

Classification: BT301.3 W35 2020 (print). | BT301.3 (epub).

Manufactured in the U.S.A.   JUNE 10, 2020

To Lizzie,
companion through life,
source of joy.

His first words were unfamiliar
even vulgar to the ear,
but hear them we did and felt their barb
scrape along our hardened imaginations.

You could say we were hooked,
and with time in his shadow
we learned to inhabit the metaphor
and play our role without shame.

Somehow he managed to touch
the bone of our souls
then with persistent melodies
draw us across unsurveyed

expanses to a country where
pallid complexions and ruddy cheeks
keep company enough with broken wits
and minds fractured by the angles of time.

Now melancholy fills our stride
and we must let our backs be broken;
but fragments of his life remain lodged within
and we will remember, and dance.

Holy Saturday (2014)

Contents

Foreword

IN *THE GALILEAN WONDERWORKER: Reassessing Jesus' Reputation for Healing and Exorcism*, Ian Wallis discusses (what we commonly refer to as) the historical Jesus in relation to healings and exorcisms. There are a number of things Wallis importantly does right, in my view. He shows that we should be analyzing such traditions in some distinction from conventional "miraculous" traditions, such as a stilling of a storm or walking on water. Indeed, healings are not necessarily what Wallis would call "biochemical" or miraculous bodily transformations. Healings and exorcisms should instead be seen in light of anthropologically informed scholarship concerning psychological and social disorders. They were often communal rather than strictly individualist in their impact, requiring broader societal support (cf. Mark 6:1–6).

It is difficult to dispute this overall point. What gives it further argumentative strength is the care and attention paid to primary sources. The combination of interdisciplinary approaches with traditional exegesis is precisely what historical Jesus studies should be doing—and I think now is. Wallis's work represents the field of historical Jesus studies that has come to terms with the importance of looking beyond its traditional strengths to nuance further how we understand the cultural and historical contexts of Jesus. In doing so, the book represents a field that is starting to resist the apologetic questions around the miraculous that have hindered historical Jesus studies and contributed to harming the critical credibility of the field. Part of the reason for this is how historical Jesus studies more broadly have increasingly become engaged over the past few decades with a range of interdisciplinary approaches and we are now starting to see the emergence of much more critically savvy scholarship. What Wallis does so successfully is deceptively simple: with his anthropologically informed argument he moves beyond mere lip service to the quest to avoid anachronism and shows how Jesus' functioned in a quite different cultural context from that of contemporary historical Jesus scholars. All the while Wallis appreciates historical change and the emergence of a movement associated with Jesus.

Wallis is not only a scholar of Christian origins. He was earlier known to me though his association with St Mark's Church in Sheffield, just down the road from the University of Sheffield where I used to work. St Mark's was well known locally for its combination of critical approaches to the Bible and progressive ideas and led to collaborations with the sometimes less-than-pious Department of Biblical Studies. Such a mix of influences (some perhaps even contradictory) come through in this book, at least they appear so to those of us familiar with the background from which Wallis's work has emerged. This is especially clear in the compassionate and empathetic reading of history presented here and shows that such readings can go hand in hand with critical scholarship.

One final point is worth making: this is a readable book. This is not such an easy thing to achieve, particularly when dealing with the complexity of the synoptic tradition and historical reconstruction. It is hoped, then, that *The Galilean Wonderworker* also achieves a wide readership beyond academic biblical studies.

James Crossley

Professor of Bible, Culture and Politics

at St Mary's Twickenham, London

Co-Academic Director of the Centre for the Critical Study of

Apocalyptic and Millenarian Movements, Panacea Charitable Trust

Preface

THIS BOOK STARTED LIFE as a pair of lectures delivered in April 2016 at a conference arranged by the then St Mark's Centre for Radical Christianity, based in Sheffield, the United Kingdom.[1] Positive feedback following that event encouraged me to take on the challenge of working the material up into a book-length manuscript. In doing so, I soon realized that the miracles of Jesus have generated a good deal of interest in recent decades at both scholarly and popular levels. Rather than replicate what others have done, I have trained my focus on addressing one particular question, namely, what are the origins of Jesus' reputation for healing and exorcism? That is to say, in the light of the evidence available to us, what is the most plausible historical reconstruction for the emergence of one of the best-attested pieces of data we possess for the founder of Christianity?

In chapter 1, we survey the evidence for Jesus the healer and exorcist before turning our attention to how this evidence, almost exclusively textual, has been interpreted, especially since the Enlightenment. Acknowledging the contribution of scientific discovery and philosophical analysis, we then explore how recent developments in these spheres have opened up fresh interpretative possibilities. In chapter 2, we turn the clock back to the first century CE and attempt to reconstruct how sickness and healing were not only understood within Israelite faith traditions, but also experienced. Against this background, in chapter 3, we take a closer look at the range of symptoms which Jesus purportedly healed, before introducing a number of insights from the field of medical anthropology which illuminate this aspect of his ministry. Chapter 4 points the spotlight on the traditions relating Jesus' healings, and pays special attention to the factors emphasized as significant within the healing process.

1. Since then, in the light of the negative and misleading associations engendered by the word *radical*, CRC has become Constructive, Responsive Christianity.

Chapter 5 is devoted to Jesus' reputation for exorcism where we examine how spirit possession was understood in the first century before assessing the dynamics of deliverance and the broader implications of exorcism.

A central contention of this book is that Jesus' healings and exorcisms only become meaningful theologically within his vision of, to employ a popular shorthand, the kingdom of God. Chapter 6 supplies the evidence for this claim and, with that, enables us to answer our initial question with some confidence. Finally, in chapter 7, we present the findings of our investigation, before offering an overview of what happened to the legacy of Jesus the healer and exorcist in the early Christian centuries. Along the way, we draw on a good deal of primary source material and attempt to engage with the relevant scholarly literature, mainly through footnotes to prevent the text from becoming overly technical.

In what follows, no attempt has been made to delve into the origins of Jesus' reputation for performing wonders within the natural world, such as stilling storms, feeding multitudes, or walking on water. Although there are some similarities between the first of these and exorcisms (as we shall note), on the whole they are very different phenomena and merit a study in their own right. More debatable, perhaps, is the omission of those traditions portraying Jesus as someone who could raise the dead. For this reason, our rationale has been presented in an *Appendix*, where we also introduce some of the interpretative challenges presented by this material.

A glance at the bibliography will demonstrate my indebtedness to scholarly research. The work of Wendy Cotter, Pieter Craffert, and Richard Horsley has been particularly helpful in gaining distance from the medical paradigm characterizing the UK, US, and much of the Western world in order to interpret the relevant biblical and early Christian material from a different worldview and perspective. I trust that their views, together with those of many others, have been represented with fidelity and respect, especially where we have disagreed. A number of people from St. Mark's Church (Broomhill, Sheffield, UK), where I used to minister, have read drafts of the early chapters and offered valuable feedback—especially Margaret Ainger, Michael Bayley, John Hillman, and Eve and Robin Saunders. I am also grateful to Professor James Crossley for supplying a foreword, as well as to the staff at Cascade Books, including Dr K. C. Hanson, Jeremy Funk, and Heather Carraher, whose input has greatly improved the manuscript. Thank you, to one and all.

Back in the early 1980s, I promised myself that one day I would attempt to write a book on Jesus' wonderworking. Since then, over twenty-five years of pastoral ministry have underlined the relational nature of disease and healing, which, in turn, alerted me to the significance of this dimension within first-century-CE Palestine, as throughout much of the ancient world. Since then, advances in medical science have transformed treatment, eradicated many illnesses, and prolonged life in ways that would have been inconceivable when Jesus ministered. Yet, at a time when we continue to view illness as a condition contracted by individuals and then to invest our energies in treating them in abstraction from the webs of relating to which they belong, there is perhaps something of contemporary significance to be garnered from the insights and practices of those who bear witness to a different approach.

Abbreviations of Primary Sources

1 Apol.	*First Apology* (Justin Martyr)
1 En.	1 Enoch
1QapGen	Genesis Apocryphon
1QM	The War Scroll
1QS	The Rule of the Community
1QSa (= 1Q28a)	The Rule of the Congregation
2 Apol.	*Second Apology* (Justin Martyr)
3Q15	The Copper Scroll
4Q174 (= 4QFlor)	Florilegium
4Q242	The Prayer of Nabonidus
4Q252 (= 4QPatrBless)	Genesis Commentary
4Q266 (= 4Q Zadokite)	Diagnosis of Skin Disease
4Q394	Miqṣ Maʿaśśê ha-Toraha
4Q444	Incantation
4Q521	The Messianic Apocalypse
11Q5	The Psalms Scroll
11Q11	The Apocryphal Psalms Scroll
11Q13 (= 11QMelchizedek)	Heavenly Prince Melchizedek
ʾAbot R. Nat.	Avot of Rabbi Nathan
Acts Andr.	Acts of Andrew
Acts John	Acts of John

Acts Pet.	Acts of Peter
Acts Pet. 12 Apos.	Acts of Peter and the Twelve Apostles
Acts Pil.	Acts of Pilate
Acts Thom.	Acts of Thomas
Adv. Nat	*Adversus Nationes* (Arnobius)
Ag. Ap.	*Against Apion* (Josephus)
Ant.	*Jewish Antiquities* (Josephus)
Apol.	*Apology* (Tertullian)
Apos. Con.	Apostolic Constitution
Autol	*To Autolycus* (Theophilus of Antioch)
b. Ber.	Berakot (Babylonian Talmud)
b. Ned.	Nedarim (Babylonian Talmud)
b. Sanh.	Sanhedrin (Babylonian Talmud)
b. Šabb.	Šabbat (Babylonian Talmud)
b. Taʿan.	Taʿanit (Babylonian Talmud)
C. Ar.	*Orations against the Arians* (Athanasisus)
Cat.	*Catechetical Lectures* (Cyril of Jerusalem)
Carn. Chr.	*The Flesh of Christ* (Tertullian)
Cels.	*Against Celsus* (Origen)
Comm. Matt.	*Commentary on Matthew* (Jerome)
Cor.	*The Crown* (Tertullian)
Descr.	*Description of Greece* (Pausanias)
Dial.	*Dialogue with Trypho* (Justin Martyr)
Did.	Didache
Disc.	*Discourses* (Epictetus)
Eccl. R.	Ecclesiastes Rabbah
Ep.	*Epigrams* (Martial)
Ep. 74	*Epistle 74* (Cyprian of Carthage)

Ep. Apos.	Epistle to the Apostles
Epit.	*Epitome of the Divine Institutes* (Lactantius)
Flor.	*Florida* (Apuleius)
Geogr.	*Geography* (Strabo)
Gig.	*On Giants* (Philo of Alexandria)
Gos. Eb.	Gospel of the Ebionites
Gos. Heb.	Gospel of the Hebrews
Gos. Jud.	Gospel of Judas
Gos. Naz.	Gospel of the Nazarenes
Gos. Nic.	Gospel of Nicodemus
Gos. Ps-Matt.	Gospel of Pseudo-Matthew
Gos. Thom.	Gospel of Thomas
Haer.	*Against Heresies* (Irenaeus)
Herm. Mand.	Shepherd of Hermas, Mandates
Herm. Sim.	Shepherd of Hermas, Similitudes
Herm. Vis.	Shepherd of Hermas, Visions
Hist.	*Roman History* (Dio Cassius)
Hist.	*Historiae* (Tacitus)
Hist. eccl.	*Ecclesiastical History* (Eusebius)
Hypoth.	*Hypothetica* (Philo of Alexandria)
Inf. Gos. Thom.	Infancy Gospel of Thomas
Ign., *Eph.*	Ignatius, *To the Ephesians*
Ign., *Pol.*	Ignatius, *To Polycarp*
Inc.	*On the Incarnation* (Athanasius)
Inst.	*The Divine Institutes* (Lactantius)
j. Ber.	Berakot (Jerusalem Talmud)
j. Demai	Demai (Jerusalem Talmud)
J.W.	*Jewish War* (Josephus)

LAB	Liber antiquitatum biblicarum
Letter	*To Arsacius, High Priest of Galatia* (Julian)
Lev. R.	Leviticus Rabbah
Life	*The Life* (Josephus)
m. Ber.	Berakot (Mishnah)
m. Neg.	Nega'im (Mishnah)
m. Yebam.	Yebamot (Mishnah)
Med.	*On Medicine* (Cornelius Celsus)
Nat.	*Natural History* (Pliny the Elder)
Nat. hom.	*Nature of Man* (Hippocrates)
Oct.	*Octavius* (Minucius Felix)
Ol.	*Olympian Odes* (Pindar)
Or.	*Orations* (Gregory of Nyssa)
Or.	*Prayer* (Tertullian)
Or. Bas.	*Oratio in laudem Basilii* (Gregory of Nazianzus)
Or. Graec.	*Oration ad Graecos* (Tatian)
Paed.	*Christ the Educator* (Clement of Alexandria)
Phaed.	*Phaedo* (Plato)
Pap. Eg.	Papyrus Egerton
Pol. *Phil.*	*To the Philippians* (Polycarp)
Pro.	*Procatechesis* (Cyril of Jerusalem)
Prob.	*That Every Good Person Is Free* (Philo of Alexandria)
Pss. Sol.	Psalms of Solomon
Pud.	*Modesty* (Tertullian)
Scap.	*To Scapula* (Tertullian)
Somn.	*On Dreams* (Philo of Alexandria)
Strom.	*Miscellanies* (Clement of Alexandria)

Symp.	*Symposium* (Plato)
T. Ab.	Testament of Abraham
T. Ash.	Testament of Asher
T. Benj.	Testament of Benjamin
T. Job	Testament of Job
Test.	*The Soul's Testimony* (Tertullian)
Tg. Isa.	Targum Isaiah
t. Hull.	Hullin (Tosefta)
T. Levi	Testament of Levi
T. Sim.	Testament of Simeon
T. Sol.	Testament of Solomon
t. Šabb.	Shabbat (Tosefta)
Trad. ap.	Apostolic Tradition
Vesp.	*Vespasianus* (Suetonius)
Vict.	*Regimen* (Hippocrates)
Virg.	*The Veiling of Virgins* (Tertullian)
Vit. Apoll.	*Vita Apollonii* (Philostratus)

Abbreviations of Secondary Sources

AB	Anchor Bible
ABD	*The Anchor Bible Dictionary.* Edited by David N. Freedman. 6 vols. New York: Doubleday, 1992
ABRL	Anchor Bible Reference Library
AGJU	Arbeiten zur Geschichte des Antiken Judentums und des Urchristentums
ANF	*The Ante-Nicene Fathers.* Edited by Alexander Roberts and James Donaldson. 10 vols. Reprint, Buffalo: Christian Literature, 1885–1896
ANRW	*Aufstieg und Niedergang der römischen Welt: Geschichte und Kultur Roms im Spiegel der neueren Forschung.* Part 2, *Principat.* Edited by Hildegard Temporini, and Wolfgang Haase. Berlin: Walter de Gruyter, 1972–
ApGos	*The Apocryphal Gospels: Texts and Translations.* Translated by Bart D. Ehrman, and Zlato Pleše. Oxford: Oxford University Press, 2011
ApNT	*The Apocryphal New Testament: A Collection of Apocryphal Christian Literature in an English Translation Based on M. R. James.* Edited by J. K. Elliott. Oxford: Clarendon, 1993
ArBib	The Aramaic Bible
ApT	*Hippolytus: A Text for Students with Introduction, Translation, Commentary and Notes.* Prepared by Geoffrey J. Cuming. Nottingham, UK: Grove, 1976

AYB   Anchor Yale Bible

BAGD   Bauer, Walter, William F. Arndt, F. Wilbur Gingrich, and Frederick W. Danker. *Greek-English Lexicon of the New Testament and Other Early Christian Literature.* 2nd ed. Chicago: University of Chicago Press; 1979

BibOr   Biblica et Orientalia

BMJ   *British Medical Journal*

BZNW   Beihefte zur Zeitschrift für die neutestamentliche Wissenschaft

CDSSE   *Complete Dead Sea Scrolls in English.* Translated with an Introduction by Geza Vermes. London: Penguin, 2011

CEQ   *The Critical Edition of Q: Synopsis including the Gospels of Matthew and Luke, Mark and Thomas with English, German, and French Translations of Q and Thomas.* Edited by James M. Robinson, et al. Hermeneia. Minneapolis: Fortress, 2000.

EHC   *Eusebius: The History of the Church from Christ to Constantine.* Translated by G. A. Williamson, revised and edited with a new introduction by Andrew Louth. London: Penguin, 1965 and 1989

HTR   *Harvard Theological Review*

HTS   Harvard Theological Studies

ICC   International Critical Commentary

IG   *Inscriptiones Graecae. Editio Minor.* Berlin: de Gruyter, 1924–

JAAR   *Journal of the American Academy of Religion*

JBL   *Journal of Biblical Literature*

JJS   *Journal of Jewish Studies*

JSNT   *Journal for the Study of the New Testament*

JSNTSup   Journal for the Study of the New Testament Supplement Series

JSP   *Journal for the Study of the Pseudepigrapha*

JTS	*Journal of Theological Studies*
LCL	Loeb Classical Library
LNTS	Library of New Testament Studies
MD	*The Mishnah: Translated from the Hebrew with Introduction and Brief Explanatory Notes.* Herbert Danby. Oxford: Oxford University Press, 1933
MR	*Midrash Rabbah.* Edited by H. Freedman and Maurice Simon. 10 vols. London: Soncino, 1939
NETS	*A New English Translation of the Septuagint and the Other Greek Translations Traditionally Included under that Title.* Edited by Albert Pietersma and Benjamin G. Wright. Oxford: Oxford University Press, 2007
NHL	*Nag Hammadi Library in English.* Edited by James M. Robinson. Leiden: Brill, 1977
NIGTC	New International Greek Testament Commentary
NovT	*Novum Testamentum*
NovTSup	Novum Testamentum Suppelements
NPNF[2]	*The Nicene and Post-Nicene Fathers,* Series 2. Edited by Philip Shaff and Henry Wace. 14 vols. Reprint, New York: Christian Literature, 1890–1900
NTL	New Testament Library
NTS	*New Testament Studies*
OTL	Old Testament Library
OTP	*Old Testament Pseudepigrapha.* Edited by James H. Charlesworth. 2 vols. Garden City, NY: Doubleday, 1983, 1985
SANT	Studien zum Alten und Neuen Testament
SBB	Stuttgarter biblische Beiträge
SBLDS	Society of Biblical Literature Dissertation Series
SemeiaSt	Semeia Studies
SNTSMS	Society for New Testament Studies Monograph Series

TDNT	*Theological Dictionary of the New Testament.* Edited by Gerhard Kittel, and Gerhard Friedrich. Translated be Geoffrey W. Bromiley. 10 vols. Grand Rapids: Eerdmans, 1964–76
WBC	Word Biblical Commentary
WUNT	Wissenschaftliche Untersuchungen zum Neuen Testament
ZNW	*Zeitschrift für die neutestamentliche Wissenschaft und die Kunde der* älteren *Kirche*

Framing the Task

AT THE CONCLUSION OF an exhaustive analysis of the gospel material portraying Jesus as a wonderworker, John Meier, a distinguished Jesus scholar with an enviable reputation for thorough research and balanced judgment, reaches the following conclusion:

> The curious upshot of our investigation is that, viewed globally, the tradition of Jesus' miracles is more firmly supported by the criteria of historicity [e.g., multiple attestation of sources and forms, coherence with sayings, etc.] than are a number of other well-known and often readily accepted traditions about his life and ministry . . . Put dramatically but with not too much exaggeration: if the miracle tradition from Jesus' public ministry were to be rejected *in toto* as unhistorical, so should every other gospel tradition about him.[1]

Meier's striking assessment is borne out by the evidence. References to Jesus' wonderworking activity[2] can be found in all the principal gospel

---

1. Meier, *Marginal Jew*, 2:630. Eric Eve makes the same point at the end of his study on Jesus' wonderworking: "Jesus' healing and exorcizing activity is so central to the presentation of his ministry in the Synoptic Gospels (most of all Mark), that were it not possible to affirm the plausibility of this going back to the historical Jesus, we should have to conclude that the Gospels were too unreliable to give us any information about the historical Jesus at all" (*Healer from Nazareth*, 164).

2. We use the term "wonderworker" or "wonderworking" throughout for two reasons. First, unlike "miracle," it doesn't prejudge the source of Jesus' abilities by inferring he was able to access supernatural powers. Second, it stresses the response to Jesus' activities—whatever he did and however he did it, Jesus caused people to wonder and, through wondering, to remember, and through remembering, to share their stories.

sources—in Mark[3] and in the hypothetical sayings source Q (*Quelle*),[4] as well as in those sources unique to the First and Third Evangelists.[5] The author of John's Gospel incorporates material from a "signs" source containing Jesus' wonders,[6] while one of the earliest New Testament manuscript fragments uncovered to date relates a healing by Jesus.[7] What is more, the sheer quantity of material militates against wholesale dismissal on the grounds of it all being secondary.[8] We should also note that references to Jesus' wonderworking can be found within different literary forms, including narratives,[9] controversies,[10] sayings,[11] and editorial

---

3. Mark 1:21–28, 29–31, 32–34, 40–44; 2:1–12; 3:1–6, 7–12, 30–33; 4:35–41; 5:1–20, 21–43; 6:30–34, 45–52, 53–55; 7:24–30, 31–37; 8:1–10, 14–21, 22–26; 10:46–52; 11:12–14, 20–25. Most scholars maintain that Mark is the earliest of the four canonical Gospels.

4. Q 7:1–10 (Luke 7:1–10//Matt 8:5–13); Q 7:18–23 (Luke 7:18–23//Matt 11:2–6); Q 10:13–15 (Luke 10:13–15//Matt 11:20–24); Q 11:14–20 (Luke 11:14–20//Matt 11:22–28). In the standard two- or four-source theories of how the Synoptic Gospels relate to one another, Q (*Quelle*: "source" in German) is the name given to the source, written or verbal, assumed to account for the material shared by Matthew and Luke, most of which is missing from Mark. The existence of Q is increasingly questioned, although at the time of writing it remains the predominant theory (see Goodacre, *Case against Q*; as well as Poirier and Peterson, *Marcan Priority*). With reference to this investigation, whether or not this common material shared by Matthew and Luke originated in a sayings gospel known as Q (unless it was created by either Matthew or Luke), it bears witness to another early source, whether written or verbal. It is convention to cite Q material according to Luke's reference.

5. Matt 4:23; 9:27–31, 32–34, 35; 9:35; 12:22; 14:14; 15:29–31; 19:2; 21:14: Luke 5:1–11; 7:11–17, 21; 9:11; 13:10–17, 32; 14:1–6; 22:51.

6. John 2:1–11, 23–25; 4:46–54; 5:1–16; 6:1–15; 9:1–34; 11:1–46.

7. Pap. Eg. 2 (Papyrus Köln), dated to around 150 CE, contains our earliest version of the cleansing of the leper recorded in Mark 1:40–44.

8. Wilkinson, *Health and Healing*, estimates, based on the Authorized Version, that 20 percent of Mark, 9 percent of Matthew, 12 percent of Luke and 13 percent of John is devoted to Jesus' wonderworking. If we restrict the search to narrative verses, the percentages increase significantly: Mark: 40 percent, Matthew: 40 percent; Luke: 35 percent; and John: 33 percent (19). Morton Kelsey records forty-one separate incidents of healing or exorcism in the Gospels (*Healing and Christianity*, 43–45).

9. E.g., Mark 1:40–45//Matt 8:1–4//Luke 5:12–16; Mark 5:21–43//Matt 9:18–26//Luke 8:40–56; Mark 10:46–52//Matt 20:29–34//Luke 18:35–43.

10. E.g., Mark 2:1–12//Matt 9:1–8//Luke 5:17–26; Mark 3:1–6//Matt 12:9–14//Luke 6:6–11; Mark 3:22–25; Q 11:14–20 (Luke 11:14–20//Matt 11:22–28).

11. E.g., Mark 2:17//Matt 9:12//Luke 5:31; Q 7:18–23 (Luke 7:18–23//Matt 11:2–6); Luke 4:23; 13:32.

summaries[12]—suggesting it was deeply embedded within the early Jesus movement's corporate memory.[13]

On top of attributing healings, exorcisms, and wonders to some of the apostles,[14] the author of Acts also refers to Jesus' performance of the same. The most explicit references fall in speeches attributed to Peter, first, when at Pentecost he bears witness to Jesus as "a man attested to you by God with deeds of power, wonders, and signs (*dynamesi kai terasi kai sēmeiois*) that God did through him among you" (Acts 2:22) and again, on the occasion of Cornelius's conversion, when he commends Jesus as one "God anointed . . . with the Holy Spirit and with power . . . he went about doing good and healing (*euergetōn kai iōmenos*) all who were oppressed by the devil, for God was with him" (Acts 10:38). Nor should we overlook those times when the apostles heal or exorcise "in the name of Jesus"[15]—a practice that wouldn't make much sense unless Jesus was a recognized authority in this sphere. In fact, the apostles' wonderworking activity in toto is largely inexplicable without Jesus' precedent and authorization to do likewise.[16]

Although the apostle Paul does not make direct reference to Jesus' wonderworking, his letters contain a number of indicators that he was not only aware of this reputation but drew on it to inform his own ministry.[17] For instance, as mentioned in the previous paragraph more generally, it would be difficult to account for Paul's mission strategy of proclamation of the gospel accompanied by powerful manifestations of the Spirit if it was not patterned on the approach of Jesus himself: "For I

12. E.g., Mark 1:32–34//Matt 8:16–17//Luke 4:40–41; Mark 3:7–12//Luke 6:17–19; Mark 6:53–56//Matt 14:34–36; Luke 7:21; 8:2.

13. "In short, multiple sources intertwine with multiple forms to give abundant testimony that the historical Jesus performed deeds deemed by himself and others to be miracles. If the multiple attestation of sources and forms does not produce reliable results here, it should be dropped as a criterion for historicity" (Meier, *Marginal Jew*, 2:622).

14. Peter (Acts 3:1–10; 5:15–16; 9:32–35, 36–41); Paul (Acts 14:8–11; 16:16–18; 19:11–12; 20:9–12; 28:8, 9); Paul and Barnabas (Acts 14:3); Ananias (Acts 9:17–19); Philip (Acts 8:6–7); Stephen (Acts 6:8); unspecified (Acts 2:43). Most scholars maintain that Luke and Acts were composed by the same person.

15. E.g., Acts 3:6, 16; 16:18; cf. Justin, *2 Apol.* 2.6; Irenaeus, *Haer.* 2.23.4.

16. Cf. Mark 3:13–19//Matt 10:1–4//Luke 6:12–16; Mark 6:7–13//Matt 10:1, 9–11, 14//Luke 9:1–6; cf. Luke 10:1–14.

17. For a full discussion of the evidence, see Twelftree, *Paul and the Miraculous*, which is summarized in Twelftree, "Miraculous in the New Testament," 332–34.

will not venture to speak of anything except what Christ has accomplished through me to win obedience from the Gentiles, by word and deed, by the power of signs and wonders (*en dynamei sēmeiōn kai teratōn*), by the power of the Spirit of God."[18] Further, in a list of spiritual gifts bestowed upon members of the believing community at Corinth can be found "healing" (*iamatōn*) and "miracle-working" (*energēmata dynameōn*; 1 Cor 12:9–10). Paul describes this community as the "body of Christ" (1 Cor 12:27), presumably to underline the continuity between the ministry of Jesus and that of his church, so we would expect the *charismata* to reflect the former. Finally, the great hymn to love in 1 Cor 13 includes one of Jesus' sayings associated with wonderworking: ". . . and if I have all faith, so as to remove mountains, but do not have love . . ." (1 Cor 13:2; cf. Mark 11:23//Matt 21:21; Matt 17:20). We cannot be sure the apostle was aware of its provenance, but in the light of references in the previous chapter to gifts of healing, miracle-working, and faith within the ecclesial body of Christ such an awareness seems likely.

The Gospel of Thomas is one of our earliest noncanonical gospels and is usually dated to somewhere around 100–120 CE. Like Q, it is a source of Jesus' sayings, 114 of them in total, which are recorded without commentary or narrative setting. Three of them, however, appear to presuppose Jesus' wonderworking activities. The first, "A prophet is not welcome in his village; a physician does not heal those who know him,"[19] is similar to a version in Mark recorded on the occasion of Jesus' return home when his healing abilities were thwarted or at least substantially reduced by the incredulity he encountered there (Mark 6:4–5; also Matt 13:57–58). The second, "No one can enter the house of the strong and take it by force unless he binds his hands. Then he will plunder his house" (35), also has its equivalent in the Synoptic Gospels where it falls within a controversy over the provenance of Jesus' exorcistic powers (Mark 3:27// Matt 12:29//Luke 11:21–22). Finally, the third takes the form of a mission charge: "And when you go into the land and walk in the countryside, if they receive you, eat whatever they place before you and heal the sick among them" (14; cf. Luke 10:9; Matt 10:1, 8//Luke 9:1, 6). Although this relates to the disciples, it implies Jesus' healing activity as well, otherwise why would they be instructed to minister in this manner?

18. Rom 15:18–19; see also 1 Cor 2:4–5; 4:20; 2 Cor 12:12; Gal 3:5; 1 Thess 1:5.
19. Gos. Thom. 31 [*ApGos*].

Unsurprisingly, we find references to Jesus' wonderworking across a range of early Christian texts,[20] which in some cases, notably the Infancy Gospel of Thomas, extend into his childhood years when, on occasion, he applies his powers in a manner more befitting a petulant child than an infant messiah.[21] The historical value of such traditions resides not so much in the access they afford to Jesus' early years as in the evidence they supply of attempts to enhance Jesus' reputation by increasing his wonderworking powers or to animate his childhood in the light of his later ministry. There would be little point claiming Jesus was a wonderworking child prodigy if his reputation for wonderworking as an adult had not been established previously.

Significantly, Josephus, a first-century Jewish historian with little if any sympathy towards Christianity, offers a brief description of Jesus referred to by scholars as the *Testimonium Flavianum*.[22] It is worth quoting in full:

> At this time there appeared Jesus, a wise man [if indeed one should call him a man]. For he was a doer of startling deeds (*paradoxōn ergōn*), a teacher of people who receive the truth with pleasure. And he gained a following both among many Jews and among many of Greek origin. [He was the Messiah.]

20. E.g., Gos. Jud. 33; Gos. Naz. [Jerome, *Comm. Matt* on 12:13]; Gos. Nic. (Acts Pil.) A 1.1; 2.5–6; 4.2; 5.1; 6.1–2; 7; 8; 14.1; Gos. Nic. (Acts Pil.) B 19; 20.1; Gos. Ps-Matt. 20.1–2; *Anaphora Pilati* 1–4; Letter of Pilate to Claudius; Letter of Tiberius to Pilate; Ep. Apos. 5–6, 21; Justin, *Dial.* 69; *1 Apol.* 30–1; Irenaeus, *Haer.* 2.31.2; Tertullian, *Apol.* 23; Origen, *Cels.* 1.38, 46; 2.48; Eusebius, *Hist. eccl.* 1.13; 2.3 (Abgar correspondence); Arnobius, *Adv. Nat.* 1.42–43; Athanasius, *Inc.* 15; 18; Gregory of Nyssa, *Or.* 23; 34.

21. For example, conjuring sparrows from clay models (2.1–5), and withering or even executing children who displeased him (3.1–3; 4.1–2). Thankfully, the infant Jesus redeems himself on other occasions by performing healings (10.1–2; 16.1–2), and resuscitations (9.1–3; 17.1–2; 18.1–2), as well as by feeding the poor (12.1–2) and offering his parents a "miraculous" helping hand (11.1–2; 13.1–2).

22. In fact, Josephus offers one further reference to Jesus, which, surprisingly, doesn't occur during his detailed discussion of John the Baptist, but when describing James, the leader of the early Jerusalem church: "And so he [Ananus, the high priest] convened the judges of the Sanhedrin and brought before them a man named James, the brother of Jesus who was called the Christ, and certain others. He accused them of having transgressed the law and delivered them up to be stoned" (*Ant.* 20.200 [LCL 456]). Further references to Jesus can be found in a Slavonic translation of Josephus's *Jewish Wars*, which emerged at the beginning of twentieth century; however, most scholars consider these to be Christian interpolations. See the discussion of van Voorst, *Jesus Outside*, 81–104.

> And when Pilate, because of an accusation made by the leading
> men among us, condemned him to the cross, those who had
> loved him previously did not cease to do so. [For he appeared to
> them on the third day, living again, just as the divine prophets
> had spoken of these and countless other wondrous things about
> him.] And up until this very day the tribe of Christians, named
> after him, has not died out.[23]

I have used the translation prepared by John Meier[24] and have adopted
his analysis of the sections, which bear the marks of being later interpolations (placed here in [square brackets]), presumably by a zealous Christian redactor desirous that this influential Jewish historian should affirm
Jesus' messiahship and resurrection. Notice how the original text refers
to Jesus as "a doer of startling deeds." The Greek word employed here,
paradoxos, is rarely used elsewhere to describe Jesus' wonderworking (cf.
Luke 5:26), which supports its authenticity. It is particularly revealing
how Josephus both draws attention to this feature without calling it into
question, and appears to acknowledge or at least imply its instrumental
role in securing Jesus a popular following—something we shall return to
later.

As our canonical Gospels record that Jesus was accused by his opponents of being demon-possessed (e.g., Mark 3:22–25; Q 11:14–20 [Luke
11:14–20//Matt 11:22–28]), so some of his later critics and detractors
continue in a similar vein. For example, in the second century, Celsus,
a Neoplatonist philosopher, penned the first comprehensive attack on
Christianity. Although that work, *True Doctrine*, does not survive, much
of the text is incorporated within the biblical scholar Origen's refutation.
Here is one of the relevant sections from *Contra Celsum*, with Celsus's
words in quotes:

> And yet he [Celsus] desires to throw discredit on them [Jesus'
> miracles], as being done by help of magic (*mageias*) and not
> by divine power; for he asserts "that he [Jesus], having been
> brought up as an illegitimate child, and having served for hire in
> Egypt, and then coming to the knowledge of certain miraculous
> powers (*dynameōn*), returned from thence to his own country,
> and by means of those powers (*dynameis*) proclaimed himself a
> god." Now I do not understand how a magician (*magos*) should
> exert himself to teach a doctrine which persuades us always to

23. Josephus, *Ant.* 18.63–64 [LCL 433].

24. Meier, *Marginal Jew*, 1:56–69.

act as if God were to judge every man for his deeds; and should have trained his disciples, whom he was to employ as the ministers of his doctrine, in the same belief.[25]

There is much of interest in this passage, but for our purposes we note the charge of magician leveled against Jesus. The source of this accusation is unclear. A Christian interpolation into the otherwise Jewish composition of the first Sibylline Oracle identifies Egypt as the place of origin for the wonderworking, incarnate son of God (1.345–59), but this reference may well postdate Origen's treatise. Equally, a version of the Infancy Gospel of Thomas includes an immature Christ working wonders in Egypt (C.1–2), yet this also is probably too late and, in any case, neither mentions magic. The third-century Acts of Thomas records that the apostle was called "a sorcerer and magician" (*pharmakos kai magos*; 107) and appears to have him casting a spell over a serpent while in Egypt in order to obtain a precious pearl (111). And, again, in the Pseudo-Clementine literature, Simon Magus, who is described in Acts as a man who "practiced magic" (*mageuō*; 8:9), is initiated into the art while in Egypt (*Homily* 2.22).

If there is anything to garner from these references, including Origen's to Celsus, it is that the link between Jesus and Egypt made by the Evangelist Matthew or one of his sources (Matt 2:23–33), especially when viewed in the light of Moses and Aaron's contest against Pharaoh's magicians and sorcerers at the time of the exodus,[26] provided a fertile source of speculation for those who wished to undermine Jesus' wonderworking abilities by calling into question the provenance of his powers. It is a tactic we come across again in the rabbinic literature, especially tractate Sanhedrin in the Babylonian Talmud, where Jesus is repeatedly portrayed as someone who "practiced magic and led Israel astray."[27] What most, if not all, of these references have in common is that they affirm Jesus' reputation for wonderworking; in the case of the rabbinic texts, they may even imply that this reputation was influential among his compatriots.

In sum, the evidence for Jesus' wonderworking is substantial. Even if some of it is apocryphal, which it almost certainly is, we would struggle to claim that it all flowed from the creative imagination of the early

25. Origen, *Cels.* [c. 175 CE] 1.38 [*ANF*]; see also 1.6, 28, 68; 2.9, 14, 16, 48–49; 6.7.

26. Exod 7:11, 22; 8:7, 18, 19; 9:11; cf. Joseph in Gen 41:8, 24.

27. b. Sanh. 43a; 107b; also b. Šabb. 104b; t. Šabb. 11.15. For a discussion of the rabbinic references to Jesus, as well as those of Josephus and Celsus, see van Voorst, *Jesus Outside*, 64–68, 75–134, and Meier, *Marginal Jew*, 1:56–111.

church without also, as Meier indicated at the outset, relinquishing hope of knowing anything about Jesus beyond the fact that he lived and was crucified.[28] Which brings us to the real challenge of a wonderworking Jesus for a post-Enlightenment worldview. Rudolf Bultmann, one of the leading New Testament scholars of the twentieth century, expressed it in these well-rehearsed terms:

> It is impossible to use electric light and the wireless and to avail ourselves of modern medical and surgical discoveries, and at the same time to believe in the New Testament world of spirits and miracles. We may think we can manage it in our own lives, but to expect others to do so is to make the Christian faith unintelligible and unacceptable to the modern world.[29]

Few aspects of Jesus' ministry are better attested than his reputation for wonderworking, and yet few details cause more difficulty for the modern mind, presenting us with a dilemma: Is a wonderworking Jesus credible within a world shaped by rational thinking and scientific inquiry? And, if not, can we be confident that our earliest sources contain any accurate information about him?

The roots of this dilemma can be traced back at least to the seventeenth century and the legacy of René Descartes (1583–1648),[30] the putative father of Western philosophy, who can perhaps be credited with inventing the category of nature as a closed system of cause and effect which could be analyzed rationally, discrete from the supernatural dimension of the mental, spiritual, and sacred—none of which, as a devout Roman Catholic, he rejected.[31] It was only a matter of time before the spotlight of rational inquiry would be trained on the Bible and, especially, the miraculous elements within it. In 1670, a Portuguese Jew, Benedict

---

28. There are a small number of scholars who maintain that the figure of Jesus of Nazareth is a fabrication. Two leading proponents of recent years are G. A. Wells (*Jesus of the Early Christians; Who Was Jesus?; The Jesus Myth*), and Robert M. Price (*Deconstructing Jesus; Incredible Shrinking*). A clear presentation of the case in favor of Jesus' nonexistence and responses to it can be found in Beilby and Eddy, *Historical Jesus*, 55–103.

29. Bultmann, "New Testament," 5.

30. For a full discussion of the figures and movements involved, see Colin Brown's treatment in *Miracles*, on which I have based this and the following paragraphs; also Keller, *Miracles in Dispute*.

31. See the insightful comments of Martin, *Corinthian Body*, 4–6, where he draws attention to how Descartes's dualism has been projected onto ancient cultures, resulting in a misconception of how the body and illness were understood.

de Spinoza (1632–1677) published anonymously for fear of reprisals, *Tractatus Theologico-Politicus*, in which he demonstrated the logical impossibility of miracles before spelling out the implications for the alleged miracles in Scripture. To quote:

> Now, as nothing is necessarily true save only by Divine decree, it is plain that the universal laws of science are decrees of God following from the necessity and perfection of the Divine nature. Hence, any event happening in nature which contravened nature's universal laws, would necessarily also contravene the Divine decree, nature, and understanding; or if anyone asserted that God acts in contravention to the laws of nature, he, *ipso facto*, would be compelled to assert that God acted against his own nature—an evident absurdity.[32]

Spinoza continues . . .

> Thus in order to interpret these scriptural miracles and understand from the narration of them how they really happened, it is necessary to know the opinions of those who first related, and have recorded them for us in writing, and to distinguish such opinions from the actual impression made upon their senses . . . For many things are narrated in Scripture as real, and were believed to be real, which were in fact only symbolical and imaginary.[33]

In hindsight, though, it proved to be a brief essay of barely 20 pages, titled "Of Miracles," published in 1748 by the Scottish philosopher David Hume (1711–1776) that was to frame the debate well into the twentieth century, in which he wrote:

> A miracle is a violation of the laws of nature; and as a firm and unalterable experience has established these laws, the proof against a miracle, from the very nature of the fact, is as entire as any argument from experience can possibly be imagined.[34]

And so miracles came to be defined out of existence by what some have claimed to constitute no more than a philosophical sleight of hand, based on questionable assumptions: a miracle is a violation of the laws of nature; the laws of nature govern the material universe; hence, miracles are

32. Spinoza, *Tractatus*, 1.81.
33. Spinoza, *Tractatus* 1.93.
34. Hume, *Human Understanding*, 114 § 90.

logically impossible.[35] Either way, Hume's definition, although contested and reformulated, increasingly became one of the presuppositions informing biblical exegesis, with far-reaching implications for the references to alleged miracles within the Gospels.

In their textbook *The Historical Jesus: A Comprehensive Guide*,[36] Gerd Theissen and Annette Merz chronicle six phases in the interpretation of Jesus' wonderworking during the ensuing centuries, although these are not necessarily mutually exclusive as there have been exponents of a number of these advocating their views concurrently. Here is a summary of their analysis:

Rationalist Interpretations

These interpretations formulated rational explanations for supernatural components within Jesus' miracles in order to make them credible to the "enlightened" mind (e.g., Carl. F. Bahrdt [1741–1792], Heinrich E. G. Paulus [1761–1851]).[37] This worked in some cases better than others. For instance, the feeding of the five thousand becomes a massive "bring and share" picnic; others, however, were less plausible as with the walking on water being facilitated by a chance deposit of floating logs that serendipitously formed themselves into a causeway over which the deftly footed Jesus was able to tiptoe. Or, Jesus standing at the secret entrance to a cave in which mountains of bread had been stashed prior to the arrival of the multitude.

Mythical Interpretations

These interpretations reconceived Jesus' miracles as mythical compositions serving kerygmatic ends. The foremost exponent here was David Strauss (1808–1874), in his magnum opus *The Life of Jesus Critically Examined*[38] (1835–1836; 4th edition, 1839–1840), in which he maintained that the miracle traditions drew on stories and hopes from the Hebrew Scriptures to reenforce Jesus' messianic status. For instance, if Elijah and Elisha fed the hungry, healed the sick, and raised the dead (1 Kgs

---

35. Keener, *Miracles*, 1:134.

36. Theissen and Merz, *Historical Jesus*, 285–91.

37. Bahrdt, *Briefe*, and *Ausführungen*; Paulus, *Leben Jesu*.

38. Strauss, *Leben Jesu*.

17:8–24; 2 Kgs 2:19–25; 4:1–5:19), then greater miracles were attributed to Jesus to demonstrate his superiority over these prophetic figures. Most of these, however, were the poetic creations of his followers, although some bear witness to actual healings that Jesus accomplished through psychosomatic means.

Comparative Interpretations

These interpretations compare the gospel miracle stories with those found in other ancient literature to demonstrate the existence of common forms with shared features, motifs, and development histories. Influenced by the "history-of-religions school," key exponents of comparative interpretations included Rudolf Bultmann (*Die Geschichte der synoptischen Tradition*, 1921) and Martin Dibelius (*Die Formgeschichte des Evangeliums*, 1919), who recognized the influence of Hellenistic miracle stories and other literature upon the gospel traditions; whereas Ludwig Bieler maintained that "miracle-worker" was a defined type in antiquity, which influenced the presentation of Jesus as a "divine man" (ΘΕΙΟΣ ΑΝΗΡ, 1935/36). Inevitably, this approach tended to reduce the weight placed upon the miracles in reconstructions of Jesus' ministry, as well as to undermine claims relating to Jesus' uniqueness or Christianity's superiority to other religions.[39]

Relativizing Interpretations

These interpretations assessed the way the gospel evangelists employ the miracle traditions to further their theological agendas rather than addressing questions over their historicity or ultimate significance. In the 1950s, the gospel evangelists came into their own as creative authors who didn't simply record inherited traditions about Jesus but redacted or edited them to serve their own purposes. Within this climate, a number of studies appeared that focused specifically on their treatment of Jesus' wonderworking. For example, Theodore Weeden maintained that by placing them within a narrative that emphasized the costliness of discipleship, Mark corrected erroneous views of Jesus derived from the miracle traditions in isolation.[40]

39. Bultmann, *History*; Dibelius, *Tradition*; Bieler, ΘΕΙΟΣ ΑΝΗΡ.
40. Weeden, "Heresy," 145–58; also Weeden, *Mark*. Other "redaction criticism"

Contextual Interpretations

These interpretations located Jesus within his first-century context and used that context to interpret the miracle traditions attributed to him. One of the landmark studies to appear in the English-speaking world during the twentieth century was *Jesus the Jew* by Geza Vermes. Within this work, as the title suggests, Jesus' Jewishness comes to the fore as his wonderworking is placed alongside that of other contemporary charismatic holy men such as Hanina ben Dosa and Honi the Circle-Drawer. Alternatively, by focusing on the accusations leveled against Jesus in the early centuries while interpreting them in the light of ancient magical texts, Morton Smith concluded that Jesus is best understood as a practitioner of magic who was successful owing to "psychological reasons" (*Jesus the Magician*, 1978).

Sociological Interpretations

These interpretations draw on insights from sociology and related disciplines to investigate the role of Jesus' wonderworking within the communities that preserved, embellished and sometimes created this material. In *Urchristliche Wundergeschichten* (1974), Gerd Theissen observes that no figure from antiquity has more miracles attributed to him or her than Jesus, before identifying their social function as a source of legitimation for protest and renewal movements within oppressive political regimes and as a means of engendering confidence in those facing challenging circumstances. Similarly, other scholars have drawn on sociological models with insightful results. John Pilch and Dieter Trunk, for example, maintain that sickness, possession, and healing are social constructs emerging from and belonging to a particular set of circumstances (not static categories), and as such must be interpreted accordingly.[41]

Yet for all these approaches to Jesus' wonderworking, with their implicit diversionary strategies, academic interest in the miraculous has, if anything, increased in recent decades. We see this in relation to the

---

studies of the miracles include (mostly, not translated into English) Matthew: Gerhardsson, *Mighty Acts*; and Held, "Miracle Stories," 165–299; Mark: Kertelge, *Wunder Jesu*; Koch, *Wundererzählungen*; and Schenke, *Wundererzählungen*; Luke: Busse, *Wunder*; and Garrett, *Demise*; John: Bultmann, *Gospel of John*; and Fortna, *Gospel of Signs*.

41. Theissen, *Miracle Stories*; Pilch, *Healing*; and Trunk, *Heiler*.

concept of miracle in general, as well as to those miracles attributed to Jesus in particular, yielding interesting developments and renewed emphases.[42] Each of the following could become a book topic in its own right and some are rather technical, but they all throw light upon our investigation, albeit in different ways.

Revision

Some philosophers and theologians are much less willing these days to draw on Hume's definition of a miracle as an event that "violates the laws of nature" out of recognition that these laws are essentially *descriptive* rather than *prescriptive*. They purport to describe the natural order, not to determine it, and are in principle open to revision. Some scientists go much further and claim that the whole notion of universal laws is fundamentally flawed on the grounds that in order to determine the course of the universe from its inception, they must have existed before the beginning of time—that is, before there was anything to determine. But where? And why these laws rather than others? And do not preexisting laws imply a purposeful universe? These are challenging questions for those who favor belief in this universe as a chance occurrence over belief in this universe as a creative act, some of whom prefer to speak of an evolving universe evolving habits through time, rather than being shaped by predetermined laws. But whether one sticks with the laws of nature while recognizing their provisional status or opts instead for evolving habits, it is possible that alleged miracles, or any inexplicable happening for that matter, bear witness to naturally occurring phenomena that our current formulations of these laws or habits cannot accommodate—phenomena that may appear extraordinary, but which are not, technically-speaking, miraculous.[43]

42. See Meier, *Marginal Jew*, 2:509–34; Twelftree, "Miraculous," 321–52, and the literature cited there.

43. Sheldrake, *Science Delusion*, 84–108; and Basinger, "What Is a Miracle?" 19–35. Eric Eve helpfully distinguishes between "miracles" and "anomalies," where the former is described as "a strikingly surprising event with apparent religious significance attributed directly or indirectly to an act of God" and the latter as "an event which would contradict some fundamental scientific principle and which would thus appear to be ruled out as impossible on our current best understanding of the way the world works" before proposing that "it may be that all sorts of things happen which we cannot explain, and there is a gap between 'we cannot explain this' and 'this is contradicted by some fundamental principle of our best current scientific theories'" (*Healer from*

Circumspection

Anthropological studies of the miraculous within different cultures have called into question the adequacy of Western scientific rationalism to account for the breadth of human experience encountered, and advocate acknowledging the contribution of other belief systems to providing a more comprehensive overview. Some go so far as to interpret refusal of the Western scientific mind-set to acknowledge the so-called enchanted world as an expression of unwarranted intellectual arrogance, and imperialism.[44] Commenting on rationalist explanations of the almost ubiquitous phenomenon of clairvoyance, the anthropologist Ronald Hutton objects, "ultimately the psychologizing of Siberian spirits is itself a statement of faith, resting upon no ultimate proof . . . It makes sense to modern westerners of otherwise uncanny or repugnant phenomena; but in its different way the native explanation made equal sense, and with as much claim to objective demonstration of evidence."[45]

Acknowledgment

In a two-volume work titled *Miracles: The Credibility of the New Testament Accounts*, which runs to over 1,200 pages, New Testament specialist Craig Keener has compiled a vast collection of reports of alleged miracles across cultures and social groupings, in the present time and through the centuries. Although readily acknowledging that not all the assembled evidence has, or could be, subject to critical scrutiny, he suggests that, at the very least, the collective force of this material demonstrates that eyewitness testimonies to alleged miracles not only exist but continue unabated throughout both the Majority World and the so-called enlightened West, where many rational and, in some cases, scientifically qualified people claim to have experienced them. Keener's research flies in the face of Bultmann's assertion mentioned earlier and challenges the conviction (prejudice?) that miracles only occur in communities informed by compatible worldviews.

Nazareth, 161).

44. Bowie, "Miracles," 167–83; also Twelftree, "Miraculous," 324–25.

45. Hutton, *Shamans,* 67, quoted in Bowie, "Miracles."

Resurgence

Although not new in itself, relational ontology has recently come to the fore across a number of disciplines, yielding some exciting work at the interface between science and theology. *Relational ontology* maintains that relations between entities, whether at a micro, subatomic or macro, whole-organism level, are ontologically more fundamental than the entities themselves, in contrast to *substantivist ontologies*, which give priority to the entities and sees relations as derivative.[46] Within theology, the context in which this has been explored most thoroughly is the Trinity, where there is a long interpretative tradition reaching back at least to the Cappadocian Fathers of the fourth century maintaining that the three members of the Godhead are constituted within their relationships to one another, and cannot be defined satisfactorily outside of those relationships (e.g., God the Father is God-the-Father-of-the-Son, God the Son is God-the-Son-of-the-Father, and so forth).[47] Equally, when applied anthropologically, the role that our relationships and interactions play in defining our identity and character, as well as in shaping our futures, comes into focus—thereby, for example, providing us with a conceptual framework for understanding the transformative nature of encounters between Jesus and those around him.[48]

Recognition

In a sense this is an extension to what has been said already under Circumspection, but the failure of scientific inquiry to explain satisfactorily fundamental experiences such as consciousness and memory, together with an increasing body of empirical research within the fields of mind-body interactions[49] and psychic studies[50] are leading some academics

46. An interdisciplinary exploration of relational ontology is provided by the collection of essays edited by John Polkinghorne, *Trinity*.

47. On social approaches to the Trinity, see, especially, Moltmann, *Trinity*; also Fiddes, *Participating*; Gunton, *Promise*; Heron, *Forgotten Trinity*, vol. 3.

48. On relational approaches to personhood, see (among many) McFadyen, *Personhood*; MacMurray, *Persons*; Schwöbel and Gunton, eds., *Persons*; Zizioulas, *Being as Communion*; and Zizioulas, *Communion and Otherness*.

49. E.g., the placebo response, epigenetics, faith healing.

50. E.g., extrasensory perception (ESP), telepathy, out-of-body experiences (OBEs), near-death experiences (NDEs), precognition, clairvoyance.

to question whether a materialist understanding of cause and effect is sufficient to account for all these phenomena. By definition, current scientific methodologies are unlikely to be able to demonstrate this, but, as precedes every major paradigm shift (cf. Thomas Kuhn), the body of evidence that cannot be accommodated within the reigning orthodoxy is mounting.[51]

These and other developments have significant implications for how we assess Jesus' reputation for wonderworking or, at the very least, invite a fresh evaluation of the evidence. In the following chapters, we will attempt to do this, hopefully less encumbered by some of the presuppositions that in the past have resulted in Jesus' reputation being either dismissed for having no historical basis or, as we have seen, explained away in one manner or another. We will also attempt to take the texts seriously in their own terms and evaluate them in light of how illness and healing were both experienced and interpreted in first-century Palestine, before locating them within Jesus' kingdom message. Where appropriate, we will draw on contemporary insights to aid in this task and clarify interpretive possibilities.

51. The is a complex and contentious area with a vast bibliography. Valuable introductions are supplied: Sheldrake, *Science Delusion*; and Hamilton, *Thought That Counts*. For engagement at a more detailed, scholarly level, see Kelly et al., *Irreducible Mind*; and Kelly et al., *Beyond Physicalism*.

Illness and Healing in Israelite Faith

NOW THAT WE'VE GAINED a little insight into some of the intellectual challenges raised by the miraculous and, by implication, Jesus' reputation for wonderworking, let us turn our attention to the milieu which gave rise to that reputation. And, perhaps, the place to start is with the following question: How was illness experienced and understood in first-century Palestine, and what sources of healing, if any, were available? As with the previous chapter, a quotation helps us to gain focus, this time from the acclaimed medical anthropologist Arthur Kleinman. In his classic study, *Patients and Healers in the Context of Culture*, he writes:

> In the same sense in which we speak of religion or language or kinship as cultural systems, we can view medicine as a cultural system, a system of symbolic meanings anchored in particular arrangements of social institutions and patterns of interpersonal interactions. In every culture, illness, the responses to it, individuals experiencing it and treating it, and the social institutions relating to it are all systematically interconnected. The totality of these interrelationships is the health care system. Put somewhat differently, the health care system, like other cultural systems, integrates the health-related components of society. These include patterns of belief about the causes of illness; norms governing choice and evaluation of treatment; socially-legitimated statuses, roles, power relationships, interaction settings, and institutions.[1]

---

1. Kleinman, *Patients and Healers*, 24.

It goes without saying that the "health care system" operating when Jesus ministered was very different from the one most of us experience today. We need to acknowledge this difference at the outset, putting to one side the assumptions we make about the nature and causes of illness, as well as those associated with diagnosis and treatment. We also need to recognize that although Kleinman's phrase resembles the United Kingdom's National Health Service or its equivalent in other developed nations, this is where the similarity ends. In fact, as we shall see, almost all of the elements we would list as characterizing our health care systems would have been unfamiliar in first-century Palestine. So, let us attempt to reconstruct the latter, critically and imaginatively, before moving on to interpret Jesus' wonderworking within this system.

We begin by focusing on what is probably the single most important ancient text we possess for our task. Scholarly consensus places the Wisdom of Ben Sira (also known as Ecclesiasticus or Sirach) in Judea, around Jerusalem, towards the beginning of the second century BCE.[2] It belongs within the sapiential tradition of wisdom writings of Israelite religion, which draws on experience, observation, and reflection, as well as Torah, to discern God's presence in life and to shape a faithful response. Composed originally in Hebrew,[3] as the prologue to the translation attested in the Septuagint (LXX) specifies, the complete text is now only available in Greek, Syriac and Latin translations. The compass of this heterogeneous work is expansive, embracing much of human existence, and in chapter 38 the author addresses our area of investigation.

> Honor a physician (*iatron*) for his services,
>> for indeed the Lord created him.
> For healing (*iasis*) is from the Most High,
>> and he will receive a gift from a king.
> A physician's (*iatrou*) skill will put up his head,
>> and in the presence of nobles he will be admired.
> The Lord created remedies (*pharmaka*) out of the earth,
>> and a prudent man will not ignore them.

2. Di Lella, "Wisdom of Ben-Sira," 931–45.

3. "You are invited, therefore, to a reading with goodwill and attention, and to exercise forbearance in cases where we may be insipid with regard to some expressions that have been the object of great care in rendering; for what was originally expressed in Hebrew does not have the same force when it is in fact rendered in another language" (NETS). This comes from the Prologue contained in the Septuagint. We have used the version contained in the Septuagint, although extant Hebrew witnesses consistently use the *rāpā'* root to render *iaomai* and its cognates.

Was not water made sweet from wood

in order that his [or "its"] strength might be known?

And it was he [i.e. the Lord] that gave skill to human beings

in order to be glorified in his marvelous deeds.

By them he [i.e. the physician] cured (*etherapeusen*) and took away his [i.e. the patient's] pain.

He who prepares unguents (*myrepsos*) will make a compound with them,

and his works will never be finished,

and peace from him is upon the surface of the earth.

Child, in your illness do not look elsewhere,

but pray to the Lord, and he will heal (*iasetai*) you.

Withdraw from error, and direct your hands,

and from all sin cleanse your heart.

Give a sweet-smell and a memorial of fine flour,

and enrich an offering [Greek uncertain].

And give a physician (*iatrō*) his place, for indeed the Lord created him,

and do not let him withdraw from you, for indeed there is need of him.

There is a time when success is in their hands as well.

For they will also petition the Lord,

that he might grant them success with rest and healing (*anapausin kai iasin*),

for the maintenance of life.

He who sins before him who made him,

may he fall into a physician's (*iatrou*) hands.[4]

The God of Health and Wholeness

The first thing to note here is the conviction that Yahweh, Israel's God, was the ultimate or final source of all healing.[5] This is a conviction characterizing ancient Israelite literature as a whole and one rooted in the perceived privileged relationship between Yahweh and the Israelite people for whom healing, as with all forms of salvation and rescue, is the divine prerogative within the covenant (Sir 2:7–11; 34:14–20; 36:1–22)—a conviction established during the deliverance of Israelite slaves from Egypt under the messiahship of Moses (cf. "I am the LORD who heals you," Exod

4. Sir 38:1–15 [NETS].

5. Avalos, *Health Care*, 33–34; and Wolff, *Anthropology*, 147–48.

15:26), and celebrated in his song at the end of Deuteronomy (32:7–10, 39; also 28:1–2), as well as in many of the psalms.[6] One consequence of this association with the covenant is that sickness, impairment, and healing tended to be interpreted theologically in the sense that a breakdown in health within the physical body was thought to reflect a breakdown in health within the covenantal body—between an Israelite and Yahweh or between Israelite and Israelite.[7]

What is more, a breakdown in health within the covenantal body was thought to result from disobedience or some other form of disordering behavior—all of which came under the umbrella of sin or transgression. While this causal relationship between sin, on the one hand, and sickness or impairment, on the other, was not universally accepted within Israelite faith traditions prior to the first century CE—think of Job's riposte—it was, if the textual evidence we possess is any guide, the dominant view as reflected in the passage from Sirach (38:9–12) and indeed in many others.[8] For example, sickness as divine punishment for transgression:

> The LORD struck the child that Uriah's wife bore to David, and it became very ill. David therefore pleaded with God for the child; David fasted, and went in and lay all night on the ground. The elders of his house stood beside him, urging him to rise from the ground; but he would not, nor did he eat food with them. On the seventh day the child died.[9]

6. The conviction that Yahweh is the restorer of peace through saving acts of rescue, deliverance and healing is ubiquitous throughout the Psalms and elsewhere (e.g., Pss 7; 18; 22; 31; 34—36; 40; 62; 71—72; 85—86; 91; 106–8; 116; 118; 144). With respect to healing, in particular, see Pss 6:2; 30:2; 41:3–4; 103:3; 107:20; 147:3.

7. Avalos, *Health Care*, 33–45; and Kee, *Medicine*, 12–16; see also the insightful discussion of the relationship between an individual body and the body politic with reference to sickness and healing in Martin, *Corinthian Body*, 139–62.

8. Interestingly, this also appears to have been the view of the apostle Paul (1 Cor 5:1–5; 10:1–11; 11:27–32), the author of the Epistle of James (Jas 5:13–16) and, quite probably, the Evangelist Luke (Luke 1:18–20, 59–64; Acts 5:1–11; 9:8–18; 12:20–23). We discuss in a later chapter whether Jesus was remembered as someone who subscribed to it as well.

9. 2 Sam 12:15–18. This case is particularly disturbing in that God's punishment doesn't fall upon the perpetrator, but on the innocent "victim" of David's transgression. Cases where there is a more direct correspondence between transgression and divine punishment, include Exod 12:12; 1 Sam 5:6; 2 Kgs 5:21–27; 2 Chr 21:12–19; 26:16–21; Hab 3:2–5; Tob 11:13–15.

And sickness as a consequence of transgression:

> Some were sick through their sinful ways,
>> and because of their iniquities endured affliction;
> they loathed any kind of food,
>> and they drew near to the gates of death.
> Then they cried to the LORD in their trouble,
>> and he saved them from their distress;
> he sent out his word and healed them,
>> and delivered them from destruction.[10]

One corollary of this link between sickness and sin is that restoration within the physical body was believed to depend upon restoration within the covenantal body—hence the need for repentance and forgiveness as a means of reordering right-relating between sufferers and Yahweh:

> Happy are those whose transgression is forgiven,
>> whose sin is covered.
> Happy are those to whom the Lord imputes no iniquity,
>> and in whose spirit there is no deceit.
>
> While I kept silence, my body wasted away
>> through my groaning all day long.
> For day and night your hand was heavy upon me;
>> my strength was dried up as by the heat of summer.
>
> Then I acknowledged my sin to you,
>> and I did not hide my iniquity;
> I said, "I will confess my transgressions to the LORD,"
>> and you forgave the guilt of my sin.[11]

What is more, sickness and impairment disordered human relationships as well. They could disrupt how a sufferer was able to participate in community life. In some cases, such as certain skin conditions, you would

10. Ps 107:17–20; also Sir 28:9–15; and 4Q242.

11. Ps 32:1–5; also "Bless the LORD, O my soul, / and do not forget all his benefits—/ who forgives all your iniquity, / who heals all your diseases" (Ps 103:3); "No one gets up from his sick-bed until all his sins are forgiven" (b. Ned. 41a); cf. "Are any among you sick? They should call for the elders of the church and have them pray over them, anointing them with oil in the name of the Lord. The prayer of faith will save the sick, and the Lord will raise them up; and anyone who has committed sins will be forgiven. Therefore confess your sins to one another, and pray for one another, so that you may be healed" (Jas 5:14–16). See Oepke, "*iaomai*," 194–203.

be rendered ritually unclean, quarantined from home and village, and excluded from corporate worship.[12] If your condition was debilitating, you would be left unable to earn a living and quite possibly forced into destitution, thrown upon the mercy of others—a source of great shame in the ancient world (cf. Sir 40:28–30)—while feeling under divine judgment and, in many cases, condemned by fellow Israelites, who would have interpreted your illness or impairment as the outcome of or punishment for wrongdoing.[13] The psalmist captures what must have been the experience of many when he described illness as a living hell: "O LORD my God, I cried to you for help, / and you have healed me. O LORD, you brought up my soul from Sheol, / restored me to life from among those gone down to the Pit . . . You have turned my mourning into dancing; / you have taken off my sackcloth and clothed me with joy."[14]

We should also spell out what to this point has been implicit, namely, that within a worldview where God is the source of all that exists, ultimately sickness, as much as healing, becomes a divine prerogative. And there are many references in the Hebrew Scriptures to Yahweh visiting disease or worse upon people, usually as a form of punishment, although sometimes as a means of proving faithfulness and fortitude (e.g., Job).[15] In addition, we find God causing disease and suffering not punitively or pastorally, but vicariously as a means of atoning for Israel's transgression. In the fourth of Isaiah's Servant Songs, Yahweh's servant is disfigured beyond recognition, "a man of suffering and acquainted with infirmity" who has "borne our infirmities and carried our diseases . . . wounded for our transgressions, / crushed for our iniquities; upon him was the punishment that made us whole, / and by his bruises we are healed." (Isa 53:3–5). This is a remarkable departure, and one which undoubtedly

12. E.g., Lev 13–14, and m. Neg. See Pilch, *Healing*, 39–54; Cotter, *Christ*, 19–41. Cotter's book offers penetrating insight into the personal and social consequences of suffering from illness in the ancient world.

13. The classic case of this in the Hebrew Scriptures is that of Job's comforters, Elipaz, Bildad, and Zophar, who interpret his extreme suffering as evidence of severe transgression now receiving commensurate divine punishment (Job 4:1–21; 8:1–22; 11:1–20; 15:1–35; 18:1–21; 20:1–29; 22:1–30; 25:1–6). While the narrative of the book of Job is almost certainly fictional, it nonetheless reflects beliefs and convictions current at the time of composition (sixth–fifth century BCE?). Avalos draws attention to how illness had economic, as well as social and religious, implications, rendering sufferers unproductive and of diminished worth (*Health Care*, 34–37).

14. Ps 30:2–3, 11.

15. E.g., Gen 20:17–18; Exod 4:11; 9:1–12; 12:29–32; Deut 28:15–22; 1 Sam 16:14–16; 2 Kgs 5:27; 2 Chr 7:12–14; Job 5:18; Jer 14:19; 30:12–17; Hos 6:1–2.

influenced early Christian attempts to make sense of Jesus' crucifixion.[16] With respect to our survey, we should note that this passage represents one of the earliest attempts to vest meaning in the experience of suffering itself, rather than seeing it as an unpleasant means to a worthwhile end or, indeed, something to be avoided at all costs.[17]

Another important development came with the recognition that at least some forms of disorder, whether within (disease) or beyond (discord) the physical body, were not divinely sanctioned but caused by an evil spiritual force operating outside of Yahweh's providence. This may reflect exposure to Zoroastrianism, a dualist religion in which the wholly good God, Ahura Mazda, is opposed by a malevolent counterpart, Angra Mainyu, although the dating of extant Persian texts calls into question whether such thoroughgoing dualism predates the Christian era.[18] So, for example, although according to 1 Samuel, Saul is tormented by an evil spirit sent by God (1 Sam 16:14–16, 23), in the book of Tobit, dating from the second or third century BCE, the demon Asmodeus works his murderous ways outside of Yahweh's behest (Tob 3:7–8; also 6:8, 17–18; 8:3).[19] And, again, in the Testament of Solomon (possibly from the first century CE), thirty-six malevolent celestial bodies (*stoicheia*) or spirits (*pneumata*) are interrogated by the king, who discovers that each is responsible for causing ailments of a particular part of the body or for disrupting the sufferer's relationships in some way (chapter 18).

Nor should we overlook how the language of sickness could be used within the Hebrew Scriptures to describe disease or disorder within the covenantal body of Israel, as right-relating with Yahweh was thought to become compromised through transgression. And, equally, how the

16. On the impact of this passage, and Isaiah as a whole upon Christianity, see Sawyer, *Fifth Gospel.*

17. The persecution of observant Jews by the Selucid king, Antiochus Epiphanes, elicited a similar response: "These [i.e. Eleazar, the seven brothers and their mother, all righteous and devout], then, who have been consecrated for the sake of God, are honored, not only with this honor, but also by the fact that because of them our enemies did not rule over our nation, the tyrant [Antiochus IV] was punished, and the homeland purified—they having become, as it were, a ransom for the sin of our nation. And through the blood of those devout ones and their death as an atoning sacrifice, divine Providence preserved Israel that previously had been mistreated" (4 Macc 17:20–22).

18. "The most important documents of Persian apocalypticism and eschatology belong to this Pahlavi literature [c. ninth century CE]. The difficulty lies in determining how far this Pahlavi literature preserves material from the pre-Christian era" (Collins, *Apocalyptic Imagination*, 37).

19. For further evidence of dualism and spirit-possession in ancient Israelite texts, see Cotter, *Miracles*, 106–27; and Witmer, *Galilean Exorcist*, 21–60.

language of healing was employed to express restoration. This is particularly pronounced in the prophetic literature as the following excerpts demonstrate:

> Return, O faithless children,
>   I will heal (√ *rāpā'/iasomai*) your faithlessness . . .

> Why have you struck us down
>   so that there is no healing (√ *rāpā'/iasis*) for us?
> We look for peace, but find no good;
> for a time of healing (√ *rāpā'/iaseōs*), but there is terror instead . . .

> For I will restore health (*'arūkāh/iama*) to you,
>   and your wounds I will heal (√ *rāpā'/iatreusō*),
>   says the LORD,
> because they have called you an outcast:
>   "It is Zion; no one cares for her!"[20]

> When Ephraim saw his sickness,
>   and Judah his wound,
> then Ephraim went to Assyria,
>   and sent to the great king.
> But he is not able to cure you
>   or heal (√ *rāpā'/iasasthai*), your wound . . .

> Come, let us return to the LORD;
>   for it is he who has torn, and he will heal (√ *rāpā'/iasetai*) us;
>   he has struck down, and he will bind us up.
> After two days he will revive us;
>   on the third day he will raise us up,
>   that we may live before him.[21]

See, the day is coming, burning like an oven, when all the arrogant and all evildoers will be stubble; the day that comes shall burn them up, says the LORD of hosts, so that it will leave them neither root nor branch. But for you who revere my name the sun of righteousness shall rise, with healing (√ *rāpā'/iasis*) in its wings. You shall go out leaping like calves from the stall.[22]

20. Jer 3:22; 14:19; 30:17; cf. 17:7–14.
21. Hos 5:13; 6:1–2; also 11:1–4.
22. Mal 4:1–2.

Channels of Divine Healing

Returning to Sir 38, the second point to note is that while acknowledging God as its ultimate source, the author recognizes how Yahweh employs intermediaries to bring healing about, notably physicians and pharmacists, as well as natural remedies.[23] This is highly significant in that self-styled physicians tended to be judged inept and exploitative in early Israelite traditions, as indeed in other ancient cultures.[24] Although there aren't many references to medical physicians in the Hebrew Scriptures, most of them are negative. For instance, King Asa of Judah (913–873 BCE) dies as a consequence of seeking their help rather than turning to Yahweh (2 Chr 16:12), while Job, in his suffering, can think of no worse aspersion to cast upon his hapless comforters than to call them "worthless physicians" (Job 13:4).[25]

The book of Tobit, usually dated around the later third or early second century BCE, is an interesting case in point. The eponymous Tobit, an exemplary Israelite, partially loses his sight as a consequence of bird excrement falling into his eyes; however, his condition worsens significantly after he consults a physician: "I did not know that there were sparrows on the wall; their fresh droppings fell into my eyes and produced white

23. It may well be that Sirach's strong advocacy of the medical arts represents the first concerted effort to accommodate them within Israelite faith by recognizing their divine origin and utility. See Allan, "Physician," 377–94. Allan also draws attention to Jubilees 10 where "in contrast to the Book of Watchers [1 Enoch 1–36], the forbidden knowledge of medicines is sanctioned here by God so that illness with its demonic origin in man being led astray, i.e. sin (v. 2), is provided with an antidote in magical remedies prescribed by a demon" (386). See also Chrysovergi, "Contrasting Views," 46–54.

24. From what we can gather, the editorial comment found in Mark's relating of Jesus' encounter with the woman suffering from chronic blood loss was true to life: "Now there was a woman who had been suffering from hemorrhages for twelve years. She had endured much under many physicians, and had spent all that she had; and she was no better, but rather grew worse" (Mark 5:25–26).

25. See also Jer 8:22; 30:12; 46:11; 51:8–9. Apart from Sir 38, the only other positive reference is Gen 50:1–3, where physicians successfully embalm Jacob's body for burial, although, to be fair, this is no measure of their therapeutic effectiveness. The occasional passing reference to the medicinal use of oil, balm, and bandages suggests that rudimentary treatments were known about, but none of these necessarily implies the work of a physician or, indeed, indicates whether their use was widespread (e.g., Isa 1:6; Jer 8:22; 51:8; Ezek 20:21). The Roman encyclopedist Celsus (25 BCE–50 CE) records a recipe for a plaster compress (*emplastra*) to be applied to "broken heads," which he attributes to a Jew (*Iudaeus*; Celsus, *Med.* 5.19.11), but this postdates Sirach.

films. I went to physicians to be healed (*tous iatrous therapeuthēnai*), but the more they treated me with ointments (*ta pharmaka*) the more my vision was obscured by the white films, until I became completely blind." (2:10)[26] Self-evidently, this verse does not show the medical profession in a good light, but it is highly questionable whether one can deduce from this the author's "fervent rejection of the medical arts" as has been claimed recently.[27] What is clear, however, is that Yahweh brings about the restoration of Tobit's sight by angelic mediation (3:17)—suggesting, perhaps, an unwillingness to acknowledge the divinely ordained nature of physicians and their remedies;[28] although this needs to be qualified by the observation that even Raphael employs the therapeutic properties of the gall of a fish to remove the films (cataracts?) from Tobit's eyes (11:7–8).

After reviewing the evidence, Howard Kee concludes, "The overall import . . . is that Yahweh is indeed the restorer and orderer of human life, individually and corporately, and no human agency, least of all physicians, can solve problems, alleviate suffering, or cure ills."[29] Given the small number of references, this is probably overstating the case as is noted by Gary Ferngren when he comments that "there is little evidence . . . to support the widespread view that the Hebrews held generally negative views of physicians or medicine."[30] In the end, however, it depends on how we account for the relative silence in the surviving sources, but judging from the clues we do possess, prior to Sirach, Kee is probably not far from the mark with respect to physicians;[31] as we shall see shortly, the

26. The NRSV, quoted here, follows the longer recension of Codex Sinaiticus rather than the shorter text reflected in the RSV: "I did not know that there were sparrows on the wall and their fresh droppings fell into my open eyes and white films formed on my eyes. I went to physicians (*iatrous*), but they did not help me."

27. Chrysovergi, "Contrasting Views," 39. Tob 2:10 is the only mention of physicians throughout the book and, although their detrimental effect upon Tobit's eyesight is mentioned, it is a brief reference that elicits neither comment nor judgment. In the light of this, Chrysovergi's claim that the "author of Tobit should have understood the rationalism of Hippocratic medicine as antagonistic to the traditional Jewish faith in healing. In other words, the rejection of secular medicine here is a veiled form of propaganda against the cultural invasion of Hellenism" (42) reaches well beyond what the evidence can support.

28. "Yet, although physicians were recognized for their healing skills, and could be consulted without fear of divine retribution, they are clearly not regarded as instruments of God's healing" (Allan, "Physician," 383).

29. Kee, *Medicine*, 17.

30. Ferngren, *Medicine*, 23.

31. It should also be noted that it wasn't only in Israel that the nascent medical profession was viewed with suspicion. Consider the following from the first century

situation may well have been different with respect to naturally occurring medicines.

Magicians

Those described, usually by others, as "magicians" or "sorcerers" fare even worse, for although their existence is acknowledged, their practices are roundly condemned within the Torah: "No one shall be found among you who makes a son or daughter pass through fire, or who practices divination, or is a soothsayer, or an augur, or a sorcerer, or one who casts spells, or who consults ghosts or spirits, or who seeks oracles from the dead. For whoever does these things is abhorrent to the LORD; it is because of such abhorrent practices that the LORD your God is driving them out before you."[32]

Although the death penalty is prescribed for occult practices in Leviticus (20:27; also 20:6), there are plenty of references in the Hebrew Scriptures, largely condemnatory, to their continuation.[33] Furthermore, in certain cases, key Israelite figures appear to be commended as exponents. For example, Joseph surpasses Egyptian magicians in being able to interpret the Pharaoh's dream correctly (Gen 41), while Moses and Aaron equipped with wonderworking (magic?) staffs are finally able to do likewise after initially being matched in performing portents by their Egyptian counterparts (Exod 7–11). In both cases, Israel's God is acknowledged as the ultimate source of such wonders (e.g., Gen 41:16; Exod 8:19), but Yahweh's mediators find themselves pitched against magicians and sorcerers, thereby inviting comparison. In the case of Daniel, the comparison is made explicit with Yahweh's faithful servant finally being crowned "chief of the magicians, enchanters, Chaldeans, and diviners" by King Nebuchadnezzar (Dan 5:11; also 4:9), having seen off his competitors (Dan 4:7–8; cf. 1:20; 2:2, 27). In these cases, what distinguishes Aaron, Daniel, Joseph, and Moses from foreign wonderworkers

---

Roman satirist, Martial (38/41–103 CE): "Diaulus used to be a doctor till recently, now he's an undertaker. What the undertaker does, the doctor used to do" (Ep. 1.47 [LCL 94]; also 5.9; 8.74; 9.96). Or the following curt injunction from Pliny the Elder (23–79 CE), the acclaimed Roman commander, naturalist, and philosopher with a keen interest in the medicinal qualities of plants: "*interdīxi tibi de medicis*—I have forbidden you to have dealings with physicians" (*Nat.* 29.7 [LCL 418]; cf. quoting Cato).

32. Deut 18:10–12; also Lev 19:26, 31.

33. E.g., 1 Sam 28; 2 Kgs 9:22; 2 Chr 33:6; Isa 2:6; 3:2–3; 47:12–13; Jer 14:14; 27:9; Ezek 13:17–23; Nah 3:4; Mal 3:5.

is not practice and application, where there is considerable overlap, but motivation and empowerment—suggesting that terms such as *magician* and *sorcerer* are as pejorative as they are descriptive in these contexts. In fact, some scholars who have compared the practices of ancient magic with the performance of miracles within a religious framework have concluded that it is all but impossible to distinguish between them at an operational level.[34]

We should also mention the episode in 1 Sam 28 where Saul, who had fallen from divine favor and was now fearful of facing the Philistine army, "inquired of the LORD" via the "conventional" means, but to no avail (v. 6). As a last resort, he manages to conjure up the spirit of the deceased Samuel via a medium from Endor, who proceeds to deliver Yahweh's judgment upon Israel's fallen king (vv. 16–19). Clearly, this does not present Saul in a good light, but it sends mixed messages about occult activity, which, on the one hand, is supposed to be a prohibited, yet, on the other, proves to be an effective means of intuiting Yahweh's mind.[35]

Physicians

Yet, for all that, we shouldn't think that the practice of medicine was denigrated or even rejected outright by everyone in the ancient world. Far from it. As those verses from Sirach affirm, some of Israelite faith from at least the second century BCE onwards not only recognized the value of medical practitioners but also believed them to be servants of God.

This positive attitude may well reflect the influence of Greek medicine, which from the fifth century BCE, through observation, dissection and surgery, had been seeking rationally and systematically to understand anatomy and organ function as well as key bodily processes such as intelligence, respiration, and circulation.[36] Of the various schools of thought that emerged prior to the Common Era, the Hippocratic tradition (cf. Hippocrates, 460–370 BCE) became preeminent for many

34. Aune, "Magic," 1510–16; and Horsley, *Jesus and Magic*, 3–19, 37–52.

35. There is also the intriguing case of a dead Moabite who is resuscitated the moment he comes into contact with the bones of Elisha: "As a man was being buried, a marauding band was seen and the man was thrown into the grave of Elisha; as soon as the man touched the bones of Elisha, he came to life and stood on his feet" (2 Kgs 13:21). Once again, occult activity (although this could have been inadvertent) delivers a "godly" outcome.

36. Helpful overviews are provided in Kee, *Medicine*, 27–66; and Martin, *Corinthian Body*, 139–62.

centuries. At this time and largely up until the nineteenth century, there was little understanding of germs or other invading substances which caused disease;[37] in fact, a case could be made that demon-possession represents one of the earliest invasive theories of disease recorded. Mostly, though, disease was thought to result not from an alien invasion but from an imbalance—for example, between the body's four humors (blood, phlegm, yellow bile, black bile)[38]—which was often deemed to be caused by external discord, thereby making the physician's task one of diagnosing the nature of the imbalance before assisting the body's restoration of harmony—in effect, aiding the body to heal itself.

Although there is no ancient source to confirm this, Hippocrates is usually credited with establishing the medical school on the Greek island of Cos in the fourth century BCE where, according to Kee, it may well have been associated with a healing center dedicated to Asclepius, which has been extensively excavated. It is possible, therefore, that medical physicians practiced their art under the patronage of the Greco-Roman deity dedicated to health—reflecting, as with Sirach, the conviction that although all healing in ultimately a divine gift, it is administered through human and natural agency. Presumably, patients would have been treated during the day by physicians and then, at night, slept within the Asclepeion (incubation), hoping to receive a healing visitation via epiphany or, asleep, through a dream or via the deity's other intermediaries—snakes and dogs.[39]

Certainly, Hippocrates didn't think it was incompatible to petition the gods at the same time as consulting a medical practitioner: "Prayer indeed is good, but while calling on the gods a man should himself lend a hand" (*Vict.* 4.87 [LCL 150]). In fact, at the end of this four-volume work, he concludes, "I have discovered regimen, with the gods' help, as far as it is possible for mere man to discover it" (4.93 [LCL 150]). What is more, it is quite conceivable that at least some of the Greek advances in

37. Martin notes that Thucydides (460–395 BCE) and Aelius Aristides (117–81 CE) were probably the first to advance invasive theories of disease (*Corinthian Body*, 149–52).

38. "The body of man has in itself blood (*haima*), phlegm (*phlegma*), yellow bile, and black bile (*cholēn xanthēn kai melainan*); these make up the nature of the body, and through these he feels pain or enjoys health. Now he enjoys the most perfect health when these elements are duly proportioned to one another in respect of compounding, power and bulk, and when they are perfectly mingled" (Hippocrates, *Nat. hom.* 4 [LCL 150]).

39. Kee, *Miracle*, 83–88.

medicine had spread to Palestine during the reign of Alexander the Great (336–323 BCE) and, possibly, during the Hellenizing reforms overseen by high-priests Jason and Menelaus in the second century BCE.

Healing Shrines

It is worth noting at this juncture that the veneration of Asclepius, in a similar way to the Egyptian cult of Isis, was enormously popular, spreading broadly throughout the Mediterranean and beyond.[40] The reason is clear enough: for once, divine beings, who were often portrayed as indifferent to the plight of humanity, were concerning themselves with the frailties of mortals, coming to their aid. It seems probable that the Asclepius cult had reached the region of Palestine sometime during or immediately prior to the first century CE,[41] raising the intriguing possibility that Jesus himself may have visited a shrine dedicated to the healing deity.

For instance, an inscription to Asclepius has been unearthed at a temple dedicated to the Phoenician deity Eshmun, at Sidon, which dates back to the second century BCE or earlier. In addition, the first-century-CE authors, Strabo (*Geogr.* 16.2.22; 17.3.14) and Pausanias (*Descr.* 7.23.7–8) both identify healing shrines to Asclepius in Phoenicia by the time of their writing. In the light of this, Mark's inclusion of Sidon within one of Jesus' itinerant missionary initiatives is suggestive (Mark 7:31; cf. 3:8).[42]

There was also a hot water spring, which both Josephus and Pliny the Elder record as being associated with healing, on the west shore of Lake Galilee at Hamath Tiberias, south of Herod Antipas's capital.[43] Vernon McCasland mentions the discovery of a bronze coin struck by the city of Tiberias in 99 CE that exhibits the bust of Emperor Trajan on one side and on the other displays Asclepius's daughter, Hygieia, who

40. Kee, *Miracle*, 78–145. The most comprehensive collection of ancient sources relating to Ascelpius we have come across, including votive tablets from the shrine at Epidaurus giving thanks for healings of various sorts, is the two-volume work by Emma and Ludwig Edelstein, *Asclepios*. For the healing cult of Isis, see Witt, *Isis*, 46–58, 185–97.

41. McCasland, "Asklepios," 221–27; and McCasland, "Religious Healing," 27–32.

42. The fullest discussion of the evidence for shrines to Asclepius in first-century Palestine is still that of Antoine Duprez, *Jésus*; however, a more balanced assessment is supplied by Yeung, *Faith*, 66–83. See also Jeremias, *Rediscovery*. A convenient and scholarly overview is supplied in Wilkinson in *Jerusalem*, 95–104.

43. Josephus, *J.W.* 2.614; *Ant.* 18.36; Pliny, *Nat.* 5.15.

"is seated on a rock beneath which water is gushing forth. She holds in her right hand the sacred serpent of Asklepios and feeds him from a phiale in her left."[44] Although the association of Hamath ("hot springs" in Hebrew) with healing predates the Common Era, the shrine could have been adopted by devotees of Asclepius following the fall of Jerusalem and subsequent increase in Roman influence throughout Palestine, yet the temple at Sidon leaves open the possibility of an earlier association. There is no reference to Hamath in the Gospels, but given how much of Jesus' ministry revolved around Lake Galilee, it would be surprising if, at the very least, he wasn't aware of its reputation.

According to the Fourth Gospel, Jesus visited and performed a healing at the pool of Bethesda[45] by the Sheep Gate near the temple in Jerusalem. The value of John as a historical source for the ministry of Jesus is currently under reassessment, and one of the reasons for this is that recent archaeological discoveries have confirmed a number of the topographical details contained therein.[46] One of these is the pool of Bethesda together with its five porticoes (John 5:1–9), although in Jesus' time it consisted of two substantial basins (north: 53 x 40 meters; south: 47 x 52 meters) divided by a thick wall, each side with its own portico.[47] This configuration, especially given the proximity of the temple and the discovery of stone steps running the full length of the west side of the southern basin, suggests use as a public *miqweh* or purification pool at some point.[48] However, archaeological excavations have uncovered the

44. McCasland, "Asklepios," 223–24; the coin was minted again in 108 CE.

45. There is considerable uncertainty over the earliest form of the Hebrew name for this location. Bruce Metzger lists no fewer than six variant readings in his *Textual Commentary*, 208. "Bethesda" has strong manuscript support, as well as possible corroboration from the *Copper Scroll* found at Qumran and written in Aramaic, which lists locations where caches of treasure had been deposited, including *Bethesdatain* (3Q15.57; the writing is not entirely legible so the *d* and *t* could be *r* and *h*, yielding *Bethesrahain*, but the former is more likely), which can be translated "house of the two springs."

46. On the reassessment of John as a historical source, see Anderson, *Fourth Gospel*; and Charlesworth, "Historical Jesus," 3–46.

47. Le Projet Béthesda, was set up in 1994 to study the site. Its preliminary findings were published in *Projet Béthesda*. An English version of Shimon Gibson's contribution, "Excavations," can be found online at https://www.academia.edu/22894959/.

48. Gibson, "Excavations," 22–29; and von Wahlde, "Archaeology," 560–66. A *miqweh* needs to be filled from water that is not drawn but flows naturally into the cistern, hence the second basin, known as a *otsar,* to act as a store. The two pools were linked by a channel and sluice.

remains of a post–70 CE sanctuary dedicated to Asclepius-Serapis, built upon an older configuration of basins and grottos, which may well have been commissioned by Hadrian as part of his reconceiving of the city as Aelia Capitolina following the quashing of the Bar Kokhba uprisings and subsequent expulsion of Jews from Judea. Votive offerings giving thanks for healing have also been found which date from the second century CE or earlier.[49] So it possible that an existing Jewish *miqweh* was transformed into a healing shrine to Asclepius at Hadrian's behest, but this would not account for the concentration of sick people by the pool noted in John's otherwise accurate description of the area. Equally, Bethesda was close to the Antonia Fortress where Roman soldiers were stationed; their presence, together with that of a significant number of traders and visitors of a cosmopolitan complexion, makes a shrine to the popular healing deity Asclepius at least plausible, as Duprez has argued.[50] What is more, at Jesus' time, Bethesda was outside the city wall where it would have caused less offense to observant Jews. On balance, Maureen Yeung's reconstruction sounds the most plausible:

> People who came to the baths for healing probably carried with them different religious convictions. Some might be Jews who were influenced by legends about Solomon. Others might be Hellenized Jews or Gentiles who were steeped in Serapis-Asclepius worship. It was in such a climate that cultural and religious exchanges took place in a most natural manner. Although there is no way of knowing whether the paralytic mentioned in John 5 was himself influenced by Asclepius, we may fairly conclude that many of his contemporaries came to the Pool because they saw the therapeutic waters as the means of Asclepius' healing.[51]

49. See Duprez, *Jésus*, chapter 1.

50. Duprez, *Jésus*, 95–7, 108–76.

51. Yeung, *Faith*, 78; she goes on to say, "Many of the Jewish sages approved the Roman introduction of public baths to the land of Israel for hygienic reasons. Hillel the Elder even regarded the washing in the bathhouse as a religious duty (*Leviticus Rabbah* 34.3). Therefore, the therapeutic baths in the land of Israel were probably a fertile ground for the interaction of the two faiths, that is, the worship of Asclepius and Jesus as saviour-healers." Earlier, Yeung refers to the fourth-century Christian travelogue known as the *Bordeaux Itinerary*, which mentions a crypt of Solomon near the pool, which, given his association with healing and exorcism (77; cf. Jesus petitioned for healing as "Son of David," Mark 10:47–48//Matt 20:30–31//Luke 18:38–39; Matt 9:27; 12:23; 15:22), adds further weight to the link between this part of Jerusalem and healing.

Medicines and Pastoral Care

Returning to Sirach, we notice that in addition to honoring physicians, the author celebrates Yahweh's provision of naturally occurring substances and their application as medicines. Here again, the author reflects a seemingly widespread practice as evidenced by the Roman naturalist Pliny the Elder, who maintained that "the true nature of each plant can only be fully understood by studying its medicinal effect, that vast and recondite work of divine power, and the greatest subject that can possibly be found."[52]

Although there is some concern over the occult origins of such knowledge within Israelite faith,[53] the Jewish historian Josephus singles out the Essenes as acknowledged practitioners of natural medicine. He writes, "They display an extraordinary interest in the writings of the ancients, singling out in particular those which make for the welfare of soul and body; with the help of these, and with a view to the treatment of diseases, they make investigations into medicinal roots and the properties of stones."[54] We should also point out that Essenes were credited with a commitment to well-being more generally.[55] While most scholars maintain that the community based at Qumran and responsible for the

52. Pliny the Elder, *Nat.* 19.62 [LCL 371]. Avalos stresses this point, drawing attention to the pharmaceutical manuals compiled by Dioscorides, Celsus, and Rufus of Ephesus (*Health Care*, 79). Schrage also cites a number of texts from rabbinic literature in which the curative qualities of flora are highlighted, in particular, with reference to healing blindness ("*typhlos*," 284).

53. Some texts associate pharmacological knowledge with the illicit union between the sons of God and the daughters of humanity narrated in Genesis 6 (e.g., 1 En. 7:1–6; Jub. 10:10–14). For further discussion, see Witmer, *Galilean Exorcist*, 35–41.

54. *J.W.* 2.134–136 [LCL 203].

55. The etymology of "Essenes" remains unclear, but one option is that it derives from the Aramaic 'asaya, meaning "healers." Geza Vermes, in particular, has championed this interpretation, drawing attention to Philo's description of a group of Jews sympathetic with the Essene way of life known as *Therapeutai*, a Greek word denoting service/worship (of God) or healing or both (*Contempl.* 2). Vermes makes a case for the Essenes as truly *therapeutai*, "worshippers of God, because they offered Him the true worship of their own spiritual healing (*therapeia*)" ("Essenes," 97–115 [98]). In addition to the evidence discussed in the text, two manuscripts have been discovered at Qumran that may reflect a particular interest in medicine. One offers a quasi-technical description of the flow of blood in arteries, while the other was initially thought to include medical notes; however, most scholars now think this scrap of leather was used by a scribe to practice letter formation, as was common in the ancient world. See Baumgarten, "4Q Zadokite," 153–65; and Naveh, "Medical Document," 52–55.

Dead Sea Scrolls was Essene, the movement was much broader. Both Josephus, and the Hellenistic Jewish philosopher Philo (25 BCE—50 CE), offer lengthy descriptions, estimating their number at approximately four thousand living in lay communities within existing settlements throughout Palestine.[56]

From what we can gather, these Essenes practiced a form of communalism—pooling their resources, partaking in shared meals and pursuing a practical piety. Philo and Josephus extol their virtues, celebrating among other qualities their simplicity of lifestyle, care for one another and compassion for those in need. It is difficult to know whether such generosity and kindness was reserved for their own, although given they lived among nonmembers this seems unlikely. Of particular interest is the way both Philo and Josephus highlight their care of the sick, the former implying that they ran rudimentary hospitals for the infirmed and elderly.[57] Philo writes:

> The sick are not neglected because they cannot provide anything, but have the cost of their treatment lying ready in the common stock, so that they can meet expenses out of the greater wealth in full security. To the elder men too is given the respect and care which real children give to their parents, and they receive from countless hands and minds a full and generous maintenance for their latter years.[58]

Assuming Josephus and Philo are reliable, albeit allowing for exaggeration, we need to color into our portrait of first-century Palestinian life the existence of lay communities of Essenes based in villages and towns, possibly running rudimentary sanatoria, where those unable to fend for themselves could be cared for and treated with dignity.

---

56. Josephus, *Ant.* 18.20, and Philo, *Prob.* 1.75. Philo places the Essenes exclusively in villages, whereas Josephus includes conurbations.

57. See Brian Capper's insightful article, "Essene Community Houses," 472–502. Following Philo's locating of Essene activity in Judaea (*Hypoth.* 11.1), Capper concludes that this network did not extend into Galilee. However, Josephus does not corroborate this—nor, for that matter, is Philo consistent as elsewhere he places Essene activity throughout "Palestinian Syria" (*hē Palaistinē Syria, Prob.* 75), which is what we have assumed here.

58. Philo, *Prob.* 87 [LCL 363]; see also Philo, *Hypoth.* 11.13, and Josephus, *J.W.* 2.136.

Exorcists

To complete the picture, mention must be made of two further and, in some cases, overlapping categories of Yahweh's mediators, namely, exorcists and religious healers.[59] We learn of the former, of course, from the Gospels themselves where Jesus challenges a delegation of Pharisees by what authority their exorcists cast out demons (Q 11:19 [Luke 11:19// Matt 12:27]). And then, again, Mark records the disciples reporting back to Jesus how they had attempted to stop someone who had been exorcising in his name (Mark 9:38–40; cf. Matt 7:22–23; Acts 19:13).

The practice of exorcism within Israelite tradition,[60] however, can be traced back at least as far as David, whose lyre-playing caused an evil spirit—sent, so it was believed, by Yahweh—to depart from Saul (1 Sam 16:14–23; cf. LAB 60). That said, according to the Genesis Apocryphon, one of the Dead Sea Scrolls from Qumran, the patriarch Abram conducted an exorcism upon the king of Egypt who had been struck down after making advances on Sarai, his wife, who had been masquerading as his sister (1QapGen 22.12–30; cf. Gen 12:10–20).

The figure from Israelite history most associated with exorcism, however, is Solomon,[61] whose unrivaled wisdom and literary creativity (1 Kgs 4:29–34; Prov 1:1; Eccl 1:1) extended through time to embrace the treatment of illness and demon possession. It is a reputation that may well be alluded to in the book of Wisdom[62] and is celebrated at length in the haggadic-styled folktale titled the Testament of Solomon (from between the first and third centuries CE) in which Israel's king is bestowed with a magic-seal ring by which he is able to subdue demons and perform other extraordinary feats. Equally, Josephus sings Solomon's praises in a

59. Neither of these is alluded to in Sir 38, which could simply be an omission, but may well reflect disapproval from the author, who had embraced a different understanding of how divine healing took place.

60. Fuller discussions of exorcism within Israelite faith traditions and beyond are supplied by Eve, *Jewish Context*, 326–49; Twelftree, *Jesus the Exorcist*, 13–52; and Witmer, *Galilean Exorcist*, 22–60.

61. Duling, "Solomon," 235–52; Duling, "Therapeutic," 392–410; and Le Donne, *Historiographical Jesus*, 137–90.

62. "For [God] gave me unerring knowledge of what exists . . . the natures of animals and the tempers of wild animals, the powers of spirits and the thoughts of human beings, the varieties of plants and the virtues of roots" (Wis 7:17, 20). As we have already noted, the pharmacological properties of plants and roots were broadly recognized and valued.

similar vein before drawing attention to a first-century Israelite exorcist by the name of Eleazar, whom he claims to have witnessed personally:

> And God granted him [Solomon] knowledge of the art used against demons for the benefit and healing of men. He also composed incantations by which illnesses are relieved, and left behind forms of exorcisms with which those possessed by demons drive them out, never to return. And this kind of cure is of very great power among us to this day, for I have seen a certain Eleazar, a countryman of mine, in the presence of Vespasian, his sons, tribunes and a number of other soldiers, free men possessed by demons, and this was the manner of the cure: he put to the nose of the possessed man a ring which had under its seal one of the roots prescribed by Solomon, and then, as the man smelled it, drew out the demon through his nostrils, and, when the man at once fell down, adjured the demon never to come back into him, speaking Solomon's name and reciting the incantations which he had composed. Then, wishing to convince the bystanders and prove to them that he had this power, Eleazar placed a cup or foot-basin full of water a little way off and commanded the demon, as it went out of the man, to overturn it and make known to the spectators that he had left the man. And when this was done, the understanding and wisdom of Solomon were clearly revealed, on account of which we have been induced to speak of these things, in order that all men may know the greatness of his nature and how God favored him, and that no one under the sun may be ignorant of the king's surpassing virtue of every kind.[63]

Further evidence of exorcism can be found in the book of Tobit previously mentioned, where a demon is expelled by the odor of burning fish entrails (Tob 8:1–3) and, again, in a poorly preserved Dead Sea Scroll that relates the prayer of a Babylonian king by the name of Nabonidus, who had suffered from an ulcer for seven years before a Judean exorcist pardoned his sins, which presumably, although this portion of the text is damaged, led to his recovery (4Q242).

Interestingly, one theory for the origin of the Jewish custom of wearing phylacteries, small boxes strapped to the forehead and inner left arm, is that they served as prophylactic amulets, affording protection from evil

---

63. Josephus, *Ant.* 8.45–49 [LCL 281].

spirits—a superstition later reinterpreted during the rabbinic era to serve a liturgical function as aids to prayer.[64]

Religious Healers

We find the following saying in the Mishnah:[65] "When Rabbi Hanina ben Dosa died, the men of (great) deeds ceased" (*Sota* 9.15). The nature of those deeds is not spelled out in that context, but elsewhere in the Mishnah and, more so, in later rabbinic literature, healings and wonders are attributed to him, becoming more and more incredible, in a comparable way to what happens to Jesus' miracles in some of the apocryphal gospels.[66] In addition to possessing a loyal donkey who goes on a hunger strike when rustled, Hanina is able to control the rain and stretch timber joists, as well as conjure up bread and, of all things, golden table legs.[67]

But the earliest traditions are much more modest, depicting him as a compassionate man of prayer whose inspired, extemporary petitions often seemed to intuit Yahweh's will. Consider this one, again from the Mishnah: "It is told concerning Rabbi Hanina ben Dosa that when he prayed for the sick he used to say, 'This one will live and this one will die.' They said to him, 'How do you know?' He replied, 'If my prayer is fluent in my mouth, I know that he (the sick person) is favored; if not, I know that (his disease) is fatal.'"[68] On the grounds that there is some historical basis to the later wonder stories attributed to him, it seems likely that Hanina was initially revered as a pious sage of discerning prayerfulness with a gift for intuiting the seriousness of patients' medical conditions.[69]

64. Fagen, "Phylacteries," 370.

65. The Mishnah is a collection of rabbinic oral tradition compiled towards the end of the second century of the Common Era but containing earlier material. Much of the contents is attributed to named rabbis, many of whom can be dated with reasonable accuracy. One of the best introductions is still Bowker, *Targums*.

66. Geza Vermes collates and evaluates all the rabbinic references to Hanina in two articles, "Hanina ben Dosa (1)," 28–50, and "Hanina ben Dosa (2)," 51–64. Vermes's contention that "charismatic holy man" was a recognized social type in first-century Palestine as exemplified by Hanina, Honi and Jesus has not won widespread support; see the discussions in Eve, *Healer from Nazareth*, 13–17; and Meier, *Marginal Jew*, 2:581–88.

67. b. Taʿan. 24b–25a; j. Demai 22a; ʾAbot R. Nat. A8.

68. m. Ber. 5:5; see also b. Ber. 34b, and j. Ber. 9d. Vermes's translations have been used.

69. "In the last analysis, all we can say with fair probability about the 'historical'

This reputation was subsequently embellished either to venerate him as a remarkable charismatic wonderworker or to subordinate him to the authorities of rabbinic Judaism. Hanina is an important figure in that he may well have been a contemporary of Jesus who, if later sources can be trusted,[70] resided in the vicinity of Sepphoris (Arav), no more than ten miles north of Nazareth.

Hope of Healing

"[The Lord's] works will never be finished, and peace from him is upon the surface of the earth." (v. 8 [NETS]; cf. "God's works will never be finished; and from him health spreads over all the earth." [NRSV]. One impression justifiably formed from Sir 38 is that Yahweh's healing ways were blossoming throughout Palestine in the second century BCE. This was almost certainly not the case. Although evidence is limited, what there is suggests that life expectancy was low throughout much of antiquity, predictably with significant variation determined by factors such as diet, sanitation, population density, political stability, geography, and climate. Unlike most advanced societies today where degenerative conditions (e.g., heart attack, cancer, stroke) are the principal killers, in first-century Galilee, like much of the ancient world, it was chronic and seasonal diseases, especially malaria, tuberculosis, and typhoid, that claimed the lives of many and left many of the survivors in a state of declining health.[71]

All this suggests that if Jesus commenced his ministry at thirty (cf. Luke 3:23), he would already have outlived a significant number of his peers and, no doubt, mourned the loss of many he held dear. What is more, he would have witnessed the diminishing effects of illness and impairment that, more often than not, went untreated. In addition to coping with debilitating symptoms, many sufferers were forced into penury and sometimes excluded from family and community life out of fear of contagion of one form or another. Then there were the judgments and scorn

---

Hanina is that he was a Palestinian Jew who lived in the 1st century AD, that he was noted for praying over the sick, and that he enjoyed the reputation of having precognition as to the results of his prayers for healing. That he lived in Galilee has no written attestation before the two Talmuds. Poverty and asceticism are likewise not attested in the earliest written traditions" (Meier, *Marginal Jew*, 2:587).

70. j. Ber. 7c; and b. Ber 34b.

71. This paragraph draws heavily on Jonathan Reed's article, "Mortality," 1:242–52. Reed provides an extensive bibliography.

of those who held such suffering to be divine punishment or comeuppance for wrongdoing. Sufferers may well have thought themselves to be accursed of God with little prospect of their circumstances improving in this life or the next.

Yet within—and, quite possibly, because of—this climate, a hope took shape that one day Yahweh would act decisively to heal Israel's wounds by freeing her from oppression and fulfilling her vocation to be a people of blessing. Unsurprisingly, restoration of physical well-being served as a potent signal or metaphor for its arrival—peace within the personal body reflecting peace within the covenantal body.[72] No one expressed this hope more lucidly than the prophet known to us as Deutero-Isaiah, composed during the Babylonian captivity of the sixth century BCE.

> The wilderness and the dry land shall be glad,
> the desert shall rejoice and blossom;
> like the crocus it shall blossom abundantly,
> and rejoice with joy and singing.
> The glory of Lebanon shall be given to it,
> the majesty of Carmel and Sharon.
> They shall see the glory of the LORD,
> the majesty of our God.
>
> Strengthen the weak hands,
> and make firm the feeble knees.
> Say to those who are of a fearful heart,
> "Be strong, do not fear!
> Here is your God.
> He will come with vengeance,
> with terrible recompense.
> He will come and save you."

72. It is possible that the language of sickness and healing is being employed metaphorically in such instances as mentioned earlier in this chapter. However, given the correlations between disorder within the human body and disorder within the covenantal body, especially as disordering behavior in the form of sin was widely identified as the cause, this seems an artificial dichotomy—a return to health within the covenantal body in the form of restored relations between Yahweh and Israel would yield a concomitant restoration of health within the bodies of Yahweh's covenantal people.

> Then the eyes of the blind shall be opened,
>
> and the ears of the deaf unstopped;
>
> then the lame shall leap like a deer,
>
> and the tongue of the speechless sing for joy.[73]

According to one tradition found in Matthew and Luke, it was to this passage, among others (Isa 26:19; 29:18; 42:7, 18; 61:1),[74] that Jesus alluded to when the disciples of John inquired whether he was "the one who is to come": "Go and tell John what you have seen and heard: the blind receive their sight, the lame walk, the lepers are cleansed, the deaf hear, the dead are raised, the poor have good news brought to them. And blessed is anyone who takes no offense at me."[75] Notice, in particular, the reference to raising the dead and preaching to the poor, along with various forms of healing, neither of which is mentioned in the Isaiah passage; in fact, while all six salvific acts can be found within the Isaiah references just mentioned, no one passage links healing with resuscitation and proclamation. However, they are found together in a fragmentary document discovered in Cave 4 at Qumran:

> . . . heaven and earth will obey his messiah . . . For he will glorify the pious on the throne of an eternal kingdom, releasing captives, giving sight to the blind and raising up those who are bo[wed down] . . . for he will heal the wounded, give life to the dead and preach good news to the poor and he will [sat]isfy the [weak] ones and lead those who have been cast out and enrich the hungry . . .[76]

The Hebrew script in this manuscript has been dated to the first century CE,[77] and therefore this document may well bear witness to the climate of hope that shaped Jesus' faith and informed his ministry. Certainly a lengthy Israelite prayer known as the Eighteen Benedictions (also *Tefillah*, *Shemoneh Esreh* or *Amidah*), which was recited daily and plausibly

---

73. Isa 35:1–6; also Isa 19:19–25; 26:19; 29:18; 61:1–2: How prevalent this embodiment of hope was in first-century Palestine is a question we shall return to in chapter 6.

74. There is no reference to the cleansing of lepers in Isaiah. Its inclusion in the Q tradition may reflect the influence of Elijah typology (cf. 2 Kgs 5) or the application of the Isaiah vision to the conditions of first-century Galilee.

75. Q 7:22–23 (Luke 7:22–23//Matt 11:4–6).

76. 4Q521 1, 7–8, 12–13.

77. Collins, "Works," 99: Collins's translation of 4Q521 has been adopted. This text will be discussed in greater detail in chapter 6.

predated the destruction of the Jerusalem temple in one form or another, reflects a similar outlook as the following petitions attest:[78]

> Forgive us, our Father, for we have sinned against You. Blot out and remove our transgressions from before Your sight, for Your mercies are manifold. You are praised, O Lord, who abundantly pardons . . . Look at our affliction, and champion our cause, and redeem us for the sake of Your Name. You are praised, O Lord, Redeemer of Israel . . . Heal us, O Lord our God, of the pain of our hearts. Remove from us grief and sighing, and bring healing for our wounds. You are praised, O Lord, who heals the sick of His people Israel.[79]

In fact, when the Eighteen Benedictions and the Lord's Prayer are placed side by side, their many similarities readily become apparent[80]—from how Yahweh is addressed ("Our Father," *abīnū*) through hallowing the divine name and establishing God's heavenly rule on earth to seeking daily sustenance, forgiveness, and protection. And, as we shall see, healing and exorcism were two ways Jesus sought to fulfil that prayer through his ministry.

78. The Mishnah attributes the following saying to Rabbi Gamaliel, a contemporary of Jesus (cf. Acts 5:34; 22:3): "A man should pray the Eighteen [Benedictions] every day" (m. Ber. 4:3 [MD]). The pre-70-CE origin of the prayer is suggested by the fourteenth petition, which assumes the Jerusalem temple is still standing ("Have compassion, O Lord . . . upon Your temple and upon Your abode."). Equally, it is generally thought that the twelfth petition (*Birkat ha-minim*), which dates from after the crucifixion when the followers of the Nazarene (i.e., Jesus) had emerged from the Jewish matrix ("May the Nazarenes and the sectarians perish as in a moment."), represents a later addition. See Instone-Brewer, "Eighteen Benedictions," 25–44. It should be noted that the date when the *Birkat ha-minim* first appeared in the *Shemoneh Esreh*, as well as its earliest wording, continue to be debated—see, especially, Langer, *Cursing the Christians?* We have used the translation prepared by Jakob Petuchowski in the book he edited with Michael Brocke, *Lord's Prayer*, 27–30. According to the Mishnah, the Tefillah was to be recited three times each day—morning, afternoon and evening (m. Ber 4:1).

79. Petuchowski, trans., "Eighteen Benedictions," benedictions 6–8.

80. Ernst Lohmeyer discusses these convergences throughout his book-length commentary, *Lord's Prayer*. Among briefer analyses, see Vögtle, "Lord's Prayer," 93–117; and Davies and Allison, *Matthew*, 1:590–99.

3

Introducing Jesus the Healer

IN THE PREVIOUS CHAPTER, we attempted to reconstruct how illness and impairment would have been experienced in first-century Palestine. We noted that while there was a growing awareness of divinely ordained intermediaries, such as physicians and medicines, Yahweh, Israel's God, was recognized as the ultimate source of all healing. We also noted that illness tended to be viewed theologically, often resulting from disordering, sinful behavior either as a consequence of wrongdoing or as divinely ordained punishment for the same—resulting in a close association between repentance, forgiveness, and healing. In a culture where disease etiology was extremely limited, certain self-destructive and life-threatening patterns of behavior came to be recognized as resulting not from sinful conduct or divine decree, but from some form of spiritual oppression, requiring exorcism as a remedy.

Further, although there was no state-sponsored healthcare system in operation, we identified the presence of self-styled physicians who may have been influenced by the Hippocratic tradition of medicine emanating from Greece or from some other school of thought (e.g., dogmatists, empiricists). It is probable that the use of naturally occurring medicines was well established, and it is possible that Essenes maintained rudimentary sanatoria in some villages and towns throughout Palestine. We reviewed evidence suggestive of the presence of exorcists, some possibly associated with the Pharisees, as well as charismatic holy men such as Hanina ben Dosa. And finally we noted how the language of illness and healing was employed, mainly by the Hebrew prophets, to describe the state of Israel's covenantal relationship and to express hope for a time when Yahweh's sovereign presence would be experienced as a blessing rather than either as an absence or, worse still, as punishment for disobedience.

In a nutshell, these are some of the defining characteristics of the culture and climate within which we must set Jesus' ministry. Before proceeding, we need to unpack further some of the implications of claiming that illness and healing were viewed theologically rather than medically. If we are correct in concluding that a breakdown in health within an Israelite's body was thought to result from or contribute to a breakdown in health within the covenantal body of Israel and its God, then illness and healing become essentially relational in nature, reflecting the state of repair within communities as well as between communities and Yahweh.[1] Within this interpretative framework, healing mediates blessing on at least three levels—personal, social, and spiritual, as sufferers are restored to health and thereby enabled to participate fully in community life, including public worship and other forms of religious practice. No longer deemed to be contagious or morally corrupt or a drain on a family's limited resources, one's life experience as a sufferer would have been transformed: onetime sufferers would have been liberated from the debilitation, stigmatization, and judgment that illness or impairment conveyed.[2]

A Follower of the Baptist

With this is mind, we turn our attention to the Gospels to reevaluate the basis for Jesus' reputation for healing and exorcism, earned within the context of his ministry—a ministry that, according to all four evangelists, began with or was preceded by an encounter with the prophet and immerser, John.[3] The fact that Jesus sought out John, underwent his

1. Although adopting a different approach, Richard Horsley also recognizes the relational aspect of Jesus' healing ministry in Horsley, *Jesus and Magic*, 119–42; and Horsley, *Jesus and the Politics*, 80–107.

2. Wendy Cotter develops this line of thinking throughout her book, *Christ*.

3. Mark 1:9–11//Matt 3:13–17//Luke 3:21–22; although John does not actually record Jesus' baptism, it can be inferred from this text: "And John testified, 'I saw the Spirit descending from heaven like a dove, and it remained on him. I myself did not know him, but the one who sent me to baptize with water said to me, "He on whom you see the Spirit descend and remain is the one who baptizes with the Holy Spirit." And I myself have seen and have testified that this is the Son of God'" (John 1:32–34). Jesus' baptism by John is also recorded in a number of the apocryphal gospels (e.g., Gos. Heb. 6; Gos. Eb. 4).

baptism, and quite possibly served as a disciple and coworker for a period suggests that he embraced John's message and program. Again, John Meier speaks for many scholars when he writes:

> While it is more difficult to discern exactly what his being baptized meant to Jesus, it (along with the events surrounding it) certainly involved a basic break with his past life, his confession that he was a member of a sinful Israel that had turned away from its God, his turning or "conversion" to a life fully dedicated to Israel's religious heritage and destiny, his acknowledgement of John as an eschatological prophet, his embrace of John's message of imminent eschatology, and his submission to the special ritual washing John alone administered and considered part of the way to salvation.[4]

The location of John's operation in Judea, along the stretch of the River Jordan associated with the initial Israelite settlement of the promised land (Josh 4; cf. Exod 14), is significant in that some of John's compatriots evidently expected another exodus-like deliverance would take place there in the imminent future. Josephus informs us of a certain Theudas (cf. Acts 5:36) who, during the procuratorship of Fadus (44–46 CE), "persuaded the majority of the masses to take up their possessions and to follow him to the Jordan River. He stated that he was a prophet and that at his command the river would be parted and would provide them an easy passage" (*Ant.* 20:97–98 [LCL 456]). Fadus swiftly dealt with this potential insurrection, killing and imprisoning many.

So the setting was associated with hope of deliverance in the minds of at least some Israelites, where John's call for radical inner repentance with ritual cleansing to escape impending judgment and undergo purification would have seemed particularly apt. Although there is considerable uncertainty over whom John expected to administer this judgment and purification ("the coming one"),[5] it seems likely he envisaged Yahweh intervening in human history once more via a messiah-like emissary

4. Meier, *Marginal Jew*, 2:129 (116–30); see also Chilton, *Jesus' Baptism*, 34–45; and Hollenbach, "Conversion," 196–219.

5. Mark 1:7//Matt 3:11//Luke 3:16//John 1:27; Matt 11:3; 7:19. Davies and Allison, *Matthew* 1:312–13, cite six options (God, Son of Man, one of John's disciples, Elijah, the messiah, no one in particular) before opting for the messiah, who John may have conceived of as an Elijah *redivivus* figure. For a fuller discussion on this and all aspects of the Baptist's message and movement see, Webb, *John the Baptizer*; Taylor, *John the Baptist*; and Wink, *John the Baptist*. For a convenient summary, consult Hollenbach, "John the Baptist."

to rescue repentant, upright Israelites from their corrupt counterparts ("snakes' litter," Q 3:7 [*CEQ*; Luke 3:7//Matt 3:7]) as well as from their godless ruler (i.e., Herod Antipas: Mark 6:17–18//Matt 14:3–4; Luke 3:19–20), with a view to being restored into a holy remnant of Israel:

> I baptize you with water; but one who is more powerful than I is coming; I am not worthy to untie the thong of his sandals. He will baptize you with the Holy Spirit and fire [or "fiery breath"]. His winnowing fork is in his hand, to clear his threshing floor and to gather the wheat into his granary; but the chaff he will burn with unquenchable fire.[6]

A major difficulty presented by the evangelists' accounts of John is that they are written from a Christian perspective where the Baptist is framed as Jesus' forerunner and inferior rather than as his mentor, and where the latter becomes the one expected by the former. These verses from the sayings source Q, however, with the probable exception of the phrase "I am not worthy to carry his sandals," are largely free from Christianizing influences. It is possible that "holy" and even "spirit" are later additions, although the linking of fire, water, and judgment is not unusual in Hebrew apocalyptic literature where we also find spirit and judgment paired.[7] While Matthew and Luke may have added "holy" from Mark's version (1:8), "spirit" needn't imply Christian influence, and it could be that what was intended here is a hendiadys, namely, not "fire and spirit," but a baptism with "fiery breath" to purify the faithful and purge away the unrepentant. Robert Webb makes the interesting suggestion that the "threshing floor" in view here is the land of Israel,[8] underlining that John's program extended beyond gathering a holy remnant to restoring a holy land where Yahweh's chosen people could dwell in covenantal fidelity.

In addition to the gospel references, Josephus supplies us with a brief account of John which, unlike his comments about Jesus, appears to be unadulterated by Christian redactors:

> For Herod had put him to death, though he was a good man and had exhorted the Jews to lead righteous lives, to practice justice towards their fellows and piety towards God and so doing to join in baptism. In his view this was a necessary preliminary if

---

6. Q 3:16–17 (Luke 3:16–17//Matt 3:11–12).

7. See Davies and Allison, *Matthew*, 2:316–17, for references. We have also taken the following hendiadys suggestion from them.

8. Webb, *John the Baptizer*, 304.

baptism was to be acceptable to God. They must not employ it to gain pardon for whatever sins they committed, but as a consecration of the body implying that the soul was already thoroughly cleansed by right behavior. When others came to join the crowds about him, because they were aroused to the highest degree by his sermons, Herod became alarmed. Eloquence that had so great an effect on mankind might lead to some form of sedition, for it looked as if they would be guided by John in everything that they did. Herod decided therefore that it would be much better to strike first and be rid of him before his work led to an uprising, than to wait for an upheaval . . .[9]

Interestingly, although Josephus cites John's popularity and influence as the reason for Herod Antipas' acting against him, Mark relates the somewhat unlikely plot whereby John's condemnation of Antipas's marriage to his brother Philip's wife resulted in the Baptist's severed head being presented to the daughter of Herodias following the daughter's mesmerizing dance, which placed the tetrarch under her spell (Mark 6:17–29; also Matt 14:3–12; cf. Luke 3:19–20). That said, Luke's ethical exhortation is entirely compatible with Josephus's portrayal of John (Luke 3:10–14). What is noteworthy for our purposes is that none of these sources refer to John carrying out healings or exorcisms (cf. John 10:41).[10] Equally, John isn't remembered for employing the language of illness and disease to describe the condition of Israel as a whole or especially egregious individuals in particular. If he had, given his message, more likely than not he would have viewed illness as a scourge, and anticipation of future judgment to be visited upon those who failed to keep covenant with Israel's God.

To recap, then, before Jesus began to earn a reputation for himself, he was impressed by the reputation of another, namely, John. From what we can gather, he was persuaded by the Baptist's reading of the present predicament and convictions about how Yahweh would remedy the situation. Like John, Jesus expected God to act decisively as judge to gather a holy remnant from a wayward and, in some cases, corrupt people—as well as, quite possibly, as vanquisher to create a holy land by driving out

9. Josephus, *Ant.* 18.116–19 [LCL 433].

10. Indirect evidence may be implied in the speculation generated by Jesus' disciples as they begin to share in his ministry of healing and deliverance: "John the baptizer has been raised from the dead; and for this reason these powers are at work in him" (Mark 6.14). However, the reference to "these powers" (*hai dynameis*) is too vague and, in the absence of more compelling evidence, proves inconclusive.

all infidels, including their Roman overlords.[11] Further, for a season, Jesus may well have worked alongside John in proclaiming this message, calling fellow Israelites to repentance, and baptizing those who responded accordingly.

Evidence That Jesus Healed

All this brings into focus one question which, as we shall see, is germane to our investigation: What caused Jesus to depart from key components of John's outlook and program? For example, why did he stop baptizing and shift emphasis away from divine judgment as a stimulus for repentance onto divine immanence as a source of blessing, especially for the marginalized and undeserving?[12] This is particularly puzzling given that baptism rapidly became the ubiquitous rite of Christian initiation,[13] and that at least some in the early Jesus movement anticipated God's immanent, cataclysmic judgment.[14] And this, in turn, leads to a second, not unrelated, question: What was the basis for Jesus' impact and popularity during his ministry? Why were people attracted to him, and on what was his reputation based? We shall leave these open for the time being and return to them as we proceed. For now, we will review the Gospel

11. Interestingly, we find a similar set expectations in the Judean work, the Psalms of Solomon (second century BCE—first century CE), chapters 17 and 18, where the Lord's messiah of Davidic stock will purge Israel of impure Gentiles, as well as cleanse wayward Israelites of their sinful ways.

12. The key point to note here is a shift in emphasis. We are not claiming that Jesus ceased to believe there would be a final reckoning orchestrated by Yahweh (e.g., Mark 8:38–9:1; 13:24–30; Luke 12:40; 17:26–27), but rather that at some point and for a reason we will suggest shortly he began to invest most of his time and energy (if the Gospels are any guide) in ministering to the presenting needs of those around him, whether or not they heeded his message. For John, anticipation of future divine reckoning was the motivation for change in the present; for Jesus, the experience of blessing in the present was the motivation for future change. Marcus Borg talks about Jesus' "Secondary Apocalyptic Gestalt," by which he means "that, in addition to whatever else Jesus was doing and teaching, he thought that God would soon intervene to vindicate or complete what Jesus had begun. But apocalyptic conviction was not the primary energy driving his mission or shaping his teaching." In the same volume, Dominic Crossan refers to an "eschatological, non-apocalyptic Jesus" where the prospect of divine consummation in the future becomes the driver for transformation in the present. See Borg, "Not an Apocalyptic Prophet," 44; and Crossan, "Not an Apocalyptic Prophet," 69.

13. E.g., Acts 2:38; Rom 6:3–4; 1 Cor 1:14–17; Heb 6:1–2; 1 Pet 3:21–22.

14. E.g., 1 Cor 15:50–52; 1 Thess 4:15–17; Jas 5:7–9; Rev 19–22.

material relating to Jesus as a healer, beginning with an overview of the symptoms he is reported to have treated:[15]

- Chronic hemorrhaging (*rhysis haimatos/pēgē haimatos/haimorreō,* also described as *mastix*—"scourge" [see below]; Mark 5:24–34// Matt 9:20–22//Luke 8:42–48)[16]

- Deafness (*kōphos;* Mark 7:31–37; also Q 7:22 [Luke 7:22//Matt 11:5]; Matt 15:29–31)[17]

- Deformed limbs (*kyllos;* Matt 15:29–31)

- Dropsy/oedema (*hdrōpikos;* Luke 14:1–6)

- Fever (*pyressō/pyretos,* from *pyr*—"fire"; hence to be "on fire," "burning up"; Mark 1:29–31//Matt 8:14–15//Luke 4:38–39; John 4:46–54)

- Lameness (*chōlos;* Q 7:22 [Luke 7:22//Matt 11:5]; Matt 15:29–31; 21:14)

- Moonstruck/"epilepsy" (*selēniazomai;* Matt 4:23–24; 17:14–20)

- Blindness (*typhlos;* Mark 10:46–52//Matt 20:29–34//Luke 18:35–43; Mark 8:22–26; John 9:1–41; also Q 7:22 [Luke 7:22//Matt 11:5]; Matt 15:29–31; 21:14; Luke 7:21)

- Paralysis/inability to walk/limb weakness (*paralytikos/paralyō;* Mark 2:1–12//Matt 9:1–8//Luke 5:17–26; Matt 8:5–13 [cf. Luke 7:1–10])

- Severed ear (*aphaireō;* Luke 22:49–51; cf. Mark 14:47//Matt 26:51–52)

- Skin eruptions/leprous conditions (*lepros/lepra/lepraō;* Mark 1:40–45//Matt 8:1–4//Luke 5:12–16//Pap. Eg. 2:11–23; Luke 17:11–19; also Q 7:22 [Luke 7:22//Matt 11:5])[18]

15. In compiling this list, I have used *BAGD,* the standard New Testament Greek lexicon, to check meanings of rare or technical terms.

16. Given it is highly unlikely that the woman received blood transfusions, the rate of blood loss can't have been life-threatening or else the duration of twelve years must be grossly overestimated. Excessive menstrual discharge may be in view here, although an inability to conceive could be the underlying concern.

17. Depending on context, *kōphos* can also mean "mute" (Matt 9:33) and even "deaf and mute" (3 Macc 4:16).

18. Contrary to van der Loos (*Miracles of Jesus,* 464–79), Wendy Cotter has demonstrated convincingly that *lepra* is unlikely to include Hansen's disease, for which another word was in use, *elephantiasis* (e.g., Pliny the Elder, *Nat.* 26.5; Cotter, *Christ,*

- Speech impediment (*mogilalos*; Mark 7:31–37)[19]

- Spinal deformation (*sygkyptō*, literally "to be bent over," also described as *astheneia*—"bodily weakness" [see below]; Luke 13:10–17).

- Wasting/withering (*xēros/xērainō*, literally "drying up"; legs: John 5:1–9; hand: Mark 3:1–6//Matt 12:9–14//Luke 6:6–11).

In addition, there are a number of more generic references where no particular symptoms are mentioned:

- Disease/illness (*nosos*; Mark 1:32–34//Luke 4:40–41; Matt 4:23–24; 9:35; Luke 6:17–19; 7:21)

- Malady/sickness (*kakōs*, literally "badly"; Mark 1:32–34//Matt 8:16–17; Mark 6:53–55//Matt 14:34–36; Luke 7:1–10)

- Weakness/sickness (*malakia*, literally "softness"; Matt 4:23–24; 9:35)

- Torment/searing pain (*basanos*; Matt 4:23–24)

- Distress/turmoil (*synechō*; Matt 4:23–24)

- Infirmity (*astheneia/astheneō*, literally "weakness"; Luke 4:40–41; 5:15; 7:1–10; 13:10–17)

- Suffering/torment (*mastix*, literally "scourge"; Mark 3:7–12; 5:24–34; Luke 7:21)

- Sick/ill (*arrōstos*, literally "powerless"; Mark 6:5; Matt 14:14)

Then there are the references to exorcisms, which we will look at in chapter 5, as well as the resuscitations or raisings from the dead, which lie beyond the scope of the present study but are recorded here for completeness.[20]

- Daughter of Jairus (Mark 5:21–24a, 35–43//Matt 9:18–19, 23–26// Luke 8:40–42, 49–56).

23–25). Bruce Chilton proposes that "outbreak" is an appropriate rendering for the Hebrew *sara'at* found in Leviticus chapters 13 and 14, stressing that the issue at stake is whether or not the body's protective layer (skin) had been compromised (*Jesus' Baptism*, 58–59; see also Pilch, *Healing*, 42–45).

19. *Mogilalos* can also mean "mute," which may be its force here as those who learn of the healing respond, "He [Jesus] has done everything well; he even makes the deaf to hear and the mute (*alalos*) to speak" (Mark 7:37; cf. *mogilalon*, 7:32). Unlike *mogilalos*, *alalos* only denotes an inability to speak.

20. See the Appendix for a brief discussion of Jesus' resuscitations, together with an explanation for why they fall outside the scope of the present investigation.

- Son of the widow of Nain (Luke 7:11–17).

- Lazarus, Jesus' friend (John 11:1–45).

- Jesus' response to John (Q 7:22 [Luke 7:22//Matt 11:5]).

Before taking a detailed look at these healing traditions, a number of preliminary observations can be made. First, with the exception of the high priest's servant who loses an ear and, possibly, the sufferer whom Matthew describes as being "moonstruck" (*selēniazomai*), these stories and summaries refer to *symptoms* rather than diagnoses.[21] As is congruent with what was said earlier about the rudimentary state of disease etiology in the ancient world, no attempt is made to explain the underlying medical condition or cause; rather, we are simply offered a brief description of the presenting malfunctions, leaving the reader to muse over how they came about. For example, Mark informs us that Peter's mother-in-law was in bed with a "fever" or, literally, was "burning up" (*pyressousa*, Mark 1:30); he does not attempt to explain why she was indisposed in this manner (malaria?).

Pieter Craffert alerts us to the dangers of projecting what he describes as our current "biomedical model" onto Jesus' healing stories in order to offer a disease etiology and diagnosis that makes sense to us.[22] He argues convincingly that health, healing, disease and illness are not universals which denote the same thing and are experienced in the same way across cultures and through time. Even where the ancient description of the underlying medical condition is similar or even identical with a contemporary understanding, its impact upon the sufferer—as well as on those people, communities, and institutions making up that person's world—would have been very different in the ancient world from today, rendering any attempt at comparison problematic, if not impossible.[23] In an similar vein, John Pilch, drawing on insights from anthropology,

21. Justin Meggitt makes a similar point when he writes, "Firstly, we do not know with any certainty what kind of disorders were suffered by those whom Jesus healed. As has long been noted, the gospels are notoriously short on detailed clinical description and medical terminology" ("Historical Jesus," 30).

22. This is something John Wilkinson, a medical physician as well as a biblical scholar, attempts in *Health and Healing*, 23–26. The problem is that there is simply no way of knowing; what is more, even if we could successfully identify an underlying condition, say, heart-failure, how that condition was understood, experienced, and managed or treated would have been radically different in the first century than today, rendering any comparison misleading.

23. Craffert, *Galilean Shaman*, 260–66.

distinguishes between *emic* and *etic* perspectives,[24] the former reflecting the "insider's" point of view with the latter the "outsider's." Applied to Jesus' healings, this distinction brings into focus two discrete interpretative tasks that can readily become blurred or merged into one, namely, attempting to reconstruct how Jesus' healing activity was experienced and interpreted by his peers and early followers (emic), and attempting to account for it in the light of twenty-first-century medical science and anthropology (etic).

Second, by far the majority of the symptoms fall within the scope of those that could have been induced by *nonbiological factors*. It would be anachronistic to describe them as psychosomatic for, as Craffert observes, mind-body dualism underpinning such a diagnosis belongs to the biomedical paradigm defining Western medicine today, which is informed by assumptions not shared by those living in first-century Palestine or, indeed, by anyone at that time. In its place, he advocates a *biopsychosocial paradigm* that rejects mind-body dualism and the prioritization of biological causation or medical intervention in favor of a wholly integrated approach where a patient isn't treated as an independent entity but as belonging to a nexus of relationships and structures, and where health and disease are modes of being that can be affected by a broad range of factors—psychological, biological, environmental, sociopolitical, cultural, and spiritual. Within this paradigm, disease reflects disintegration or "disequilibrium" within the sufferer's world, and healing occurs when balance is restored or, to use his phrase, where there is "successful psychobiological adaption to the environment."[25]

Much of this is in line with the approach we are adopting in this book, but Craffert helpfully coins the phrase "culture-specific syndrome" to describe "conditions that are reactive to psychosocial and cultural circumstances." He draws a comparison with what is described in the *Diagnostic and Statistical Manual of Mental Disorders* (DSM-IV) as "somatization disorder" where no biological or organic cause has been identified. It is worth quoting his summary of the *Manual's* list of symptoms or conditions that can fall within this syndrome:

> According to the DSM-IV (see DSM-IV 1994, 446–50) *somatization disorder* covers a whole spectrum of bodily sites of pain or discomfort (head, abdomen, back, joints, extremities, chest,

24. Pilch, *Healing*.
25. Craffert, *Galilean Shaman*, 266–78.

and rectum), while the clinical symptoms listed include nausea, vomiting, diarrhea, intolerance of food, excessive menstrual bleeding, urinary retention, sexual dysfunctions, paralysis, blindness, deafness, seizures, amnesia, fainting, difficulty swallowing, a lump in the throat, and hallucinations.[26]

What is more, Craffert draws attention to modern diseases of civilization or affluence (e.g., obesity, hypertension, cardiovascular disease, some forms of cancer) where "although pathogenic organisms or genetic predispositions might be present in some of these conditions, their onset cannot be divorced from the culturally constituted environmental and psychological conditions."[27] Clearly there are similarities here with his proposed culture-specific syndromes of the first century, and it is significant that most of the symptoms Jesus is recorded as having treated fall within the reach of somatization disorder. It is important to stress that symptoms induced by nonbiological factors are no less real or debilitating; equally and significantly, it would be entirely congruent if patients suffering these symptoms were healed through nonbiological factors as well.[28] Recent research into the placebo response[29] demonstrates beyond reasonable doubt the therapeutically effective contribution made by nonphysical factors such as trust, expectation, and symbolic intervention,

26. Craffert, *Galilean Shaman*, 274; see also the book by consultant neurologist, Suzanne O'Sullivan, *All in Your Head*.

27. Craffert, *Galilean Shaman*, 274.

28. Meggitt, "Historical Jesus," rejects such nonphysical etiologies, claiming that "if the success of Jesus was limited to those individuals presenting with symptoms that have a psychosomatic basis alone surely such a pattern should be discernible in the records" (31). However, is this not in fact what we have? For example, we have no records of Jesus supplying missing body parts or mending broken bones or healing gaping wounds. It is true that Luke records him restoring the severed ear of one of his arrestors (Luke 22:49–51), but given that this detail is missing from the other Synoptics (Mark 14:47//Matt 26:51–52), it is probably redactional. Meggitt also draws attention to two cases where it is claimed that sufferers were born with their symptoms (Mark 9:21; John 9:1). Again, this is not persuasive given that emphasizing the length/extent of suffering is a recognized characteristic of the miracle genre and, as such, may well be a secondary embellishment. See Bultmann, *History*, 221; and Theissen, *Miracle Stories*, 51–52.

29. "The 'placebo response' may most usefully be defined as a change in a person's health status that is caused by the symbolic aspects of a therapeutic intervention . . . I have offered a definition of 'placebo response' without attempting first to define a placebo. This approach is important because the most fruitful accounts of placebo response do not restrict the term solely to circumstances in which an actual placebo is employed" (Brody, "Ritual," 151).

when exercised within certain relationships and frameworks of meaning, to the treatment of a broad range of medical conditions. Justin Meggitt, surveying recent literature, observes:

> Placebo-induced symptom relief has been reported in an impressively wide range of illnesses, including allergies, angina pectoris, asthma, cancer, cerebral infarction, depression, diabetes, enuresis, neurosis, ocular pathology, Parkinsonism, prostatic hyperplasia, schizophrenia, skin diseases, ulcers and warts and so on . . . Indeed, as it stands it appears that placebo responses can be seen in virtually all conditions (although the clinical data has tended to be focused, for historical reasons, upon symptoms related to pain). The point to note here is that placebos have been shown to effect not just a patient's subjective *perception* of a symptom (such as pain) but also in bodily processes that are objectively observable and measurable.[30]

Self-evidently, the medical term "culture-specific syndrome" is as anachronistic to a first-century milieu as "psychosomatic disorder"; however, as we have already demonstrated, there was by then a growing appreciation of how someone's body could be affected by factors influencing that person's outlook and sense of well-being. We mentioned earlier that the idea of alien substances (antigens, bacteria, viruses) invading the body was largely unknown in the ancient world; disease was thought to reflect imbalance or disorder within a person's constitution—in the case of the Hippocratic tradition, represented by the four humors. What is more, the body's imbalance or disorder could reflect or be caused by, among other things, dis-ease within the covenantal or societal body to which the sufferer belonged. Hence, as a consequence of this reciprocal dynamic, changing a patient's external "climate" was recognized as a means of affecting the internal climate as well. An obvious instance of this, already alluded to, is when a penitent recognizes the disruption in relationships caused by wrongdoing, seeks to assuage guilt by restoring right-relating with Yahweh and other affected parties through repentance, and then experiences a restoration in physical health as a consequence (cf. Ps 32).

Third, most of the symptoms treated by Jesus are of a *chronic, debilitating nature*, which would have left sufferers incapable of earning

---

30. Meggitt, "Historical Jesus," 33. The literature relating to the placebo response is vast, including the following volumes: Frank and Frank, *Persuasion and Healing*; Shapiro and Shapiro, *Powerful Placebo*; Guess et al., *Science*; Moerman, *Meaning*: Dispenza, *Placebo*.

a living within an agrarian economy where most employment outside of conurbations involved physical exertion and manual labor. Further, their ability to contribute to family and community life would have been seriously impaired, and, in cases where symptoms rendered a sufferer ritually unclean, curtailed altogether. Richard Horsley highlights both the communal and socioeconomic impact of these illnesses upon rural life. He writes:

> All of them are fundamentally debilitating in the socio-econom-ic as well as the personal sense. The sicknesses that appear in the earliest gospel texts all consist of some kind of serious disabling of the basic personal functions necessary for productive social life in an agrarian society. That blind Bar-Timaeus had become a beggar beside the road, for example, gives a clear indication of how blindness left people utterly incapable of productive activity and normal participation in family and community. Blindness, deafness, paralyzed legs, withered hands, and demon possession are all long-term disablings of the most fundamental functions of personal and social life, without which a person cannot func-tion in social-economic life and without which a society cannot long survive.[31]

Seeing bodily disease as symptomatic of societal disease chimes with what we were saying earlier about the dynamic and reciprocal nature of the relationship between the individual Israelite and the covenantal community. Horsley pushes beyond this when he claims that the kind of illnesses Jesus treated not only evidenced malaise within Israelite village life but also characterized "peoples impacted by colonial/imperial inva-sion or conquest." In this way, he locates Jesus' healing ministry within its first-century political context, suggesting that the diseases he healed were manifestations of an oppressed people experiencing social disintegration under Roman hegemony. But, equally, if there was a political dimension to sickness, then presumably there was also a political dimension to Jesus' response: "healings and exorcisms are the principal manifestations of the renewal of Israel under the direct kingship of God."[32]

Fourth, all the symptoms Jesus heals entailed *restoring the func-tionality of existing body parts or organs* rather than replacing defective ones or even generating missing members ex nihilo. We do not find in the Gospels the equivalent of the following inscription discovered at

31. Horsley, *Jesus and the Politics,* 98; see also Horsley, *Jesus and Magic,* 119–42.
32. Horsley, *Jesus and the Politics,* 106, 99–100.

Epidaurus in the Peloponnese concerning a blind man with a missing eyeball who approached the shrine of Asclepius, seeking healing:

> A man came as a supplicant to the god. He was so blind that of one of his eyes he had only the eyelids left—within them was nothing, but they were entirely empty. Some of those in the temple laughed at his silliness to think that he could recover his sight when one of his eyes had not even a trace of the ball, but only the socket. As he slept a vision appeared to him. It seemed to him that the god prepared some drug, then, opening his eyelids, poured it into them. When day came he departed with the sight of both eyes restored.[33]

This omission, of course, is open to multiple explanations—for example, Jesus may not have been approached by anyone with a missing body part or with one beyond repair—but it does seem significant that he has been remembered principally as a restorer of health rather than as a conjurer or magician.[34] As we shall see, this resonates with the motivation for and meaning of these bodily restorations within Jesus' overall kingdom vision.

Fifth, although not a comment on the range of symptoms Jesus is reputed to have healed, it is worth noting at this stage that Jesus *didn't consider healing or exorcism to be his exclusive prerogative*—an inference that can be drawn from the well-attested recollection that Jesus called apprentices to work alongside him who, as part of this, were also expected to heal and exorcise.[35] On two occasions Mark records how Jesus authorized

---

33. *IG* 4.121–22 (Stele 1.9), quoted in Cotter, *Miracles*, 17. The inscription is preserved on a stone stele dated to the third or fourth century BCE. A similar feat is also recorded for the Neo-Pythagorean Apollonius of Tyana (c. 15–100 CE; Philostratus, *Vit. Apoll.* 3.39).

34. This is disputed, of course, notably by Morton Smith in *Jesus the Magician*. However, Richard Horsley has convincingly argued that concepts of miracle and magic are products of Enlightenment thinking with no immediate correlates within the Israelite faith tradition: "Jesus was not performing miracles or practicing magic. To apply these concepts to the healing and exorcism (stories) of Jesus is to modernize him. The investigations in these chapters indicate that the concept of miracle and magic under which the healing and exorcist (stories) of Jesus have been classified and interpreted are the products of Enlightenment reason shaped by (natural and social) scientific perspective. The concept of miracle and especially the concept of magic were also influenced by colonial and orientalist attitudes. Interpretation of Jesus and the field of New Testament studies in general somehow became stuck in these modern constructs" (Horsley, *Jesus and Magic*, 163).

35. On whether Jesus called disciples to share in his mission and whether this

disciples to cast out demons (*ta daimonia*, 3:15) or unclean spirits (*tōn pneumatōn tōn akathartōn*, 6:7), while Jesus' mission charge recorded in Q includes the injunction to "cure the sick (*therapeuete tous en autē asthenountas*)."[36] On top of this, Mark narrates one healing-exorcism where Jesus intervenes after the disciples had proved ineffective, which concludes with a mini case review (9:14–29). Additionally, as mentioned in chapter 1, it would be difficult to account for why healings and exorcisms were attributed to the apostles in the early Christian movement if Jesus hadn't authorized such ministry when alive.

Recognition that Jesus expected at least the inner core of disciples to share in his ministry of both proclaiming the proximity of God's reign and demonstrating its dawning through healings and exorcisms, suggests that such acts reflect not so much his particular genius or anointing as what becomes possible when someone inhabits his worldview—that is, participates in his vision of Yahweh's sovereign presence informing what is possible in the here and now, shaping the future. Evidently, Jesus was challenged to perform wonders to establish his theological credentials, and before long the early church was putting them to work in this way,[37] but initially they served a different purpose—manifestations of covenantal promise fulfilled.

An Applicable Distinction?

Before proceeding further, we need to introduce a technical distinction between *disease* and *illness* that has been employed by some New Testament scholars when interpreting Jesus' wonderworking. In normal

---

included exorcism and healing see Meier, *Marginal Jew*, 3:40–197; and Twelftree, *Name of Jesus*, 49–54.

36. Q 10:9 (Luke 10:9). The authors of the critical edition of Q reconstruct the mission charge principally from Luke 9 and Matt 10, finding corroboration for the inclusion of this injunction in the Gospel of Thomas 14:4: "And when you go into the land and walk in the countryside, if they receive you, eat whatever they place before you and heal the sick among them" (*CEQ*, 174–75). There are also additional references to healing and exorcism in Matthew (e.g., 10:1, 8) and Luke (e.g., 9:1, 6).

37. Mark 8:11–12; Q 11:29–32 (Luke 11:29–32//Matt 12:38–42); Matt 16:1–4; Luke 11:15–16. This outlook, which is already evident within the Synoptic Gospels in nascent form (e.g., Q 7:18–23 [Luke 7:18–23//Matt 11:2–6]; Matt 8:16–17), clearly characterizes John's approach and can be found in Acts (e.g., 2:22; 10:38), as well as in many other early Christian writings. See Lampe, "Miracles," 205–18, Wiles, "Miracles," 221–34, and Brown, *Miracles*, 3–20.

parlance, of course, these words are used interchangeably; however, within the discipline of medical anthropology they are often distinguished, where *disease* relates to the biological, mental, or psychological malfunctioning of the body, and *illness* denotes the personal and social responses to such malfunctioning.[38] To use a contemporary example, those who contract AIDS suffer not only from a pernicious viral infection, a disease, but also, in many cases, regrettably from the opprobrium surrounding this condition in certain quarters as well as, sometimes, from a sense of guilt or judgment—that is, from an illness.

This distinction has significant implications for our investigation. For instance, it is possible to heal an illness and not cure the underlying disease—we could challenge the prejudices associated with AIDS, while affirming the humanity of sufferers, without recourse to antiretroviral drugs. Equally, we could cure a disease, but still be unable to heal the illness—let's say a cure for AIDS had been found and had been administered successfully to a patient, others may still choose to be hostile, judgmental, and closed.

In a number of publications, John Dominic Crossan has drawn on this distinction to conclude that Jesus earned a reputation for healing illness without curing disease. Commenting on Jesus' encounter with a leper narrated in Mark 1, he writes with characteristic eloquence and rhetorical force:

> Was he [Jesus] curing the disease through an intervention in the physical world, or was he healing the illness through an intervention in the social world? I presume that Jesus, who did not and could not cure that disease or any other one, healed the poor man's illness by refusing to accept the disease's ritual uncleanness and social ostracization . . . By healing the illness without curing the disease, Jesus acted as an alternative boundary keeper in a way subversive to the established procedures of his society . . . Jesus heals by refusing to accept traditional and official sanctions against the diseased person. Jesus heals him, in other words, by taking him into a community of the

---

38. "*Disease* refers to a malfunctioning of biological and/or psychological processes, while the term *illness* refers to the psychological experience and meaning of perceived disease. Illness includes secondary personal and social responses to the primary malfunctioning (disease) in the individual's physiological or psychological status" (Kleinman, *Patients and Healers*, 72); also Eisenberg, "Disease and Illness," 7–23; Pilch, *Healing*, 24–25; and Young, "Anthropologies," 257–85.

marginalized and disenfranchised—into, in fact, the Kingdom of God.[39]

Self-evidentially, this explanation is highly attractive to the modern liberal Western mind, but does it account for all the evidence and related issues convincingly? For a number of reasons, I remain unpersuaded.[40] To begin with, it is highly questionable whether the distinction between curing a disease and healing an illness would have been recognized in first-century Palestine where, as we have seen, there was little understanding of the biomedical basis for illness.[41] Nor was illness individualized as it is today. When Jesus lived, the principal diagnostic judgment was whether or not members were able to fulfil their roles within family and community.[42] Where there are high levels of mutual interdependence, illness carries consequences for all parties, whether in terms of contagion, lost labor or income, childlessness, time and energy diverted into care—as well as, if it could be afforded, expense through seeking medical assistance (cf. Mark 5:26). Within such an environment, Crossan's distinction all but dissolves for most ailments because whether a sufferer was banished from a village community or cared for within it, the implications for the other members remained largely the same.

Second, let us return to the two questions we introduced earlier in the chapter: (i) What caused Jesus to depart from key emphases within John the Baptist's outlook and program? (ii) What was the basis for Jesus' impact and popularity during his ministry? To a measure, both of these take us into the realm of speculation, eliciting qualified and multifaceted responses. However, Jesus' capacity for engendering healing, for curing disease, is surely the most plausible explanation in each case. In the first instance, it supplies a reason for why Jesus departed from his mentor John's reading of the present time and convictions about how God would

39. Crossan, *Jesus*, 82–83; also Crossan, *Historical Jesus*, 320–26; and Crossan, *Birth of Christianity*, 293–304.

40. See also the discussion in Henriksen and Sandnes, *Jesus as Healer*, 26–40.

41. Pieter Craffert maintains this distinction is inappropriate for a first-century context in that it is "a perfect replication of the Cartesian dualism in disguise with *disease* the actual (material) cause of sickness and illness only the subjective (mind) experience thereof" (*Galilean Shaman*, 263 [italics original]).

42. A good example of this is Jesus' healing of Peter's mother-in-law. Mark informs us that once the fever had abated, "she began to serve them" (Mark 1:31). And, again, in the Q tradition, where a centurion approaches Jesus concerning his ailing servant whose illness presumably prevented him from serving his master (Q 7:1–10 [Luke 7:1–10//Matt 8:5–13]).

act in the future.[43] Jesus' ability to inspire healing, when interpreted through the lens of those expectations identifying such acts as indicative of Yahweh's presence and good favor,[44] led him to conclude that God's reign was underway and that Israel would be restored as a community of blessing with a vocation to bless.[45] This reconstruction becomes unworkable if Jesus' healings amounted to no more than encouraging communities to take better care of their ailing members.

But, more so, it is difficult to see how encouraging communities to welcome ailing members back into the fold would account for his appeal and popularity. Surely Jesus must have been doing more than that to have attracted so much attention among ordinary people who had next to no access to health provision and for whom illness was, as we have seen, a debilitating curse and one that impacted detrimentally upon family and community members as well[46]—people who, in most cases, appear to have shown little interest in Jesus' message, but who were attracted by rumors of Jesus' healing powers.[47] Although clearly editorial, the sum-

43. Paul Hollenbach speaks of Jesus' "conversion" and wholesale departure from the Baptist's agenda precipitated by his spiritual anointing at baptism, inspiring a this-worldly ministry of healing and exorcism (Hollenbach, "Conversion," 196–219). For the present writer, Hollenbach overstates the divergence between Jesus and John; what is more, assuming Jesus' baptism took place at the outset of his time with John, it is difficult to see how this could have been the moment when his spiritual anointing started to take him in a different direction. Bruce Chilton constructs a more plausible scenario for Jesus' moving beyond the Baptist's repentance-baptism program to embrace healing as a means of restoring the purity of Israel (Chilton, Jesus' Baptism, 58–97).

44. E.g., Isa 35:1–6; 61:1–2; 4Q521; Eighteen Benedictions; these were discussed in the final section of chapter 2.

45. Jesus' vision, informing his mission and ministry, will be discussed in detail below.

46. Richard Horsley and Neil Silberman develop this approach in Message, 43–64; also Eve, Healer from Nazareth, 141–44.

47. With the exception of Mary Magdalene (Luke 8:1–3) and possibly the Geresene demoniac (Mark 5:1–20), blind Bartimaeus (Mark 10:46–52), and the Samaritan leper who returned to give thanks (Luke 17:11–19), the evangelists give little indication that any of those healed by Jesus were interested in him for any other reason. In contrast to the practice of some of the apostles as related in the apocryphal gospels, Jesus didn't make belief in his message a prerequisite to healing (cf. "When the apostle [Thomas] heard this from the captain he felt very sorry for him. And he said to him, 'Do you believe that Jesus can heal?' And the captain said, 'Yes.' And the apostle said, 'Commit yourself to Jesus, and he will heal and help them [his demon-possessed wife and daughter].' The captain said, 'Show him to me, that I may ask him and believe in him.' And the apostle said, 'He appears not to these bodily eyes, but is only found with the eyes of the mind.' And the captain lifted up his voice and said, 'I believe in you,

maries of Jesus' ministry composed by the evangelists capture the gist of what plausibly took place. For instance:

> That evening, at sundown, they brought to him all who were sick or possessed with demons. And the whole city was gathered around the door. And he cured many who were sick with various diseases, and cast out many demons; and he would not permit the demons to speak, because they knew him . . . And wherever he went, into villages or cities or farms, they laid the sick in the marketplaces, and begged him that they might touch even the fringe of his cloak; and all who touched it were healed.[48]

We should also point out that by no means all the medical symptoms mentioned in the Gospels rendered sufferers ritually unclean or were socially isolating in the sense of excluding sufferers from their communities. According to Leviticus, some skin conditions fell into this category, as did female genital discharges of blood (chs. 13–14; 15:25–30); but most of those treated by Jesus didn't, and, in any case, it is debatable how rigorously these Levitical stipulations where enforced in first-century Galilee.[49] What is more, Jesus conducted an itinerant ministry,[50] and it is difficult to envisage how an itinerant with no institutionally endorsed authority would have been in a position to persuade villagers and townspeople to risk the survival of their communities by reintegrating members thought to be suffering from threatening conditions who had been quarantined for the purpose of containment. For as much as Jesus earned a reputation for charismatic authority (Mark 1:27; 2:10), there is no explicit evidence of him exercising it in this way, nor does it seem plausible.

So, as attractive as Crossan's proposal may appear, it fails on a number of counts,[51] which inclines us to the view that at the source of Jesus'

Jesus, and I beseech and ask of you, help my little faith, which I have towards you.'" Acts Thom. 65 [*ApNT*]; also 150 and Acts John 23).

48. Mark 1:32–34; 6:56.

49. For example, the prospect of a cleansed leper, who had suffered the diminishing effects of the disease for what could have been years (social isolation, destitution, placement under God's perceived curse) making a six-day round trip to Jerusalem through hostile territory (Samaria) to purchase the prescribed sacrifice seems highly unlikely. It is also questionable whether Israelite women with genital discharges would have been quarantined in first-century Galilee; see Collins, *Mark*, 283–84, and the literature cited there.

50. On Jesus as a wandering charismatic, see Theissen, *First Followers*, 8–16; and Theissen, *Social Reality*, 33–59.

51. That said, the distinction between disease and illness is a valuable one, for some

reputation for healing were encounters with diseased sufferers whose symptoms abated or ceased to be so debilitating as a consequence of those engagements. In the following chapters we will look at the nature of those encounters and seek to identify effective factors within the healing dynamic.

We conclude this one by reflecting on whether Jesus' healings would have been thought of as miraculous in a Humean sense of the word. The answer is almost certainly no, for the simple reason that the distinction between natural and supernatural had yet to be drawn. As we have seen, Yahweh was believed to be the source of all healing, and whether God's healing power was thought to be any more evident in Jesus' ministry than in a physician's administration of naturally occurring medicines is, as Sir 38 demonstrates, difficult to tell. Why? Because the distinction resides not at the level of *final cause*, where all healing was thought to flow from God, but of *intermediary or proximate cause*, where there was little more appreciation of how a medicinal plant aided recovery than an intervention by Jesus. Both were equally wondrous and rare; both eloquent expressions of Yahweh's covenantal faithfulness and care.

---

of the symptoms treated by Jesus did convey significant consequences. The obvious example is the one cited by Crossan, leprosy, although this is more likely to refer to conditions where the skin was broken in some way rather than to Hansen's disease (Pilch, *Healing*, 39–54). In addition to having to manage the symptoms, sufferers were also rendered ritually unclean and, depending on the severity, would be quarantined until a priest established whether the condition had abated (cf. Lev 13–14)—hence, Jesus' instruction to lepers who approached him to subject themselves to priestly examination (Mark 1:44; Luke 17:44)—another detail that doesn't sit easily with Crossan's proposal. We can only imagine the devastating impact this condition must have visited upon sufferers—in some cases, the priest's "diagnosis" would have been tantamount to a death sentence.

4

The Dynamics of Jesus' Healings

It is not our intention in this study to analyze each healing or exorcism story in turn with a view to assessing whether it corresponds to an incident occurring in Jesus' ministry. That task has been undertaken by others; while others, again, consider it beyond what the evidence permits.[1] Our focus is somewhat different, namely, to identify those key elements composing the healing dynamic as borne witness to within these traditions—those components consistently highlighted as being significant in shaping the outcome. In doing so, we are seeking to gain an appreciation of how Jesus' healings and exorcisms were conceived, whether in terms of the means by which they came about or the characteristics of the resulting state or the significance attributed to what had taken place.

Such an exercise, like any act of interpretation, draws on presuppositions that will shape our approach, inform its execution, and affect the outcome. For example, if, following Spinoza and Hume, we were to believe that miracles are logically impossible, then however ancient and well-attested references to Jesus' wonderworking may be, an alternative account for their emergence would need to be sought.[2] If, on the

1. The most comprehensive treatments in English, adopting different perspectives, are van der Loos, *Miracles of Jesus*; and Meier, *Marginal Jew*, 2:509–1038.

2. This is the approach adopted by Theissen and Merz: "On the one hand miracles are attested in so many old strata of tradition that there is no doubt about their historical background. On the other hand they seem to us to be an unhistorical 'gleam' born of longing and poetry which has attached itself to the historical figure of Jesus . . . In our view the historical challenge lies in differentiating in a convincing way—i.e. in explaining the relatively early rise of a miracle tradition with a great degree of wishful thinking and poetry without discrediting the whole Jesus tradition. Here the approach

other hand, we were able to entertain the possibility of miracles, then we would approach those same accounts with an open mind.[3] A third option, alluded to in chapter 1, acknowledges the possibility of extraordinary events occurring that, although currently inexplicable in terms of cause and effect, need not be miraculous—constituting, instead, natural potentialities yet to be fully understood. For example, the extraordinary effectiveness of the placebo response in certain circumstances is now so well documented that the pressing question is no longer whether it can yield significant therapeutic benefit, but how.[4] What is more, whereas biomedical science has advanced beyond recognition since the first century, there is no reason why the so-called placebo response would have been any less effective then than now. In fact, a strong case could be made for the opposite view, along the lines that in the absence of cures and with a greater propensity for trust, especially when invested in one with a growing reputation for healing, there would be greater openness to such a phenomenon. In the light of this, it seems intellectually reasonable and exegetically responsible to interpret the relevant biblical texts with this option firmly in mind.

Self-evidently, the presuppositions adopted here are unlikely to have been shared by Jesus. Equally, we cannot be confident that those of Jesus were shared, for example, by the evangelists. What we can say, however, is that traditions relating Jesus' wonderworking were transmitted orally and later committed to writing by persons of different experience, cultural background, presuppositions, and worldview who nonetheless deemed them to be not only meaningful and significant but also worthy of commendation—as well as, in some cases, emulation. This is unlikely

---

cannot be to regard the objectively probable as historical and the objectively improbable as unhistorical. Rather, it is necessary to explain how the two can lie so closely together in the tradition and can nevertheless be distinguished for good reason" (*Historical Jesus*, 281–82).

3. This is the approach adopted by van der Loos: "Our investigation into the miraculous power of Jesus and the miracles performed by Him has revealed that the definition of miracle which we gave at the end of the Introduction reproduces every facet. In His miracles as direct deeds Jesus revealed to mankind, with an intention, a new observable reality, which can only be fully understood by faith. In this new reality, outside and against the known laws of order and regularity in nature, he proclaimed His freedom, power and love as the Son and Lord sent by the Father" (*Miracles of Jesus*, 706).

4. In addition to the literature cited in chapter 3, see Benson and Epstein, "Placebo Effect," 1225–27; Hamilton, *Thought That Counts*; Lipton, *Biology of Belief*, 117–47; and Spiegel, "Placebos," 927–28.

to have happened had they been judged to be unbelievable, incomprehensible, or plain irrelevant. Their transferrability in this way suggests that they resonated with communities of faith who were able to relate to them personally, perhaps because those nascent churches included the kinds of people who benefitted from Jesus' wonderworking, or because those healing narratives bore witness to the kinds of experiences that characterized some of their members. For example, the fact that the story of Jesus' encounter with a woman suffering from chronic blood loss was preserved may well reflect the existence of early groups of Christ-followers inclusive of women, some of whom were infirmed and had found a measure of healing through encountering their risen Lord.[5]

A great deal of research into how social or collective memory functions within predominantly oral communities has taken place over recent decades, yielding insights that both aid our task and set limits to what is achievable in terms of historical reconstruction.[6] For instance, social groupings tend to remember what they can relate to and apply in some way within their corporate identity, which suggests that stories and sayings about Jesus' healings or exorcisms were not considered miraculous in the sense that they were freakish events that couldn't be accommodated within a group's worldview. They were clearly considered meaningful and worthwhile, fulfilling a valuable purpose. By the time some of those traditions had been integrated within the Christian community or communities reflected in the Fourth Gospel, they served as signs of Jesus' identity within God's saving purposes and celebrations of the new life that comes through belief in him.[7] But other traditions included in the earlier Mark and Q suggest a different role, framing the kind of happenings that become possible among those who, however briefly, enter into Jesus' kingdom vision and participate in its realization. Within this context, they disclose the kinds of qualities, perceptions, and practices that in Jesus' company engender release from the debilitating effects of disease and oppression.

5. I have developed this line of thinking in Wallis, "New Directions," 349–56.

6. Helpful reviews of this research and its relevance for Jesus studies are supplied in Eve, *Behind the Gospels*; and Rodriguez, *Oral Tradition*.

7. E.g., "Jesus did this, the first of his signs, in Cana of Galilee, and revealed his glory; and his disciples believed in him . . . many believed in his name because they saw the signs that he was doing . . . Now Jesus did many other signs in the presence of his disciples, which are not written in this book. But these are written so that you may come to believe that Jesus is the Messiah, the Son of God, and that through believing you may have life in his name" (John 2:11, 23; 20:30–31; also 4:48; 6:30; 7:31; 12:37).

In a recent book, Wendy Cotter draws on her extensive knowledge of ancient Greco-Roman literature to present some of Jesus' wonder stories in a different light. Contrary to the early form-critics, who tended to focus on the miraculous components of these traditions or their edifying quality or polemical function,[8] she maintains that a number of the wonder stories resemble another literary form, *exemplary anecdotes*, where considerable attention is paid to characterization as a means of highlighting those qualities—whether exhibited by Jesus, the sufferers, or those around them—that are worthy of emulation, thereby revealing their role within the early Jesus movement. She expresses it in this way:

> Once we recognize that the miracle story is not simply the attestation of a work of power by Jesus, but that it is placed in a context designed to reveal something of Jesus' virtue, his soul, then we can say that this effort of the narrators addresses and serves a community *Sitz im Leben* [setting in life]. The various petitioners who approached Jesus are those who belong to the world of his followers, and mirror the range of petitioners who will come to them for help, care, and intercession in their problems, or maybe just for alms . . . The portrait of Jesus in the miracle-story encounters calls for the abandonment of judgment, rejection, reproof, or denial on any grounds, and call (sic) the followers to look beneath the externals to the desperate need, the anxiety, the shame, the abuse, and the social rejection that explain their externals. It calls on the followers to feel compassion, understanding, and more.[9]

We will engage with Cotter's study throughout this chapter, but before moving on we should draw attention to another insight from recent memory studies and, this time, to one that requires us to qualify what is knowable about Jesus of Nazareth or, rather, how it is knowable. Given that neither Jesus nor his earliest disciples left written records of what he did or said or of other people's reactions to him, for the first generation or so after him death, Jesus was accessible only via memories of him communicated orally. Scholarly opinion over the reliability of these memories as sources of information about Jesus, some of which have survived in written form within the Gospels and elsewhere, varies enormously— from those who stress that they are rooted in eyewitness testimony to

8. E.g., Bultmann, *History*, 209–44; Dibelius, *Tradition*, 70–132; and Taylor, *Formation*, 119–41.

9. Cotter, *Christ*, 9.

those who concentrate on the frailties of memory and the vagaries of oral transmission.[10] In reaching a judgment, however, we need to acknowledge that memory is an interpretative process. We don't remember something as a pure datum, unadulterated by subjective appropriation, to be interpreted at a later stage; rather, as all experience is subjective, so remembering is also subjective in the sense that it entails integrating personal experience of something or someone within existing cognitive and emotional associations. This means that the only Jesus available to us is the remembered Jesus, and those memories disclose as much about *why* he was remembered as *what* was remembered.[11] For example, following Wendy Cotter's lead, Jesus' healings may have been remembered not so much for their capacity to induce wonder or to confirm Jesus' special status before God, as for their exemplary and emulative function in delimiting instincts, emotions, and behaviors that characterize persons and communities wishing to participate in Jesus' continuing kingdom vision and ministry.

So what do the traditions outlined in the previous chapter disclose about the healing dynamic in terms of active ingredients? The first point to make is that there is considerable variation, not simply between healings and exorcisms, where there is also considerable overlap,[12] but within each of these groupings. Although this makes analysis more complex, it suggests that Jesus has been remembered as someone whose approach to healing wasn't prescriptive or formulaic[13] but flexible and extemporary—shaped by each particular set of circumstances. What is more, there is little evidence of attempts to standardize Jesus' "technique" when these stories were transmitted orally or finally written down, to the extent that different traditions present him treating what appear to be identical symptoms in significantly different ways. For example, when Jesus encounters a blind man at Bethsaida, he administers saliva to his eyes and lays hands upon them twice before full sight is restored (Mark 8:22–26); then, at Jericho, when blind Bartimaeus finally manages to catch his attention, Jesus asks him what he was seeking before pronouncing him

10. For the former position see Bauckham, *Eyewitnesses*; and for the latter, Ehrman, *Jesus*.

11. Le Donne explores the implications of this insight in Le Donne, *Historical Jesus*.

12. In certain traditions, possession by an evil or unclean spirit is cited as the cause of presenting symptoms (e.g., Mark 9:14–29; Matt 12:22).

13. Cf. Hanina ben Dosa, "If my prayer is fluent in my mouth, I know that he (the sick person) is favoured; if not, I know that (his disease) is fatal" (m. Ber. 5:5 [Vermes]).

healed (Mark 10:46–52). And there is further variation in the accounts found exclusively in Matthew (9:27–31; 12:22) and John (9:1–7).

In fact, the only common denominator running across all the wonder stories in the Gospels, with the exception of the sufferer, is Jesus himself, although even he isn't always present at the scene of the healing or exorcism, as with the Roman centurion's servant (Q 7:1–10 [Luke 7:1–10//Matt 8:5–13]) or the daughter of a Syrophoenician woman (Mark 7:24–30). More often than not, though, he is. Further, one of the most striking points to note is that for all Jesus understood his healing ministry within the context of Yahweh's will for Israel, and for as much as the intensity and intimacy of Jesus' relationship with God is stressed within the Gospels,[14] on no occasion within their healing and exorcism accounts is he ever recorded as praying.[15] The closest we come to it is a prayer-like gesture ("Then looking up to heaven," Mark 7:34). One implication of this is that the healing dynamic is located firmly within personal interactions and relationships, on the horizontal plain. Not infrequently, God is acknowledged as the ultimate source of healing,[16] but healings are realized through the agency of Jesus, who, as we shall see, acts as a kind of catalyst who enables sufferers to participate in their own healing.

14. This is celebrated especially in the baptism (Mark 1:9–11//Matt 3:13–17//Luke 3:21–22) and transfiguration accounts (Mark 9:2–8//Matt 18:1–8//Luke 9:28–36), as well as in the Lord's Prayer (Q 11:2–4 [Luke 11:2–4//Matt 6:9–13//Didache 8]) and elsewhere (e.g., Mark 12:1–12; Q 10:21–22 [Luke 10:21–22//Matt 11:25–27]; Luke 10:18).

15. By contrast, as Gerd Theissen points out (*Miracle Stories*, 65), prayer regularly accompanies the apostles' healings in Acts (9:40; 28:8) and on at least one recorded occasion was commended by Jesus to his disciples following their ineffectiveness (Mark 9:29), although this may well be a redactional gloss (cf. Mark 11:24). Karl Sandnes's proposal that Jesus' instruction to the unsuccessful disciples, "This kind can come out only through prayer [and fasting]" (Mark 9:29), reflects preparatory rituals practiced by early Christian healers seems plausible (Henriksen and Sandnes, *Jesus as Healer*, 55–58). However, when he goes on to claim that "Jesus therefore appears unique in not using these preparatory rituals" (57), he is on less sure ground. For one thing, the synoptic evangelists do record Jesus withdrawing from ministry to pray (e.g., Mark 1:35; Mark 6:46//Matt 14:23; also Luke 3:21; 6:12; 9:18, 28–29; 11:1; 22:32), as well as at key moments (e.g., Mark 14:32–42//Matt 26:36–46//Luke 22:40–46). For another, preparatory rituals, in a comparable way to the practices of healing and exorcism themselves, may well have been adopted by early Christ-followers precisely because they characterized Jesus' activity.

16. This usually takes the form of praise or thanksgiving following the healing, which is emphasized especially in Luke (e.g., Mark 2:12; Matt 9:8; 15:31; Luke 5:25; 7:16; 8:39; 9:43; 17:18; 18:43).

As we turn to those vital ingredients, it will be helpful to keep in mind Wendy Cotter's insights about Jesus' wonderworking traditions previously mentioned, because if their purpose is primarily exhortatory and didactic, through making visible qualities and behaviors worthy of emulation, then we shouldn't be surprised if different accounts focus on different aspects in a not-dissimilar way to how Jesus' Beatitudes were intended to be understood—while each commends a particular way of being, they are not meant to be mutually exclusive, but complementary in the sense that together they constitute an embodiment of holy living. So with the traditions under review, cumulatively they make visible the motivations, responses, and practices characterizing Jesus' healings. But, more than that, they also reflect the motivations, responses, and practices of communities who integrated these stories within their corporate memory—deeming them to be worthy of emulation. For this reason, they afford insight into the common life of these communities.

Personal Encounter and Relationships

One detail that is pronounced in many of these narratives is how sufferers struggle to reach Jesus: friends of a paralyzed man dig up a roof (Mark 2:1–4), a woman with a flow of blood burrows through the crowd (Mark 5:24–28), a Syrophoenician humbles herself before a foreigner who initially insults her (Mark 7:25–27), blind Bartimaeus makes a nuisance of himself to gain attention (Mark 10:46–49), a centurion within Rome's occupying forces condescends to begging for help from a menial Israelite (Q 7:1–9 [Luke 7:1–9//Matt 8:5–6]). There are a number of reasons why this is stressed,[17] but we are concerned here with the manner in which it highlights the subsequent encounter between Jesus and the sufferer or, in some cases, the sufferer's advocate. It may seem obvious to us now, but at a time when disease was feared and sufferers given a wide berth to avoid contamination of one form or another, the fact that Jesus invested himself personally in the well-being of people he did not know and, to do so, for no financial gain, with all the attendant risks, would have been considered extraordinary, if somewhat ill-advised.

The importance of *personal encounter* is exemplified in a number of accounts, but none more than the healing of a woman suffering from chronic blood loss (Mark 5:23–34//Matt 9:19–22//Luke 8:42–48). Mark

17. See Theissen, *Miracle Stories*, 52–53.

and Luke's versions, in particular, narrate how the encounter develops from anonymous contact with Jesus' clothing to a face-to-face exchange.[18] Interestingly, the words used suggest a broadening of her healing as a consequence, from a physical cure through the stemming of a flow of blood ("and she felt in her body that she was healed of her disease," *kai egnō tō sōmati hoti iatai apo tēs mastigos*, Mark 5:29) to a fuller sense of wholeness and peace realized in the presence of Jesus and within the community gathered around him ("your faith has made you well [*or* saved you]; go in peace," *hē pistis sou sesōken se, hypage eis eirēnē*, Mark 5:34).[19]

In addition to the sheer immediacy of personal encounter, its intensity is heightened further in some instances through the inclusion of *pleas for help* (e.g., "If you choose, you can make me clean." "Jesus, Son of David, have mercy on me!"),[20] as petitioners bare their souls before Jesus. Occasionally, the *exposed and vulnerable* nature of healing encounters is emphasized through the inclusion of dialogue as between Jesus and a Syrophoenician woman with a demon-possessed daughter (Mark 7:24–30). The narrative explores how both parties find themselves in unfamiliar territory, drawn into liminal space. It takes place in the region of Tyre, outside Israel, as Jesus, a male Israelite, is approached in private (in a Gentile dwelling?) by a Gentile woman who bows before him, pleading for assistance. Already, a number of cultural boundaries have been crossed, before Jesus addresses her: "Let the children be fed first, for it is

18. In line with his treatment of the healing traditions more generally, Matthew has edited the story line so that the healing only occurs once Jesus has addressed the woman, thereby stressing the importance of belief in Jesus as a prerequisite. He appears uncomfortable with the saying "Your faith has made you well/saved you," presumably because it places too much emphasis upon faith, rather than upon Jesus, as the agent of transformation. He omits it altogether from the other Markan context where it appears (10:46–52) and elsewhere employs a "reformed" version, "According to your faith let it be done to you," (8:13; 9:29; 15:28). See Held, "Miracle Stories," 178–81.

19. For a detailed analysis of this line of thinking, see Wallis, "Redaction-Critical Analysis," 23–68, and the literature cited there; also Yeung, *Faith*, 170–95.

20. E.g., "If you choose, you can make me clean" (Mark 1:40). "My little daughter is at the point of death. Come and lay your hands on her, so that she may be made well, and live" (Mark 5:23). "Teacher, I brought you my son; he has a spirit that makes him unable to speak; and whenever it seizes him, it dashes him down; and he foams and grinds his teeth and becomes rigid; and I asked your disciples to cast it out, but they could not do so" (Mark 9:17–18). "Jesus, Son of David, have mercy on me" (Mark 10:47–48; also Matt 9:27; Luke 17:13)! "Lord, my servant is lying at home paralyzed, in terrible distress" (Matt 8:6).

not fair to take the children's food and throw it to the dogs" (Mark 7:27). Despite scholarly attempts to lessen its force, there can be little doubt that an insult is intended here as Jesus, at best, feels bound by the limits of his mission (cf. Mark 3:13–19; Matt 10:6; 15:24), but more likely discloses a prejudice shared by many compatriots.[21] Yet, undeterred, she responds with wisdom and wit: "Sir, even the dogs under the table eat the children's crumbs," precipitating a change of mind on Jesus' part as he accedes to her request—"For saying that, you may go—the demon has left your daughter" (Mark 7:28–29). Given the portrayal of Jesus as a rude bigot who is outwitted by the recipient of his bigotry, it is surprising this narrative was preserved within Christian communities that venerated Jesus; unless, of course, it served a different function, namely, to highlight key qualities within the healing dynamic, such as openness and vulnerability, compassion and conviction, tenacity and risk-taking.[22]

Sometimes the healing encounter takes on a tactile quality as *bodily contact* is made, usually in the form of touch:

> [Jesus] came and took her by the hand and lifted her up. Then the fever left her, and she began to serve them. (Mark 1:31)

> Moved with pity, Jesus stretched out his hand and touched him, and said to him, "I do choose. Be made clean!" (Mark 1:41)

> He told his disciples to have a boat ready for him because of the crowd, so that they would not crush him; for he had cured many, so that all who had diseases pressed upon him to touch him. (Mark 3:9–10)

21. See Cotter, *Christ,* who discusses all the options before convincingly making the case for an insult (148–54). She also captures the meaning of the woman's response when she writes: "Drawing on her mother's experience of feeding children, she points out to him [Jesus] that even as the children are served, their messy eating results in the crumbs of bread falling where the house dogs snap them up. So even though she does not serve the children's food to the dogs, they still manage to eat some of it simultaneously. Seen in a wider symbolism, her answer addresses the fact that Jews and pagans live together in God's world, and yet God nourishes the pagans as he does the Jews" (156).

22. "Here Jesus shows that virtue of *praos,* that meekness which recognizes the truth that a subordinate speaks; and also there is the virtue of *epieikeia,* that understanding which comes from listening to another, considered inferior, and recognizing the wisdom in that person's words . . . The story seems to present an example of the *ēpios* of Jesus, his readiness to listen" (Cotter, *Christ,* 159–60).

Then one of the leaders of the synagogue named Jairus came and, when he saw him, fell at his feet and begged him repeatedly, "My little daughter is at the point of death. Come and lay your hands on her, so that she may be made well, and live" . . . He took her by the hand and said to her, "Talitha cum," which means, "Little girl, get up!" (Mark 5:22–23, 41) . . . She had heard about Jesus, and came up behind him in the crowd and touched his cloak, for she said, "If I but touch his clothes, I will be made well." (Mark 5:27–28)

They brought to him a deaf man who had an impediment in his speech; and they begged him to lay his hand on him. He took him aside in private, away from the crowd, and put his fingers into his ears, and he spat and touched his tongue. (Mark 7:32–33)

They came to Bethsaida. Some people brought a blind man to him and begged him to touch him . . . (Mark 8:22)

Then [Jesus] touched their eyes and said, "According to your faith let it be done to you." (Matt 9:29)

Moved with compassion, Jesus touched their eyes. Immediately they regained their sight and followed him. (Matt 20:34)

Then he came forward and touched the bier, and the bearers stood still. And he said, "Young man, I say to you, rise!" (Luke 7:14)

The *laying on of hands* was an established practice within Israelite faith where it could serve a number of functions.[23] For example, on the inauguration of the Day of Atonement, Aaron is instructed by God to "lay both his hands on the head of the live goat, and confess over it all the iniquities of the people of Israel, and all their transgressions, all their sins, putting them on the head of the goat, and sending it away into the wilderness" (Lev 16:21). Here, the gesture is the means by which guilt is transferred, but the laying on of hands could also be used to mediate blessing, as when Jacob blesses Manasseh and Ephraim (Gen 48:14–22), or to bestow authority, as when Moses ordains Joshua (Num 27:18–20; Deut 34:9) or Elisha commissions Joash (2 Kgs 13:15–17). Although there are established links between intentional touch and healing in the

23. For a detailed discussion, see Lohse, "*cheir*," 424–34.

Greco-Roman world, there is limited evidence of this association in the Hebrew Scriptures and other Israelite literature.[24] A reference can be found, however, in the Genesis Apocryphon (between the first century BCE and the second century CE), where Abram is petitioned to lay hands on Pharaoh, who had been afflicted as a punishment for making advances on Sarai: "So I prayed [for him] . . . and I laid my hands on his [head]; and the scourge departed from him and the evil [spirit] was expelled [from him], and he lived." (20.29 [CDSSE]).[25] This suggests that the practice may have been in operation around the time of Jesus, especially among Essenes who, as noted previously, took a keen interest in healing.[26]

Focusing on the first three of these applications in order to throw light on the fourth, we discover that central to each are the processes of *donation* and *transference* as the possessor bestows guilt, blessing, or authority upon the recipient and is thereby *diminished* as a consequence. In the case of the first, that diminishment is beneficial in the sense that all Israel is relieved of its culpability for transgression; but with respect to the second and third, it entails personal loss whether of possessions bequeathed through blessing or influence surrendered through the transfer of authority. Evidentially, there is an implicit sacramental dimension at

24. E.g., "It seemed to him that, as he was playing at dice below the Temple and was about to cast the dice, the god appeared, sprang up on his hand, and stretched out his [the suppliant's] fingers. When the god had stepped aside it seemed to him [the suppliant] that he [the god] bent his hand and stretched out all his fingers one by one. When he had straightened them all, the god asked him if he would still be incredulous of the inscriptions on the tablets in the Temple . . . Alcetas of Halieis. The blind man saw a dream. It seemed to him that the god [Asclepius] came up to him and with his fingers opened his eyes, and that he first saw the trees in the sanctuary. At daybreak he walked out sound" (*IG* 4.1.121–122 [Epidaurus Stele 1.3 and 1.18]). "However when they massaged with their hands his [a hunter lamed through combat with a lion] hip, the youth immediately recovered his upright gate . . . but merely touching her and whispering in secret some spell over her, at once woke up the maiden from her seeming death" (Philostratus, *Vit. Apoll.* 3.39 and 4.45); cf. "So Elisha died, and they buried him. Now bands of Moabites used to invade the land in the spring of the year. As a man was being buried, a marauding band was seen and the man was thrown into the grave of Elisha; as soon as the man touched the bones of Elisha, he came to life and stood on his feet" (2 Kgs 13:20–21). For further texts, see Cotter, *Miracles*, 11–53.

25. There is also an allusion to it in Elisha's healing of Namaan. While the Hebrew refers to the prophet "waving his hand" over the king, the Septuagint translates this as "laying his hand" (*kai epithēsei tēn cheira autou*) in order to heal; however, as this occurs in Namaan's protest over what Elisha failed to do, it doesn't really count as an actual occurrence.

26. Flusser, "Healing," 107–8.

play here which, though mediated through a physical action, transcends it to communicate something essential which affects the beneficiaries substantially. A change that gains significance from the interpretive context in which it takes place, with implications for others who participate in that context: the ritual of atonement through which Israelites gain absolution; the inheritance of goodwill with responsibility to disseminate; the appointment to public office to be exercised on behalf of the Israelite people.

Interestingly, much of this analysis resonates with the healing dynamic at play in Jesus' ministry as portrayed in the Gospels. For example, the idea of healing as *gift* or *donation* is highlighted by the recognition that, unlike physicians, Jesus healed without leveling a charge (cf. Mark 5:26). In particular, it is captured in the following exchange: "'If you wish to you are able to cleanse me.' Moved with compassion, stretching out his hand, [Jesus] touched him and said, 'I do so wish, be cleansed.'" (Mark 1:40–41; my translation); or, again, "'What do you want me to do for you?' The blind man said to him, 'My teacher, let me see again.' Jesus said to him, 'Go; your faith has made you well.' Immediately he regained his sight and followed him on the way" (Mark 10:51–52).

Healing as *transference* and ensuing *diminishment* find expression in Jesus' encounter with the woman suffering from chronic blood loss: "She had heard about Jesus, and came up behind him in the crowd and touched his cloak, for she said, 'If I but touch his clothes, I will be made well.' Immediately her hemorrhage stopped; and she felt in her body that she was healed of her disease. Immediately aware that power had gone forth from him, Jesus turned about in the crowd and said, 'Who touched my clothes?'" (Mark 5:27–30). The transference of power or energy is also implied in those cases where stress is placed upon the importance of not simply being near Jesus, but making personal contact with him as with Jairus's daughter ("My little daughter is at the point of death. Come and lay your hands on her, so that she may be made well, and live." Mark 5:23) or the blind man at Bethsaida ("Some people brought a blind man to him and begged him to touch him" Mark 8:22; also Mark 3:9–10; 7:32). Equally, the impact of healing upon the healer (a kind of diminishment) is accented in Luke's editorial comment "And all in the crowd were trying to touch him, for power came out from him and healed all of them" (6:19) and, perhaps, in the taunt leveled at Jesus during the crucifixion: "He saved others; he cannot save himself" (Mark 15:31). The Greek word translated here as "save," *sōzō*, can also be rendered "heal" or "cure" and is frequently used with this sense in the Gospels.[27] So this insult could be translated "He healed others; he cannot save himself" or, to maintain the play on the same word, "He rescued others (from illness and oppression); he cannot rescue himself (from death)."

Occasionally, touch is accompanied by the use of *saliva*, administered either directly or after being made into a paste:

> [Jesus] took [the deaf mute] aside in private, away from the crowd, and put his fingers into his ears, and he spat (*ptusas*) and touched his tongue. (Mark 7:33)

> [Jesus] took the blind man by the hand and led him out of the village; and when he had put saliva on his eyes (*ptusas*, literally, "spitting into his eyes") and laid his hands on him, he asked him, "Can you see anything?" (Mark 8:23)

> When he had said this, he spat (*eptusen*) on the ground and made mud with the saliva (*ptusmatos*) and spread the mud on the man's eyes. (John 9:6)

In the Hebrew Scriptures, spitting and spittle tend to carry negative connotations,[28] but throughout the ancient world the curative properties of saliva were widely recognized.[29] In some cases, its potency was derived from the status or significance of the donor, whether Asclepius's sacred dogs and serpents in the shrine at Epidaurus licking the wounds of hopeful suppliants[30] or the Emperor Vespasian (69–79 CE) deigning to moisten the cheeks and eyes of a blind man at Alexandria.[31] In fact, Eric Eve has recently proposed that the attribution to Jesus of the use of saliva was a later addition to demonstrate his superiority to the emperor.[32] Whether or not this was the case, it would be impossible to determine with any confidence why Jesus would have used it beyond the recognition that he believed it contributed to the healing dynamic in some way.

27. E.g., Matt 9:22; Mark 3:4; 5:34; 5:56; 10:52; Luke 6:9; 7:3; 8:48; 17:19; 18:42.

28. E.g., Num 12:14; Deut 25:9; 1 Sam 21:13; Job 17:6; 30:10; Sir 26:22.

29. See the discussions in Collins, *Mark*, 370–71; Hull, *Hellenistic Magic*, 76–78; and van der Loos, *Miracles of Jesus*, 306–13, for references.

30. Edelstein and Edelstein, *Asclepios*, 423:17, 20, 26.

31. Tacitus, *Hist.* 4.81; also Suetonius, *Vesp.* 7.2, and Cassius Dio, *Hist.* 65.8.

32. Eric Eve maintains that spittle is superfluous within the healings of Mark 7 and 8, where Jesus is approached to *touch* the sufferers with a view to healing them. This he duly does; but, in addition, he administers spittle which isn't requested and which was, at best, partially effective—suggesting a later addition ("Spit in Your Eye," 1–17).

As we would expect, the seminal encounter within the gospel healing stories is between Jesus and the sufferer; however, the importance of other relationships is also recognized, in particular, the role of the intercessor or intermediary, which can assume different forms. In some instances, such as the four stretcher-bearers, their commitment to the well-being of a paralyzed friend took them to extreme lengths in order that he might encounter Jesus (Mark 2:1–12).[33] In other cases, they serve as petitioners or advocates, supplying the umbilical between Jesus and the patient, who exhibit vital qualities within the healing dynamic: the Roman centurion is commended for his exemplary trust in Jesus' authority (Q 7:1–10 [Luke 7:1–10//Matt 8:5–13); the Syrophoenician mother for her shrewdness and tenacity (Mark 7:24–30). Additional reinforcing roles include those who offer encouragement: "Take heart; get up, he is calling you" (Mark 10:49). In sum, all these participants, as Richard Horsley recognizes, bear witness to *the relational nature* of the healings associated with Jesus: "The healings happen through the relation and interaction between the sufferer and Jesus, or through the wider relations between the sufferer, the support network, and Jesus."[34] And if during his ministry, then also within the communities that continued to inhabit these stories and make them their own.

Authority

In a sense, pretty much all the features highlighted as significant within the healing dynamic alluded to in the Gospels are aspects of personal relating in one way or another. This is certainly the case with respect to authority.[35] Different kinds of authority were in existence in first-century Palestine, including *delegated authority*, exercised by officials of powerful institutions such as the Roman Empire (e.g., Pontius Pilate) or the

33. Simon and Andrew, Jairus and the father of the "epileptic" boy are permutations of this role (Mark 1:29–31; 5:22–24, 35–43; 9:14–29; see also Mark 6:54–56; 7:32; Matt 9:32–33; 12:22; 15:29–31; John 11:1–44).

34. Horsley, *Jesus and Magic*, 141.

35. The root idea behind the Greek word *exousia* is freedom to act unimpeded. Often it goes hand in hand with *dynamis*, power, for the obvious reason that, without the latter, the former remains largely hypothetical in many circumstances. See Foerster, "*exestin*," 560–75: According to Foerster, there is no close Hebrew (cf. *memshālāh* = "rule, dominion, realm," from *māshal* = "to rule, have dominion, reign") or Aramaic (cf *shālat* = "to rule, have power over") equivalent to *exousia*.

Jerusalem temple (e.g., the high priest); *acquired authority*, resulting from expertise in interpreting Torah (e.g., Scribes) or administering natural medicines (e.g., Essenes); and *kinship authority*, assumed by senior members of a family (e.g., a father) or community (e.g., the ruler of a synagogue). Jesus, like his mentor John, didn't readily fall into any of these categories and, unsurprisingly, the source of his authority was a matter of controversy (Mark 3:22-27; 11:27-33; cf. Mark 1:21-28).

As the narratives relating his baptism affirm, Jesus was believed to be a charismatic in the sense that he was inspired by a gratuitous spiritual energy emanating from Yahweh (Mark 1:10; John 1:32-33; cf. Mark 1:8, 12).[36] There are strong resonances between the Synoptic accounts and various Hebrew Scriptures, including the voice from heaven (cf. "Here is my servant, whom I uphold, / my chosen, in whom my soul delights; / I have put my spirit upon him; / he will bring forth justice to the nations," Isa 42:1) and the correspondence between John's anointing his disciple, Jesus, and Elijah's anointing his disciple, Elisha (2 Kgs 2:1-15; cf. Mark 1:9-11), which is made all the stronger with the identification of the Baptist as Elijah *redivivus* (Mark 9:11-13; Matt 11:14; Luke 1:17; cf. Mal 4:5).[37] In both instances, the bestowal of God's spirit is emphasized.

On top of this and perhaps more important are the traditions in which Jesus is accused of being possessed by Beelzebul, the ruler of demons, by whose authority he was able to control lesser demons.[38] Signifi-

36. Dunn, *Jesus and the Spirit*, 68-92. There is considerable scholarly debate over whether the sociological construct of *charismatic* as defined by Max Weber and many others is an appropriate interpretative category for Jesus (see the review article by Piovanelli, "Jesus' Charismatic Authority," 395-427; also Johnson, *Religious Experience*). Space does not permit a detailed engagement in this debate here, but we would wish to stress that Jesus was remembered as possessing *charisma* which did not originate in formal learning or institutional mandate (cf. Mark 1:21-28)—charisma which found expression through his preaching and teaching, healing and exorcising, challenging and disputing, forgiving and blessing, as well as through winning allegiance and recruiting disciples. In this respect, we can speak about *charisma* as a quality or capacity which Jesus possessed innately or acquired. *Charisma* also needs to be recognised for what it is and, as such, only becomes manifest through relationships with those who acknowledge it and choose to be open to its influence. In this respect, *charisma* and authority are closely linked.

37. For scriptural allusions in the accounts of Jesus' baptism (Matt 3:13-17//Mark 1:9-11//Luke 3:21-22), see Meier, *Marginal Jew*, 2:106-16.

38. There appear to have been versions of this controversy, including the parable of the house divided, in both Mark (Mark 3:22-25) and Q (Q 11:14-20 [Luke 11:14-20// Matt 11:22-28]), with Matthew expanding the material further (Matt 10:24-25). See the discussions in Twelftree, *Jesus the Exorcist*, 98-113; and Witmer, *Galilean Exorcist*,

cantly, the issue at stake is not whether his ministry was animated by a spiritual presence, which seems to be taken for granted; rather, Jesus is concerned to demonstrate its provenance—namely, that he was inspired by Yahweh's spirit and not by some malevolent counterpart (Q 11:14–20 [Luke 11:14–20//Matt 12:22–28]; cf. John 7:20; 8:48–52; 10:20–21).

With respect to wonderworking, Jesus was remembered for exercising *charismatic authority* in one of two ways: *coercively*, with respect to exorcising unclean or evil spirits, who were forcibly banished; *consensually*, with respect to various healing scenarios. We will examine the former in a subsequent chapter and focus on the latter here. At least two modes of permissive authority are attributed to Jesus. The first takes the form of *pronouncing forgiveness*. In chapter 2, we noted the link within Israelite faith traditions between illness and transgression, pointing out that any scar or breach in covenantal relationship with Yahweh or another Israelite caused by sin could lead to bodily disease or disorder, either as a consequence of wrongdoing or as divine punishment for the same. Although not universally accepted, this link would have been widely acknowledged within first-century Palestine. In truth, Jesus may well have been sympathetic himself. For example, one of the earliest New Testament manuscripts discovered to date, Papyrus Egerton 2 (150–200 CE), includes a version of the healing of a leper found in the Synoptics (Mark 1:40–44//Matt 8:2–4//Luke 5:12–16). It differs in a number of respects and merits reproduction in full:

> And behold, a leper approached him [Jesus] and said, "Teacher Jesus, while I was traveling with some lepers and eating with them at the inn, I myself contracted leprosy. If, then, you are willing, I will be made clean." Then the Lord said to him, "I am willing: be clean." Immediately the leprosy left him. Jesus said to him, "Go, show yourself to the priests and make an offering for your cleansing as Moses commanded; and sin no more . . ."[39]

The text breaks off at this point and while no causal link is made explicit, the implication of Jesus' closing direction is that sin was responsible for the sufferer's former ailment, which, if the passage discloses his wrongdoing, must have been a failure to observe the Torah's requirement for lepers to be quarantined ("while I was travelling with some lepers and eating with them in an inn"; cf. Lev 13). The author of the Fourth

---

109–29.

39. Papyrus Egerton 2, fragment 2 [*ApGos*].

Gospel records a similar command on the occasion of Jesus' healing of a paralyzed man by the pool at Bethesda in chapter 5, "See, you have been made well! Do not sin any more, so that nothing worse happens to you" (5:14). Both of these passages imply that Jesus' healings were a form of forgiveness; otherwise his imperatives to refrain from transgression would lack force. In fact, "and sin no more"/"Do not sin any more" are translations of the same Greek phrase (*mēketi hamartane*), which may serve as a form of absolution by means of which Jesus releases sufferers from the grip of sinful habits or behavior. Here, we see Jesus exercising consensual or permissive authority, where his capacity to influence the lives of the leper and the blind person is a measure of his persuasiveness, coupled with their willingness to trust him and inhabit their new identities among the healed forgiven.

Further evidence that Jesus was remembered as someone who recognized a link between sickness and sin is supplied by the healing of a paralyzed man (Mark 2:1–12). The narrative as it stands is complex, including both a healing and a controversy story, concluding with an apothegm or pithy saying. Rudolf Bultmann maintained that it should be understood as an amalgamation of two traditions—verses 5b-10 representing a secondary interpolation,[40] although Joanna Dewey has subsequently defended its literary integrity[41]—certainly it is not the only one of Jesus' healings to generate disputation. In fact, in this context as elsewhere, Jesus appears to use healing to make a theological point. An obvious further example is whether such activity constituted work and, as such, lay outside of faithful Sabbath observance as prescribed in the Torah.[42] In this case of Mark 2, Jesus is concerned to demonstrate that forgiveness, like healing, is another divine prerogative mediated by human agency. Just as Yahweh uses physicians and healers to restore right-relating within the physical body, so Yahweh uses ministers[43] to restore right-relating within the covenantal body.

40. Bultmann, *History*, 14–16, 383.

41. Dewey, *Markan Public Debate*; see also Collins, *Mark*, 184–89.

42. E.g., Mark 3:1–6; Luke 13:10–17; John 5:1–18; cf. Exod 16:23–30; 20:8–11; 31:12–18; 35:1–3.

43. The meaning of the slightly awkward phrase "the son of the man" (*ho huios tou anthrōpou*) is hotly contested. Elsewhere it can denote a third party (e.g., Mark 8:38; 13:26; 14:62) or can refer to Jesus himself (e.g., Mark 8:31; 9:31; 10:33–34, 45; 14:21, 41); here it could serve as a self-reference, but some scholars, notably Geza Vermes (*Jesus the Jew*, 160–91), claim that it should be understood as a generic circumlocution for humanity as a whole. For a reassessment of all the evidence and interpretative

Whether this story illustrates the later rabbinic saying "No one gets up from his sick-bed until all his sins are forgiven." (b. Ned. 41a), or whether Jesus, aware that a causal link was widely acknowledged, made use of it here to push home his point is difficult to decide. Certainly, forgiveness and healing are not conflated, but Jesus' initial response to the paralyzed man of pronouncing forgiveness strongly suggests that he recognized the connection. Once again, this passage presents Jesus exercising consensual or permissive authority, which is only as effective as it is persuasive. Unless Jesus' utterances—"Son, your sins are forgiven . . . I say to you, stand up, take your mat and go to your home" (Mark 2:5, 11)— serve as magic spells with coercive force, they are able to perform what they connote only with the cooperation of the recipient, who chooses to embrace the identity they communicate—of an Israelite healed, forgiven, and free to participate fruitfully within the life of the community on which he had formerly been heavily dependent.

Before moving on, we should balance the evidence for Jesus being remembered as recognizing an association between illness and disease with that which suggests he challenged it. The clearest reference comes in the Fourth Gospel where the narrative relating the healing of a blind man begins thus: "As he [Jesus] walked along, he saw a man blind from birth. His disciples asked him, 'Rabbi, who sinned, this man or his parents, that he was born blind?' Jesus answered, 'Neither this man nor his parents sinned; he was born blind so that God's works might be revealed in him'" (John 9:1–3; cf. Mark 8:22–26). In cases where someone was born with an impairment, culpability was vested in the parents or in a previous generation of descendants, according to the precedent set by Exod 20:5 (cf. Deut 5:9), although some later Rabbis maintained that infants could even sin in the womb.[44] Although John's Jesus appears to challenge the consensus over the causes of illness and impairment, it is reinforced elsewhere (e.g., John 5:14) and even in this instance it is unclear whether the saying implies any more than a temporary suspension in service of a higher goal (cf. John 11:4). John Meier may well be correct when he identifies the earliest stratum of this healing tradition within verses 1, 6–7, to which the dialogue between Jesus and his disciples was added at a later stage, thereby shifting the focus from the cause of the man's blindness onto its purpose, namely, making manifest God's glory—a characteristically

---

options, see Hurtado and Owen, eds., *Son of Man*.

44. See Beasley-Murray, *John*, 154–55, for references.

Johannine theme.[45] So it is questionable whether the views expressed here can be attributed to Jesus with any confidence.

This leaves one further passage which is only found in Luke, although it could plausibly have been inherited by him from an earlier source. It is not concerned with the causes of sickness and impairment directly, but with those of suffering and untimely death:

> At that very time there were some present who told him [Jesus] about the Galileans whose blood Pilate had mingled with their sacrifices. He asked them, "Do you think that because these Galileans suffered in this way they were worse sinners than all other Galileans? No, I tell you; but unless you repent, you will all perish as they did. Or those eighteen who were killed when the tower of Siloam fell on them—do you think that they were worse offenders than all the others living in Jerusalem? No, I tell you; but unless you repent, you will all perish just as they did."[46]

The passage alludes to events that cannot be corroborated from any other ancient source. That said, the theological convictions communicated are not dependent on the historicity of the incidents. But those convictions are unclear. On the one hand, these verses seem to reject any causal link between transgressions committed by the two groups in view and their tragic demise. Yet, on the other, their tragic demise then supplies the motivation for repentance, which implies correlation.[47] Perhaps the best that can be said is that the author of these verses wished to emphasize how the unpredictable, even capricious nature of human existence is reason enough for maintaining communion or right-relating with God at all times.[48]

In the light of this evidence, it seems probable that Jesus was not remembered as someone who challenged the consensus with respect to whether illness or impairment resulted from transgression. However, he was remembered as someone who challenged what constituted transgression, rejecting attempts by the Pharisees and others to divert attention

45. Meier, *Marginal Jew*, 2:694–98; see also Bultmann, *Gospel of John*, 330–33.

46. Luke 13:1–5.

47. "A connection between sin and calamity has a firm background in Jewish thought . . . and is implicitly accepted by Jesus here. Jesus will, however, dispute the possibility of determining the degree of sinfulness from the experience of calamity and will shift the focus away from the passing of judgement on others to the need to put one's own house in order" (Nolland, *Luke*, 2:718).

48. See Fitzmyer, *Luke*, 2:1004–6.

away from the core commandments by focusing on secondary embellish-ments or matters of ritual purity (cf. "the tradition of the elders," Mark 7:3, 5). This came into focus, in particular, around Jesus' practice of eating with morally compromised characters ("tax collectors and sinners," Mark 2:15–17; Q 7:33–34 [Luke 7:33–34//Matt 11:18–19]), as well as refraining from public fasting (Mark 2:18–20; cf. Matt 6:16–18) and hand-washing before meals (Mark 7:1–9)—stressing, in the case of the latter, that defile-ment was not a contagion from without, but a corruption from within: "It is what comes out of a person that defiles. For it is from within, from the human heart, that evil intentions come: fornication, theft, murder, adultery, avarice, wickedness, deceit, licentiousness, envy, slander, pride, folly. All these evil things come from within, and they defile a person" (Mark 7:20–23).[49]

The second mode of consensual or permissive authority exercised by Jesus is the *healing utterance*. In contrast to exorcisms, where his com-mands carry coercive force as demons and unclean spirits are banished against their will, in the case of the healing stories the effectiveness of Jesus' words is dependent on the cooperation of patients, which, in turn, is an expression of their trust in him. There is little conformity over what Jesus says or how his words contribute to the outcome. In some instances, they simply declare what has already taken place, or is about to, by other means. To the woman whose chronic bleeding ceased the moment she made contact with his garment Jesus confides, "Daughter, your faith has made you well; go in peace, and be healed of your disease" (Mark 5:34), whilst to another, crippled for eighteen years, he says, "Woman, you are set free from your ailment" (Luke 13:12) before laying hands upon her. In these cases, referring back to the distinction made earlier between heal-ing an illness and curing a disease, Jesus' utterances operate more at the level of healing rather than curing, confirming a change in the sufferer's status as a person no longer defined by their symptoms, with all that im-plied socially and theologically.

Although more characteristic of Jesus' exorcisms and resuscitations,[50] in other accounts Jesus' words take the form of commands, performing

49. Jesus' attitude towards the Torah and the interpretative traditions which would eventually be collected together and codified during the second century into the Mish-nah is complex and need not detain us here. For a thorough discussion of the relevant texts and issues raised, see Meier, *Marginal Jew*, 4:26–477.

50. Exorcisms: "Be silent, and come out of him!" (Mark 1:25); "Come out of the man, you unclean spirit!" (Mark 5:8); "You spirit that keeps this boy from speaking

what they express. When a man suffering from a skin condition asks to be made clean, Jesus replies, "I do choose. Be made clean!" (Mark 1:41). And, again, when supporters seek his help for a deaf person with a speech impediment, Jesus places fingers in his ears and saliva upon his tongue before pronouncing, "Ephphatha," which is the Aramaic for "Be opened" (Mark 7:34). What is unclear in both of these accounts is to whom the command is directed. In cases of possession, it was evidently thought that Jesus was addressing the persona of the malevolent spiritual oppressor; but where no such oppressor is identified, it appears that Jesus was expecting either the ailing part of the anatomy, which seems unlikely, or the sufferers themselves to obey his words, implying they had some control over their conditions or, at least, how they were experienced.[51] Particularly striking is the paradox of Jesus commanding a deaf person to hear! As difficult as it is now for us to appreciate the dynamics at play here, these texts bear witness to the conviction that Jesus' words were authoritative for sufferers, enabling them to find healing either within their symptoms or through their alleviation.

In further instances, healing results from being willing to trust Jesus and to put that trust to the test by responding to his bidding. Here, Jesus' words are not performatory in the sense that they effect healing; rather they elicit a particular response in sufferers and advocates who are thereby enabled to move beyond a presenting past in order to participate in an unfolding future—one intimately related to Jesus. The person who was paralyzed and had to be stretchered into Jesus' company is empowered to take responsibility for his own departure: "I say to you, stand up, take your mat and go to your home" (Mark 2:11). The man with a withered hand risks contravening Sabbath regulations by obeying Jesus' command in the hope that healing would ensue: "'Stretch out your hand.' He stretched it out, and his hand was restored" (Mark 3:5). The Syro-Phoenician woman, who had demonstrated humility, tenacity, and forbearance in approaching Jesus and refusing to take no for an answer, is finally challenged to let go her struggle and entrust herself to a different reality: "Go (home); on account of this saying the demon has gone

and hearing, I command you, come out of him, and never enter him again!" (Mark 9:23–25); resuscitations: "'Talitha cum,' which means, 'Little girl, get up!'" (Mark 5:41); "Young man, I say to you, rise!" (Luke 7:14); cf. "Peace! Be still!" (Mark 4:39).

51. Cf. Matthew's formulation "let it be done for you (*genēthētō soi/hymin*)," which stresses the final cause of healing, namely, Yahweh, and does not speculate over how God brings it about (8:13; 9:29; 15:28).

out of your daughter" (Mark 7:29; Collins's translation, *Mark*, 364). Little wonder Matthew makes explicit what is only implicit within the Markan narrative: "Woman, great is your faith!" (Matt 15:28). Finally, it is as the ten "lepers" heed Jesus' command to subject themselves to the scrutiny of priests ("Go and show yourselves to the priests." Luke 17:14), who had previously pronounced them unclean, that their purity is restored.

With the possible exception of the two occurrences where the Aramaic is supplied as well as the Greek translation,[52] there is little in the healing narratives reviewed to suggest that Jesus' words exerted coercive authority in a quasi-magical sense of manipulating participants against their wills; rather, they became powerful within a healing dynamic where hope-filled sufferers were invited to participate in a different reality (one prescribed by Jesus' kingdom vision) and, in his company, to discover the wherewithal to do so. In this respect, Jesus is remembered as someone whose words uttered within the context of trusting, expectant encounters were authoritative in that they energized recipients to embrace an identity unconstrained by their ailments or impairments.

Character and Motivation

As mentioned previously, Wendy Cotter has recently offered a reassessment of the gospel wonder stories, stressing that a number of the earliest accounts highlight qualities of Jesus that were considered to be worthy of emulation. This is a key observation and one which suggests that these accounts served primarily a *didactic or exhortatory function* for would-be followers, creating common ground between Jesus and his disciples, rather than an *apologetic function* in which Jesus' uniqueness was emphasized, thereby calling forth veneration rather than emulation. Certainly there are accounts where Jesus is petitioned to show mercy (e.g., "Jesus, Son of David, have mercy on me [*eleēson me*]," Mark 10:47–48),[53] but

---

52. It should be noted that Mark uses transliterations of Semitic languages elsewhere and, when he does, supplies a translation in Greek: "Then they brought Jesus to the place called Golgotha (which means the place of a skull) . . . At three o'clock Jesus cried out with a loud voice, "*Eloi, Eloi, lema sabachthani*?" which means, 'My God, my God, why have you forsaken me?'" (Mark 15:22, 34).

53. This is a form of petition preferred by Matthew (9:27; 15:22; 20:30–31; cf. Luke 18:38–39) where it carries messianic connotations, stressing Jesus' unique role within God's plan of salvation; see Duling, "Therapeutic," 392–410.

relatively few where his motivations are explicitly mentioned.[54] A case in point is his encounter with a "leper" where Mark states that Jesus was moved with either compassion (*splagchnistheis*) or anger (*orgistheis*, Mark 1:41). Both readings have significant manuscript support,[55] making it difficult to judge between them—either way, the text bears witness to Jesus being motivated by a very human emotion.

Cotter's contention, however, is that the narrative form of exemplary anecdote, into which a number of Jesus' earliest wonder stories fall, illustrates those virtues worthy of imitation by seeing them in practice, rendering their naming superfluous. For example, commenting on the same healing narrative, she concludes, "Certainly, Jesus invites the description of *praos* ("meekness"). Jesus, instead of taking offense at the man's proximity and demanding more distance, or challenging his insinuation of a capricious ministry, sees only the man's terrible need and shows him that compassion and *ēpios* ('gentleness') that become this anecdote's lesson for the listener."[56] Or, again, with reference to Jesus' encounter with a blind beggar (Mark 10:46–52), "Thus, it is not only Jesus' *philantrōpia*, *praos* and *epieikia* that are modelled here for the would-be follower, but also the boldness of Bartimaeus in the actual practical ramifications of them."[57] Importantly, as this case demonstrates, Cotter maintains it is not only Jesus who acts as an exemplar, but also those who seek his help—an observation we will develop in the next section. Before doing so, however, we should note some of the other virtues celebrated in the ancient world that she identifies in the eight gospel narratives under review: *epieikia* ("true fairness and understanding"), *ēpios* ("gentleness"), *philanthrōpia* ("loving concern for others"), *praos* ("meekness"), and *praotēs* ("inner restraint").[58]

---

54. E.g., Matt 9:36 (compassion; editorial/general overview), Matt 14:14 (compassion; editorial/healing referenced), Matt 20:34 (compassion; healing of two blind men), Mark 5:19 (mercy; Gerasene demoniac), Mark 8:2 (compassion; feeding of the four thousand), Luke 7:13 (compassion; resuscitation at Nain).

55. See Metzger, *Textual Commentary*, 76–77.

56. Cotter, *Christ*, 41.

57. Cotter, *Christ*, 75.

58. E.g., Mark 1:40–45 (*praos, praotēs, ēpios*); Mark 2:1–12 (*philantrōpia, praos, praotēs, epieikia*); Mark 4:35–41 (*philanthrōpia*); Mark 6:45–52 (*praos*); Mark 7:24–30 (*ēpios*); Mark 9:14–29 (*philantrōpia, epieikia*); Mark 10:46–52 (*philantrōpia, praos, praotēs, epieikia*); Luke 7:1–10 (*epieikia*).

Faith

The quality or virtue receiving most attention in the gospel healing and, to a lesser extent, exorcism traditions is faith (*pistis*).[59] Although its presence can be implied in almost every incidence, we will focus on those where it is explicitly mentioned on the basis that these cases were considered to be particularly noteworthy examples. As you would expect, the faith of sufferers is identified, but in relatively few places. If we put to one side those references unique to Matthew, which, reflecting his theology and style, were probably coined by him,[60] there are only three occasions, all of the same saying, "your faith has made you well" (*hē pistis sou sesōken se*, Mark 5:34; 10:52; Luke 17:19; cf. Luke 7:50). We will look at this memorable formulation in more detail shortly, but here we note how it emphasizes the *effective role* attributed to faith within the healing process, a dimension emphasized further in the first of these accounts where the healing occurs before the sufferer's encounter with Jesus (Mark 5:29)—his subsequent words declaring what had already taken place. In the light of this, it could be argued that faith in these instances is exercised by patients, who, in some measure, become their own healers.[61]

The faith of supporters is also highlighted and is manifested in various ways.[62] There are traditions where faith is encouraged or celebrated in petitioners who approach Jesus on behalf of someone for whom they are personally concerned. The centurion pleads for his servant, recognizing Jesus' authority to heal, and elicits the response, "I tell you, not even in Israel have I found such faith (*pistin*)" (Q 7:9 [CEQ; Luke 7:9//Matt

59. See the discussions of Theissen, *Miracle Stories*, 129–40, and Ebeling, "Jesus and Faith," 201–46; also my *Faith of Jesus Christ*, 24–64.

60. "Go; let it be done for you according to your faith (*episteusas*)" (8:13). "Do you believe (*pisteuete*) that I am able to do this? . . . According to your faith (*pistin*) let it be done to you" (9:28–29). "Woman, great is your faith (*pistis*)! Let it be done for you as you wish" (15:28). Cf. "You of little faith (*oligopiste*), why did you doubt?" (14:31). "You of little faith (*oligopistoi*), why are you talking about having no bread?" (16:8). See Held, "Miracle Stories," 275–96, who stresses the petitionary nature of faith in Matthew's Gospel, as reflected in these references.

61. "Unlike the disciples, who were unable to calm the storm because of their lack of trust or faith (4:40), this woman was able to heal herself by the power of her faith. By availing herself of the power of Jesus, she has saved herself from her torment and is able, as Jesus confirms, to go in peace" (Collins, *Mark*, 284). I explore this in more detail in "Redaction-Critical Analysis," 22–68.

62. See Christopher Marshall's discussion of the "faith of minor characters" in Marshall, *Faith as a Theme*, 79–133.

8:10]). Having approached the disciples on behalf of his deranged son, who had been unable to help, the father exclaims, "I believe (*pisteuō*); help my unbelief (*apistia*)!" (Mark 9:24). Eventually a resuscitation rather than a healing, we should also mention Jairus who sought Jesus' assistance for his dying daughter and, becoming despondent at the news of her demise, is exhorted, "Do not fear, only believe (*pisteue*)." (Mark 5:36; also Luke 8:50).

In each of these scenarios, faith is identified with concrete action which emerges from the hopelessness of the situation and yet an unwillingness to be defined by it, coupled with a readiness to invest trust in Jesus. As such, it possesses a *subversive dimension* transcending the constraints of the presenting circumstances in order to expose sufferers to a climate of hope and opportunity associated with Jesus, where healing becomes possible. This is graphically demonstrated in the case of a paralytic whose friends, refusing to accept Jesus was out of reach, vandalize a roof covering to ensure that encounter takes place; the accompanying editorial comment is revealing, "When Jesus saw *their* faith (*pistin*), he said to the paralytic, 'Son, your sins are forgiven'" (Mark 2:5; also Matt 9:2//Luke 5:20; italics added).

Its absence is another way in which the importance of faith within the healing dynamic is acknowledged. The foremost example is in an account of Jesus returning to his home town of Nazareth where he was greeted with incredulity, and, as a consequence, his healing ministry was largely, if not wholly, ineffectual. Mark records that "he was amazed at their unbelief (*apistian*)" (Mark 6:6; also Matt 13:58). In addition, when the disciples had been unable to help a boy oppressed by an unclean spirit, Jesus despairs, "You faithless (*apistos*) generation, how much longer must I be among you? How much longer must I put up with you?" (Mark 9:19; also Matt 17:17//Luke 9:41).

Less obvious are references to the faith of healers—although, as previously mentioned, the saying "Your faith has made you well" is suggestive in this respect. Possibly, the strongest case can be found in the Markan account of a boy oppressed by an unclean spirit (Mark 9:14–29), which we will consider here for the sake of completeness.[63] If you recall, when Jesus was elsewhere, the father approached some of the disciples, who subsequently had been unable to restore his son to health. On learning of the situation, Jesus admonishes those whom he describes as a "faithless

63. A fuller treatment of this passage can be found in Wallis, *Faith of Jesus Christ*, 27–36.

generation (*genea apistos*)," which would almost certainly have included his impotent followers, but probably not the father whose faith, like the stretcher-bearers of the paralytic, is demonstrated by his approaching Jesus for assistance in the first place. The father subsequently describes his son's plight to Jesus before pleading, "if you are able to do anything (*ei ti dynē*), have pity on us and help us" (9:22)—evidently, less confident now. In response, Jesus repeats his equivocation, "If you [i.e. Jesus] are able (*to ei dynē*)," before disclosing the grounds for his confidence in being able to succeed where the disciples had faltered, "All things become possible for the one who believes (*panta dynata tō pisteuonti*, my translation)" (9:23). Given that Jesus had, in effect, just been challenged by the despairing father, it is difficult to think that he didn't include himself among those called to exercise faith—constituting the "missing ingredient" in the healing dynamic which, now present, is able to make possible what had previously proved unrealizable.[64] The father's following confession, "I believe; help my unbelief!" (9:24) doesn't amount to a coming to faith—he wouldn't have been there without believing Jesus could help—rather, it is a cry for faith to be strengthened, in the company of its finest exemplar.[65]

This interpretation gains support from two sayings, possibly variants, which extol faith's potential for mediating the divine prerogative.[66]

64. Marshall is surely incorrect when he concludes, "It is the *father's* faith which is the key to the boy's cure" (Marshall, *Faith as a Theme*, 122; italics original). Clearly, the father's faith had been stretched (cf. "I believe; help my unbelief") following the disciples' failure precipitated by their lack of faith (cf. "You faithless generation"), but it was Jesus' faith that made up what was lacking in the healing dynamic (cf. "All things become possible for the one who believes"). Jesus' response to the disciples' question about their ineffectiveness, "This kind can come out only through prayer [and fasting]" (Mark 9:29), looks secondly. For one thing, no reference is made in the narrative to Jesus doing either; for another, it reads like an interpretative gloss informed by Mark 11:24: "So I tell you, whatever you ask for in prayer, believe that you have received it, and it will be yours." See Marcus, *Mark 8–16*, 665–66.

65. I have discussed the evidence for Jesus' faith in Wallis, *Faith of Jesus Christ*, as well as in Wallis, "Before Big Bang," 12–19; and in Wallis, "Jesus the Believer," 10–17.

66. On the one hand, Mark 11:23 and Matt 21:21, and, on the other, Luke 17:6 and Matt 17:20, appear to be variants of two different sayings; what is less clear is whether Jesus coined one form, which was subsequently adapted through oral transmission and the evangelists' redaction (Telford, *Barren Temple*, 95–27), or whether he is responsible for two or more of these final versions (Davies and Allison, *Matthew*, 2:726–27). I incline towards the latter, with versions preserved in Mark and Q, not least because it is difficult to account for why the "mustard seed" metaphor, so central to Matt 17:20 and Luke 17:6, would have been omitted from Mark 11:23 and Matt 21:21.

The first follows Jesus' cursing of a fig tree en route to the Jerusalem temple and forms part of his response to the disciples who draw attention to the tree's subsequent demise:

> Have faith in God (*echete pistin theou*). Truly I tell you, if you say to this mountain, "Be taken up and thrown into the sea," and if you do not doubt in your heart, but believe (*pisteuē*) that what you say will come to pass, it will be done for you. So I tell you, whatever you ask for in prayer, believe that you have received it (*pisteuete hoti elabete*), and it will be yours. (Mark 11:22–24)

Within the Markan redaction, the cursing and subsequent withering of the fig tree symbolize Jesus' judgment upon the temple and its ensuing fate,[67] as "this mountain (*tō orei toutō*)" becomes the temple mount; however, the saying need not be so specific and lends itself to a more general application. Mountain-moving, like health-restoring, is impossible for humans, unless they able to participate in divine creativity or mediate divine power. Significantly, the leveling of mountains is associated in Hebrew literature with the consummation of Yahweh's saving purposes and, therefore, is an apt metaphor for the emergence of God's reign, which, as we shall see, is a central conviction underpinning Jesus' ministry.[68] Although now framed as praying faith ("Have faith in God ... whatever you ask for in prayer, believe that you have received it, and it will be yours."), the central force of the saying ("If you say to this mountain, 'Be taken up and thrown into the sea,' and if you do not doubt in your heart, but believe that what you say will come to pass . . .") is performatory rather than petitionary—as were Jesus' healing words that, rather than praying to Yahweh for assistance, exercise the divine prerogative.

The second version of this saying may well have been inherited by Matthew and Luke from Q, although their renderings differ considerably with Luke's version usually thought to be closer to their source:[69]

> If you had faith the size of a mustard seed (*ei echete pistin hōs kokkon sinapeōs*), you could say to this mulberry tree, "Be uprooted and planted in the sea," and it would obey you. (Luke 17:6)

67. Telford, *Barren Temple*, 39–68, 238–39; but this has recently been challenged in Esler, "Withered Fig Tree," 41–67.

68. I present the evidence in *Faith of Jesus Christ*, 49–52.

69. Robinson et al., eds., *Critical Edition of Q*, 492–93.

For truly I tell you, if you have faith the size of a mustard seed (*ean echēte pistin hōs kokkon sinapeōs*), you will say to this mountain, "Move from here to there," and it will move; and nothing will be impossible for you. (Matt 17:20)

The examples cited differ in each case (mulberry tree, mountain), but both liken faith to a mustard seed—another striking metaphor that can be understood quantitatively (stressing how little faith is needed to be effective) or qualitatively, (stressing not the smallness of the mustard seed but its renowned creative potential). Either interpretation is possible, although, given that in the Markan version faith is incompatible with "doubt" (*diakrinō*, Mark 11:23; also *distazō*, Matt 14:31) and elsewhere with "fear" (*phobeomai*, Mark 5:36) and "timidity" (*deilos*, Mark 4:40), the qualitative reading of the mustard-seed metaphor seems more probable (cf. Mark 4:31).[70] This logion doesn't refer specifically to healing or exorcism, although Matthew makes the association by appending it to his relating of a boy possessed by a demon (17:14–21);[71] however, given that, as with Mark 11:23, moving mountains and uprooting trees, like restoring health, were thought to be Yahweh's domain, this saying becomes relevant to our investigation for the way it advocates faith's role as a means of mediating the divine prerogative.[72]

A similar conviction is affirmed in the stilling-of-the-storm narrative where the disciples are admonished for their lack of faith, "Why are you so timid? Have you no faith?" (*ti deiloi este; oupō echete pistin*,

70. See Wallis, *Faith of Jesus Christ*, 55.

71. It is true that in Matthew's version the disciples are admonished for their littleness or poverty of faith (*dia tēn oligopistian hymōn*, 17:20), which may appear to favour a quantitative interpretation for the mustard seed metaphor; however, the evangelist uses *oligopistos/ia* elsewhere in relation to the disciples' failure to perform or discern the miraculous (Matt 8:26; 14:31; 16:8; cf. Q 12:28 [Luke 12:28//Matt 6:30]), suggesting that it may denote not so much a paucity of faith in general, but the lack of a particular quality of faith necessary for mediating the divine will. The apostle Paul makes a similar distinction when he includes faith in a list of spiritual giftings exercised within the Corinthian Christian community (1 Cor 12:9). Self-evidently, he does not mean by this that only some Corinthian Christians were believers, but rather that only those so anointed possessed "mountain-moving faith" (1 Cor 13:2). See Wallis, *Faith of Jesus Christ*, 33–36.

72. Davies and Allison note that mountain-moving was a "proverbial expression for the impossible or improbable" in Israelite literature (Davies and Allison, *Matthew*, 2:727). Bernard Brandon Scott (*Hear then the Parable*, 380–81) draws attention to how mustard was renowned in the ancient world for its curative properties (e.g., Pliny the Elder, *Nat.* 20.87).

my translation; Mark 4:40; also Luke 8:25; cf. "of little faith," *oligopistoi*, Matt 8:26). Jesus' admonishment implies that if the disciples had possessed the requisite faith, then they would have been able to restore calm themselves.[73] Interestingly, although healing illness and subduing storms appear to us to be very different undertakings, this will almost certainly not have been the case in the first century when they would both have been understood in terms of restoring balance—balance in the body's inner relations (cf. phlegm, blood, yellow bile, black bile) and balance in relations between the natural elements (cf. fire, air, earth, water). In both cases, peace as harmonious relating is the sought-after outcome.

"Your faith has made you well"

Now that we've acknowledged the important role attributed to faith within the healing dynamic and explored the range of participants who exercised it, we turn our attention to how faith was understood within these contexts by focusing on the most recorded saying attributed to Jesus in the Gospels—*hē pistis sou sesōken se*, a form eminently memorable in both Greek and Aramaic, which can be translated, "your trust (or 'faith') has rescued you (or 'saved you' or 'healed you' or, possibly, 'made you well' or 'made you whole')." It occurs in four narrative settings—three relating to Jesus' encounters with those deemed to be sick (i.e., experiencing "disorder within the personal body"): a woman suffering from chronic blood loss, Mark 5:34//Matt 9:22//Luke 8:48; a blind man named Bartimaeus, Mark 10:52//Luke 18:42; a Samaritan leper, Luke 17:17; and a fourth with one judged to be sinful (i.e., experiencing "disorder within the covenantal body"; a "sinful" woman, Luke 7:50).[74]

The saying is unusual in that while containing familiar words denoting central themes within both Israelite religion and Christianity, *faith* and *salvation*, it orientates them in an unexpected manner. The subject of the verb "to save" is not Yahweh, as you would expect; it isn't even Jesus; it is, rather, the person's "faith," albeit engendered by Jesus, which in his presence enabled exponents to experience "healing." We should also caution that the semantics of *pistis* ("trust," "faith," "belief," "creed," and so

73. I have explored this further in Wallis, "Relating," 346–51.

74. In the following discussion of this saying, I have drawn on material previously published, especially Wallis, "Redation-Critical Analysis; and Wallis, "New Directions," 349–56.

forth), as with *sōzō* ("rescue," "heal," "save," and the like), are broad,[75] so meaning must be discerned from context rather than imported from a lexicon.

Where, then, is faith to be found? This simple answer is among *outsiders*: a woman (presumably Israelite) forced to the margins by a debilitating condition that rendered her ritually unclean and likely curtailed her social interactions significantly (Mark 5:24–34; cf. Lev 15:19–33); a blind man who, unable to earn a living, reduced to begging and penury, in all likelihood barred from temple, and possibly synagogue, worship (Mark 10:46–52; cf. 2 Sam 5:8; 1QSa 2:5–6; m. Hag. 1:1); a female city-dweller, deemed by religious authorities to be a moral hazard and bad company (Luke 7:36–50); ten "lepers," at least one a Samaritan, quarantined owing to their ritual contagion (Luke 17:11–19; cf. Lev 13–14). Further, given the associations explored earlier between disease, impairment, and sin, sick people came under the judgment of many and would have been ostracized as a consequence.

And what counts for faith among such unlikely exemplars? In all four traditions, faith means *radical trust in Jesus expressed through personal investment and concrete action*: the chronic sufferer ploughs through the crowd undeterred by the ramifications; the blind man throws off his livelihood and pleads for mercy; the penitent risks opprobrium and spends a fortune on costly ointment; the "lepers," while still diseased, set off in search of a priest, expectant of a positive verdict (cf. Lev 13–14). Each of these initiatives embodies a readiness to abandon a former way of being so as to be renewed in some manner in relation to Jesus. In this way, although implicit, these narratives reflect belief in him, however inchoate—confidence, at least, in his trustworthiness as a minister of Yahweh, from whom all healing and forgiveness was believed to flow.[76] Faith also entails radical *boundary-crossing*[77] whether in terms of gender, purity,

75. See the entries in BAGD.

76. However, Yeung overstates the case when she claims that the saying "Your faith has saved you," demonstrates Jesus' "demand for faith in his own person" and "can be regarded as an authoritative declaration of his special identity and an implicit demand for faith in his own person" (*Faith*, 194). In none of the four traditions does Jesus make faith a prerequisite, nor does the saying frame Jesus as the "healer." In contrast to the Fourth Gospel, faith in the Synoptics is rarely ever expressed as belief in Jesus (cf. Matt 18:6 and, possibly, Mark 9:42); more often than not, the object of faith is left open and, in many cases, the focus is on how faith is manifested rather than on whom it is focused. See Ebeling, "Jesus and Faith," 201–46.

77. I've borrowed this phrase from Gerd Theissen; see his discussion of the

race, illness, morality, or (possibly) class, as outsiders find in Jesus a capacity to transcend taboos and social conventions.[78]

And what of *sōzō*? Healing is clearly central, although as we have seen, it is a complex, multidimensional phenomenon of which the underlying medical condition is only one factor. Assuming these traditions originate in actual events, they still do not afford access to the inner experiences of those involved, nor can we be confident of their diagnoses—we are simply informed of how participants appeared and how they responded. But we can be confident that these testimonies of transformation were sufficiently significant to have been remembered, celebrated, embellished, and shared. And in this iterative process they came to serve, and indeed continue to do so, as prisms through which others were able to relate to Jesus with life-changing effect, thereby redrawing the boundaries of Israel to embrace all who found healing in his presence or through his name.

Further, although not directly relevant to our investigation, the four traditions attesting this saying bear witness to communities capable of embracing considerable diversity, where members, unencumbered by many of the religious and socioeconomic boundaries defining existence and fostering division, find common ground in Jesus. Communities capable of including, even with a bias towards, the marginalized where faith and salvation are not conceived as tightly prescribed categories, delimiting particular sets of beliefs or experiences, but encompass a broad spectrum of responses and transformations rooted in and emerging from the particularity of members' circumstances. There are commonalities (faith as radical trust in Jesus with life-changing implications; salvation as encountering Jesus through release from life-threatening or life-diminishing symptoms, restoration of right-relating and social interaction; and so forth), but they are animated personally, lending themselves to multiple embodiments.

---

faith-motif in Theissen, *Miracle Stories*, 129–40.

78. Other expressions of faith include profession (Mark 5:33; 10:47–48), devotion/worship (Luke 7:37–38; 17:16–18), petition (Mark 10:51), and discipleship (Mark 10:52).

Concluding Observations

So far in this chapter we have focused on those elements that are high-lighted within the narratives, sayings and editorial comments relating to Jesus' healing ministry that either contribute to a beneficial outcome or hinder one being reached in some way. What is surprising is how little emphasis is placed upon *the role of Yahweh's spirit or power*. It is true that all four canonical Gospels confirm that Jesus was inspired by God's spirit and that divine inspiration was the motivation for his ministry,[79] but rarely is there any reference to Yahweh's spirit or power within a heal-ing context. Frequently, his wonders are described as "deeds of power" (*dynameis*), yet never by Jesus himself.[80] On one occasion, Jesus becomes aware of a depletion in power when touched intentionally, expectantly, and anonymously by a woman suffering from chronic blood loss (Mark 5:30), although this detail is not stressed to elevate Jesus' status as a wonderworker or mediator of spiritual energy, but to occasion a deeper encounter between both parties, yielding a fuller sense of wholeness. By contrast, as is characteristic of both his Gospel and Acts, Luke goes out of his way to accentuate the divine resourcing of Jesus. For instance, he alone records that Jesus was "filled with the power of the Spirit" (*en tē dynamei tou pneumatos*, Luke 4:14) at the commencement of his min-istry and correlates this to both Jesus' and the disciples' wonderworking activities;[81] yet these references are clearly secondary and reflect a later interpretative phase.

The situation is even more marked with respect to *Yahweh's spirit*, which is particularly striking given the number of references to malevo-lent spirits.[82] Again, Luke repeatedly affirms that Jesus was animated by

79. This is clearly affirmed in the accounts of Jesus' baptism, with the bestowal of the holy spirit (Mark 1:10//Matt 3:16//Luke 3:21–22) which is also recorded in the Fourth Gospel although there is no explicit reference to the baptism itself (John 1:32–34). The Baptist's proclamation about the "coming one" who will baptize in the "holy spirit" is also relevant here (Mark 1:7–8//Matt 3:11–12//Luke 3:15–16).

80. E.g., Mark 6:2, 5//Matt 11:54, 58; Matt 7:22; Q 10:13–15 (Luke 10:13–15//Matt 11:20–24); Luke 10:13; 19:37; Acts 2:22; 8:13; 19:11; cf. Mark 6:14//Matt 14:2. Mark does attribute to Jesus the following saying in response to news of an exorcist who was casting out demons in his name: "Do not stop him; for no one who does a deed of power (*dynamin*) in my name will be able soon afterward to speak evil of me" (Mark 9:39). However, the most plausible setting for this would be the life of the early Jesus movement, rather than the ministry of its founder (see Collins, *Mark*, 448).

81. Jesus: Luke 5:17; 6:19; Acts 10:38; disciples: Luke 9:1; 10:19; Acts 3:12; 4:7; 6:8.

82. E.g., "unclean spirit/s" (*pneuma akatharton*): Mark 1:23, 26, 27//Luke 4:33, 36;

divine spirit (Luke 1:80; 4:1, 14, 18), but outside of the baptism account, Mark refrains from doing so. He speaks of Jesus' own spirit (Mark 2:8; 8:12; cf. John 13:21); he even records the accusation that Jesus was possessed by an unclean spirit (Mark 3:30; also 3:22), but Mark makes no further mention of Jesus being inspired by Yahweh's spirit, not even in relation to his healings or exorcisms. The one possible exception to this silence within our earliest sources is the Q version of the Beelzebul controversy; however, the Matthean and Lukan renderings differ over one keyword: "And if I by Beelzebul cast out demons, your sons, by whom do they cast «them» out? This is why they will be your judges. But if it is by the finger (Matthew: "spirit") of God that I cast out demons, then there has come upon you God's reign." (Q 11:19–20 [*CEQ*; Luke 11:19–20// Matt 12:27–28]). Most scholars conclude that it is easier to account for Matthew replacing "finger" with "spirit" than Luke doing vice versa, so "finger of God (*en daktylō theou*) is probably the more primitive reading, leaving Matthew responsible for the link between God's spirit and Jesus' exorcisms.[83]

In the light of these observations, we would have to conclude that little attempt has been made in our earliest sources, Mark and Q, to heighten the supernatural component within the healing dynamic, not even with respect to exorcisms. Jesus is presented in these traditions neither as a divine figure (*theios anēr*) with access to limitless power nor as a divine messenger seeking authentication for his mission, although his wonderworking would come to be seen in such a light. We only need to compare the healing accounts in Mark and Q with those contained in, for example, the Infancy Gospel of Thomas to recognize the difference:

> Some days later Jesus was playing on a flat roof top of a house, and one of the children playing with him fell from the roof and died. When the other children saw what had happened, they ran away, so that Jesus stood there alone. When the parents of the one who died arrived they accused him of throwing him down. But Jesus said, "I certainly did not throw him down." But they continued to abuse him verbally. Jesus leapt down from the

---

Mark 3:11, 30; Mark 5:2, 8, 12, 13//Luke 8:29; Mark 6:7//Matt 10:1; Mark 7:25; Mark 9:25 (cf. Mark 9:17, 20//Luke 9:39); Q 11:24 (Luke 11:24//Matt 12:43); Luke 6:18; evil spirit/s (*pneuma ponēron*): Q 11:26 (Luke 11:26//Matt 12:45); Luke 7:21; 8:2. Then there are all the references to demon/s (*daimonion/a*; approximately sixty across all four Gospels).

83. Davies and Allison conveniently summarize all the arguments in *Matthew*, 2:339–41.

roof and stood beside the child's corpse, and with a loud voice he cried out, "Zenon!" (for that was his name) "rise up and tell me: did I throw you down?" Right away he rose and said, "Not at all, Lord! You did not throw me down, but you have raised me up!" When they saw this they were astounded. The parents of the child glorified God for the sign that had occurred, and they worshipped Jesus . . . After these things, and infant in Joseph's neighborhood became sick and died; and his mother was weeping loudly. When Jesus heard the outburst of sorrow and the disturbance, he ran up quickly and found the child dead. He touched its breast, saying "I say to you, young child, do not die but live, and be with your mother." Immediately the child opened its eyes and laughed. Jesus said to the woman, "Take him, give him milk, and remember me." When the crowd standing there saw what had happened, it was amazed. The people said, "Truly this child is either a god or an angel of God, for his every word is an accomplished deed." Jesus then left from there to play with the other children.[84]

Yet even the Johannine presentation of Jesus' wonderworking as signs (*sēmeia*) pointing to his true identity and grounds for belief in him is alien to these earliest traditions in Mark and Q, where Jesus' healings and exorcisms do not serve as expressions of his divine status or of his exclusive role within God's kingdom; rather, they constitute manifestations of the kingdom itself and, as such, characterize those who share Jesus' convictions about the immanence of Yahweh's reign and choose to participate in its emergence. It is entirely congruent, therefore, that the vital ingredients within the healing dynamic are expressions of, as we have seen, a quality of human being that Jesus embodied personally and engendered in others. These testimonies of transformation bear witness neither to magic nor to miracles, but to what becomes possible when people come to see themselves in relation to a different paradigm, animated by a different vision of human being in relation to the divine and its associated potentialities.

84. Inf. Gos. Thom. 9.1–3; 17.1–2 [*ApGos*].

5

Jesus the Exorcist

IN THIS CHAPTER OUR attention turns to Jesus' reputation for performing exorcisms. As we have already pointed out, such a reputation was by no means unique in the ancient world,[1] nor was it one that Jesus considered to be exclusively his own prerogative. In chapter 3, we noted how those recruited to serve as apprentices were expected not only to preach his kingdom message but also to demonstrate its proximity through, above all, performing exorcisms (Mark 3:15; 6:7; Matt 10:8), and that the Synoptics record at least one incidence of the disciples attempting to do so (Mark 9:14–29)[2]—suggesting exorcising, like healing, was an activity characteristic of those who shared Jesus' convictions about Yahweh's

---

1. E.g., 1QapGen 20.12–30; 4Q242; Tob 8:1–3; Josephus, *Ant.* 8.45–49; Q 11:19 (Luke 11:19//Matt 12:27); Mark 9:38–40; cf. Matt 7:22–23; Acts 19:13.

2. See also, Mark's editorial comment, "So they [the disciples] went out and proclaimed that all should repent. They cast out many demons, and anointed with oil many who were sick and cured them" (6:12–13//Luke 9:6), the longer "secondary" ending to his gospel, "And he [resurrected Jesus] said to them, 'Go into all the world and proclaim the good news to the whole creation . . . And these signs will accompany those who believe: by using my name they will cast out demons . . .'" (16:15–17), and Luke's account of the return of the Seventy, "The seventy returned with joy, saying, 'Lord, in your name even the demons submit to us!' He said to them, 'I watched Satan fall from heaven like a flash of lightning. See, I have given you authority to tread on snakes and scorpions, and over all the power of the enemy; and nothing will hurt you. Nevertheless, do not rejoice at this, that the spirits submit to you, but rejoice that your names are written in heaven'" (10:17–20). It is possible that Peter's authorization to "bind" and "loose" should also be understood in this light (Matt 16:17–19; cf. 18:18); see Hiers, "Binding," 233–50; and Evans, "Jesus and the Spirits," 154.

kingdom and, perhaps more importantly, were willing to put those convictions to the test through following his lead and living in their light.

Equally noteworthy is the observation, again made previously, that healings and exorcisms cannot always be distinguished at the level of presenting symptoms, but only in terms of their etiology or treatment or, in some cases, both. In several instances, sufferers present with physical maladies that, unlike in other healing accounts, are attributed to alien or oppressive forces and, as we shall see, dealt with accordingly. For example, a boy rendered deaf and dumb, given over to convulsions, was deemed to be possessed by an "unclean spirit" that is forcefully expelled (Mark 9:25–26; cf. 9:17, 20).[3] Or, again, a Q tradition attributes muteness to demonic activity,[4] while Luke records Jesus describing a woman unable to stand upright as "a daughter of Abraham whom Satan bound for eighteen long years" (Luke 13:16).[5]

In addition to these narratives are those where either no symptoms are recorded, such as with the daughter of a Syrophoenician woman (Mark 7:24–30//Matt 15:21–28), or those mentioned are interpreted as indicative of possession, or at least oppression, by a malevolent presence variously identified as a "demon" (*diamonion*), "unclean spirit" (*pneuma akatharton*) or, occasionally in Matthew and Luke, as an "evil spirit" (*pneuma ponēron*).[6] The synoptic evangelists appear to use the first two of these terms interchangeably, sometimes employing both in the same

3. Interestingly, Matthew initially describes the boy as being "moonstruck" (*selēniazomai*, 17:15), which is misleadingly translated in some modern versions as "epileptic" (e.g., RSV, NRSV). The invasive and oppressive source of the presenting symptoms is underlined later in Matthew's text where he records that Jesus both rebuked and expelled the menacing demon (17:18).

4. This case is complicated by the fact that Matthew records two versions of what appears to be the same Q tradition (Q 11:14–15 [Luke 11:14–15//Matt 12:22–24// Matt 9:32–34). The latter is probably a "redactional doublet" (see Davies and Allison, *Matthew*, 2:138–39).

5. Witmer suggests that certain symptoms may have been associated with unclean spirits in first-century Palestine (Witmer, *Galilean Exorcist*, 146, 190).

6. "Unclean spirit/s" (*pneuma akatharton*): Mark 1:23, 26, 27//Luke 4:33, 36; Mark 3:11, 30; Mark 5:2, 8, 12, 13//Luke 8:29; Mark 6:7//Matt 10:1; Mark 7:25; Mark 9:25 (cf. Mark 9:17, 20//Luke 9:39); Q 11:24 (Luke 11:24//Matt 12:43); Luke 6:18; "evil spirit/s" (*pneuma ponēron*): Q 11:26 (Luke 11:26//Matt 12:45); Luke 7:21; 8:2; plus, over sixty references to "demons" (*daimonia*) across all four Gospels. On one occasion, Luke uses a conflated version, "spirit of an unclean demon" (*pneuma daimoniou akathartou*, 4:33).

narrative;[7] while in others, Matthew or Luke replaces Mark's rendering with one of the alternatives.[8]

These designations merit closer attention as their meaning is far from obvious. Consider, for example, "demon" (*daimonion*), which occurs only occasionally in the Septuagint where it translates several Hebrew words.[9] In most cases, "demons," as well as comparable figures such as *lilith*, *sā'irim* (goat-demons), and, possibly, *'āz'azēl*, are contrasted with Yahweh and deemed to be incompatible with covenantal faithfulness.[10] As such, they represent forms of idolatry which compromise allegiance to and worship of the one true God. For instance, reflecting on the wilderness sojourns following the exodus, Moses bemoans that "[t]hey [Israelites] sacrificed to demons (*shēdim*; LXX, *daimonios*), not God (*'elohah*; LXX, *theō*), to deities (*'elohim*; LXX, *theois*) they had never known, to new ones recently arrived, whom your ancestors had not feared."[11] In describing demons as "gods," this verse bears witness to a conviction affirmed elsewhere in the Hebrew Scriptures, namely, that although other deities and forms of spiritual mediation exist, they should be shunned in favor of exclusive devotion to Yahweh:

7. E.g., Mark 5:1-20; 6:6-13; 7:24-30.

8. E.g., Mark 1:26 (unclean spirit)//Luke 4:35 (demon); Mark 1:39 (demon)//Luke 4:44 (unclean spirit); Mark 3:15 (demon)//Matt 10:1 (unclean spirit); Mark 5:2 (unclean spirit)//Luke 8:27 (demon); Mark 7:25 (unclean spirit)//Matt 15:22 (demon); Mark 9:25 (unclean spirit)//Matt 17:18 (demon).

9. I.e., *gad* (coriander [sic!], fortune), Isa 65:11; *'elil* (worthless, idol), Ps 95:5; *qeteb* (disaster), Ps 90:6 (MT Ps 91:6); *shēd* (demon), Deut 32:17; Ps 105:37 (MT 106:37); *sā'ir* (male goat, satyr, demon), Isa 13:21; 34:14; no Hebrew equivalent, Isa 65:3.

10. E.g., "Wildcats shall meet with hyenas, goat-demons (*sā'ir*; LXX, *daimonia*) shall call to each other; there too Lilith (*lilith*; LXX, *onokentauroi*) shall repose, and find a place to rest" (Isa 34:14). On one occasion, *sā'ir* is translated as *daimonia* in the LXX (Isa 13:21), while elsewhere it is rendered by *mataios* ("vain," "useless," "worthless"; Lev 17:7; 2 Chr 11:15; cf. "and Aaron shall cast lots on the two goats, one lot for the LORD and the other lot for Azazel (*'āz'azēl*; LXX, *apopompaiō*) . . . but the goat on which the lot fell for Azazel (*'āz'azēl*; LXX, *apopompaiou*) shall be presented alive before the LORD to make atonement over it, that it may be sent away into the wilderness to Azazel (*'āz'azēl*; LXX, *apopompēn*) . . . The one who sets the goat free for Azazel (*'āz'azēl*; LXX, *ton chimaron ton diestalmenon*) shall wash his clothes and bathe his body in water, and afterward may come into the camp" (Lev 16:8, 10, 26).

11. Deut 32:17; also "Happy are we, O Israel, for we know what is pleasing to God. Take courage, my people, who perpetuate Israel's name! It was not for destruction that you were sold to the nations, but you were handed over to your enemies because you angered God. For you provoked the one who made you by sacrificing to demons and not to God (*thusantes daimoniois kai ou theō*)" (Bar 4:4-7; also 4:35).

I am the LORD your God, who brought you out of the land of
Egypt, out of the house of slavery; you shall have no other gods
before me. (Exod 20:2-3)

For the LORD your God is God of gods and Lord of lords, the
great God, mighty and awesome, who is not partial and takes no
bribe, who executes justice for the orphan and the widow, and
who loves the strangers, providing them food and clothing. You
shall also love the stranger, for you were strangers in the land
of Egypt. You shall fear the Lord your God; him alone you shall
worship; to him you shall hold fast, and by his name you shall
swear. (Deut 10:17-20)

No one shall be found among you who makes a son or daughter
pass through fire, or who practices divination, or is a soothsayer,
or an augur, or a sorcerer. (Deut 18:10; also Exod 22:18; Lev
19:26; Num 23:23; cf. Deut 12:31; 2 Kgs 17:17; 21:6; Isa 65:2-5)

Do not turn to mediums or wizards; do not seek them out to
be defiled by them. I am the LORD your God. (Lev 19:31; also
18:21; 20:6; cf. 1 Sam 28:1-14)

This pursuit of a thoroughgoing monotheism may well account for
the paucity of references to demons and the like in the Hebrew Scriptures
in the sense that, where Yahweh is believed to reign supreme, everything
else is ultimately of divine origin, even evil. And from what we can gather,
it was attempting to account theologically for the existence of suffering
and moral evil, together with possible exposure to dualistic religious systems such as Zoroastrianism, that led to the emergence of malevolent
forces and their personifications within Israelite faith.[12] This development stands in contrast to the classical world where demons tended not
to be cast in a pejorative light, but denoted deities or, more frequently,
divine mediators between humans and the gods.[13] This excerpt from

12. "It is a debatable point among scholars in what specific ways and to what extent Persian influence made itself felt among the Jews; but it can hardly be denied
that the apocalyptic teaching, for example, concerning such matters as 'the two ages',
the determinism of historical events, angelology and demonology, the notion of the
final judgement and eschatological ideas generally owes much to this source" (Russell,
Method and Message, 19, also 235-62; but note the cautionary comments of Collins,
Apocalyptic Imagination, 37).

13. E.g., "Their Olympic victories to date have, it seems, already been reported; and
those to come I would declare clearly when they occur. At this point I am hopeful, but
with the god (*daimōn*) is the outcome. But if their family fortune should continue, we

Plato (428/7–348/7 BCE), which relates a dialogue between Socrates and a philosopher-prophetess from the Greek city of Mantinea by the name of Diotima, is characteristic of many ancient authors:

> "So you see," she said, "you are a person who does not consider Love to be a god."
>
> "What then," I asked, "can Love be? A mortal?"
>
> "Anything but that."
>
> "Well what?"
>
> "As I previously suggested, between a mortal and an immortal."
>
> "And what is that, Diotima?"
>
> "A great spirit (*daimōn megas*), Socrates: for the whole of the spiritual is between divine and mortal (*to daimonion metaxu esti theou te kai thnētou*)."
>
> "Possessing what power?" I asked.
>
> "Interpreting and transporting human things to the gods and divine things to men; entreaties and sacrifices from below, and ordinances and requitals from above: being midway between, it makes each to supplement the other, so that the whole is combined in one. Through it are conveyed all divination and priestcraft concerning sacrifice and ritual and incantations, and all soothsaying and sorcery. God with man does not mingle: but the spiritual is the means of all society and converse of men with gods and of gods with men, whether waking or asleep. Whosoever has skill in these affairs is a spiritual man (*ta toiauta sophos diamonios anēr*); to have it in other matters, as in common arts and crafts, is for the mechanical. Many and multifarious are these spirits (*hoi daimones polloi*), and one of them is Love."[14]

In fact, as Werner Foerster observes,[15] the emergence of angels within Israelite religion provided the conceptual framework for

will leave it to Zeus and Enyalius to accomplish" (Pindar [518–438 BCE], *Ol.* 13.101–107 [LCL 56]). "Think the matter over more carefully, know yourself, ask the Deity (*to daimonion*), do not attempt the task without God (*theou*). For if God so advises you, be assured that He wishes you either to become great, or to receive many stripes" (Epictetus [55–135 CE], *Disc.* 3.22.53 [LCL 218]).

14. Plato, *Symp.* 202e [LCL 166]; also *Phaedr.* 246e.

15. "The Greek *daimōn* concept embraces the forces which mediate between God and men. It is characteristic of the Old Testament that a special name was coined describing such powers as God's messengers, i.e. *malāk > angelos*. In this way a linguistic and material basis was given for dualism within the spirit world, and the way was thus prepared for later development. It is particularly important to realize that the actual

embracing dualistic worldviews in which the struggle between good and evil was rehearsed not only on earth but also in spiritual realms. David Russell explains the rationale in these terms:

> God had entrusted the government of the world to the care of his angelic rulers, but they had rebelled against him and had stolen it from his control. The world was no longer God's kingdom; it lay in the hands of evil cosmic forces which were bent on the destruction of mankind and of the world itself.[16]

Whether or not Israelite faith and subsequently Christianity embraced a thoroughgoing dualism in which two equally powerful forces were locked in cosmic combat in perpetuity, there is ample evidence that both traditions accommodated a relativized form where, although Yahweh's sovereignty would ultimately be vindicated, the present time was characterized by celestial skirmishes between benevolent and malevolent forces populating history.[17] Within such a scenario, angels and demons

---

workings of destructive powers, which in the Greek world are attributed to *daimones*, are in the Old Testament ascribed to the rule of God . . . Old Testament monotheism is thus maintained, since no powers to which man might turn in any matter is outside the one God of Israel" (Foerster, "*daimōn*," 11).

16. Russell, *Method and Message*, 267. Clearly, this is a generalization. One of the key interpretive issues relates to whether the present time where evil appeared to flourish unabated was nevertheless authorized by Yahweh or beyond Yahweh's control. Different texts, mainly apocalyptic in genre, espoused different positions, although there was convergence around the conviction that Yahweh's will would ultimately prevail, usually through the agency of a mediator variously envisaged. Robert Webb outlines five intermediary archetypes (e.g., Davidic King/Messiah; Aaronic Messiah; Angelic Prince Michael/Melchizedek; Human-like Figure/Son of Man; Elijah-redivivus), before concluding "that Yahweh, as Israel's God, was not on a par with the other expected figures of judgment and restoration, because Yahweh was the prime figure behind all of them . . . By concentrating upon Yahweh, the author was stressing the theological necessity for divine involvement as the prime cause behind the eschatological judgment and restoration being hoped for. At the same time, by emphasizing other expected figures, the author was expressing the realization that Yahweh worked through these figures as his agents to bring about the historical and terrestrial expectations described" (*John the Baptizer*, 259–60, also 219–60).

17. E.g., "He [God] has created man to govern the world, and has appointed for him two spirits in which to walk until the time of His visitation: the spirits of truth and injustice. Those born of truth spring from a fountain of light, but those born of injustice spring from a source of darkness. All the children of righteousness are ruled by the Prince of Light and walk in the ways of light, but all the children of injustice are ruled by the Angel of Darkness and walk in the ways of darkness" (1QS 3:17–23 [*CDSSE*]). Dualist thinking is pronounced in several Dead Sea Scrolls, as well as various intertestamental works; see Witmer, *Galilean Exorcist*, 35–41, and, more broadly,

as, indeed, sacred spirit and evil/unclean spirits, were the mediators and prosecutors of this attrition, who possessed the potential to infect each human heart and fuel conflict at every level of human intercourse. A case in point is the book of Tobit (from the third or second century BCE) where these intermediaries are at work for good or ill, as the following passage illustrates:

> But the angel said to the young man, "Catch hold of the fish and hang on to it!" So the young man grasped the fish and drew it up on the land. Then the angel said to him, "Cut open the fish and take out its gall, heart, and liver. Keep them with you, but throw away the intestines. For its gall, heart, and liver are useful as medicine (*eis pharmakon chrēsimon*)." So after cutting open the fish the young man gathered together the gall, heart, and liver; then he roasted and ate some of the fish, and kept some to be salted. The two continued on their way together until they were near Media. Then the young man questioned the angel and said to him, "Brother Azariah, what medicinal value (*to pharmakon*) is there in the fish's heart and liver, and in the gall?" He replied, "As for the fish's heart and liver, you must burn them to make a smoke in the presence of a man or woman afflicted by a demon or evil spirit (*daimoniou ē pneumatos ponērou*), and every affliction will flee away and never remain with that person any longer. And as for the gall, anoint a person's eyes where white films have appeared on them; blow upon them, upon the white films, and the eyes will be healed (*hugiainousin*; cf. *iathēsetai*)."[18]

Interestingly, although Josephus (37–circa 100 CE) can employ *daimonion* in either a neutral or positive sense to denote deity, divine providence, or the spirits of the departed,[19] he can also use it with respect

---

Wink, *Unmasking the Powers*.

18. Tob [Sinaiticus] 6:4–9; on *daimonion*, see also 3:8, 17; 6:14, 16, 17; 8:3.

19. E.g., "for the Deity (*to daimonion*) conversed with him (John Hyrcanus), and he was not ignorant of anything that was to come afterward." (*J.W.* 1.69 [LCL 203]; also 6.429; cf. 5.502); "for Divine Providence (*to daimonion*) had in reality conferred upon him [Herod the Great] a great many outward advantages for his happiness, even beyond his hopes" (*Ant.* 16.76 [LCL 410]; also *daimonion*: *Ant.* 13.314; 19.60; *J.W.* 1.82; 1.331, 370, 373, 376, 613; 2.457; 3.341; 4.76, 217, 501, 622; 5.377; 7.82, 159, 318; *Life* 1.402; *daimōn*: *Ant.* 14.291; *J.W.* 1.556; 4.41; cf. *J.W.* 2.259; 4.649); "As these men said thus, and called upon Alexander's ghost (*tous Alexandrou daimonas*) for pity of those already slain, and those in danger of it" (*Ant.* 13.416 [LCL 365]; also *daimōn*: 13.317; *J.W.* 1.521, 599, 607; 6.47; *daimonion*: *J.W.* 1.84; 16.210; *Ag. Ap.* 2.263).

to evil forces working at variance to God's will and saving purposes.[20] For example, in the episode narrated in 1 Sam 16, where Saul, having fallen from divine favor, is tormented by an "evil spirit" (*ruach rā'āh*; LXX *pneuma ponēron*) sent from Yahweh (16:14–23), Josephus—perhaps, recognizing the incongruity in the biblical text caused by the divine provenance of conflicting species of spirits—concludes that the king had become demon-possessed:

> So Samuel, when he had given him these admonitions, went away. But the Divine Power (*to theion*) departed from Saul, and moved to David; who, upon this removal of the Divine Spirit (*tou theou pneumatos*) to him, began to prophesy; but as for Saul, some strange and demoniac disorders (*pathē tina kai daimonia*) came upon him, and brought upon him such suffocation as were ready to choke him; for which the physicians (*tous iatrous*) could find no other remedy (*therapeian*) but this: that if any person could charm (*exadein dynamenos*) those passions by singing, and playing upon the harp, they advised them to inquire for such a one, and to observe when these demons (*ta daimonia*) came upon him and disturbed him, and to take care that such a person might stand over him, and play upon the harp, and recite hymns to him.[21]

20. This development from classical usage is something that the influential Alexandrian Jew Philo (25 BCE–50 CE) seems reticent to follow, preferring to place angels, demons, spirits, and the like under the same umbrella of intermediaries: "So if you realize that souls (*psychas*) and demons (*daimonas*) and angels (*angelous*) are but different names for the same one underlying object, you will cast from you that most grievous burden, the fear of demons or superstition (*deisidaimonian*) . . . And so, too, you also will not go wrong if you reckon as angels, not only those who are worthy of the name, who are as ambassadors backwards and forwards between men and God and are rendered sacred and inviolate by reason of that glorious and blameless ministry, but also those who are unholy and unworthy of the title" (*Gig.* 1.16–18 [LCL 227]; also Philo, *Somn.* 1:140–41).

21. Josephus, *Ant.* 6.166, 168 [LCL 490]; also "Consider these things [Jonathan to Saul], and change your mind to a more merciful temper, and do no mischief to a man, who, in the first place, has done us the greatest kindness of preserving you; for when an evil spirit and demons (*tou ponērou pneumatos kai tōn daimoniōn*) had seized upon you, he cast them out (*exebalen*), and procured rest to your soul from their incursions: and, in the second place, has avenged us of our enemies; for it is a base thing to forget such benefits" (*Ant.* 6.211 [LCL 490]; also 6.214; 8.45–48; 13.415; cf. *J.W.* 7.185, 389; *Ag. Ap.* 2.263).

Like *demon*, *evil spirit* occurs infrequently in the Hebrew Scriptures and the writings of the Second Temple period,[22] yet *unclean spirit* is even rarer.[23] With respect to the latter, it is important to recognize, as Jonathan Klawans has recently reiterated, that ritual and moral impurity were "understood as two distinct but analogous perceptions of contagion" in this literature.[24] One consequence of this is that moral defilement through sexual impropriety, bloodshed, or idolatry did not of itself render the sinner ritually impure, any more than becoming ritually impure through contact with human corpses or animal carcasses or developing certain skin conditions or discharging various bodily emissions rendered someone morally defiled. That said, what remains opaque is whether *unclean* in "unclean spirit" denotes moral impurity or ritual impurity or both.

Professor Collins proposes that this term, presumably along with "evil spirit," should be understood in the light of the speculation over the origins of evil rooted in the story about how the "sons of God" fall from grace through sexual relations with the "daughters of humanity" (Gen 6:1–4).[25] In 1 Enoch (from the second century BCE to the first century CE), the patriarch is instructed by God to rebuke these "watchers" in the following terms: "For what reason have you abandoned the high, holy, and eternal heaven; and slept with women and defiled yourselves with the daughters of the people . . . ? Surely you, you [used to be] holy, spiritual, the living ones, [possessing] eternal life; but (now) you have defiled yourselves with women." (15:3–4 [*OTP*]). Likewise, in the book of Jubilees (from the second century BCE), one of the three causes of the flood is given as "the fornication which the Watchers, apart from the mandate of their authority, fornicated with the daughters of men and took for themselves wives from all whom they chose and made a beginning of impurity" (7:21). Collins's reconstruction seems plausible despite the lack of verbal correspondence and suggests that *unclean* in "unclean spirit"

22. In some instances, the "evil spirit" (*ruach rā'āh*; LXX *pneuma ponēron*) is sent by Yahweh (e.g., Judg 9:23; 1 Sam 16:14–16, 23; 19:9), while in other later texts it constitutes an independent, opposing force (e.g., Hos 12:1 [LXX]; Tob 6:8; 1 En. 15:8; T.Sim. 3:5; 4:9; T. Levi 5:6; 18:12; T. Ash. 1:9; 6:5; T. Sol. [A] 13:6; 22:10; [C] 1:2).

23. In the Hebrew Scriptures, "unclean spirit" occurs only in Zech 13:2 (*ruach hatemāh*, LXX *to pneuma to akatharton*; see also: 11Q5 19.15; 4Q444; T. Benj. 5:2; T. Sol. 3:7).

24. Klawans, *Impurity*, 158. However, Klawans notes that these perceptions are collapsed into one within many of the sectarian documents among the Dead Sea Scrolls (67–91).

25. Collins, *Mark*, 167–68.

denotes moral defilement rather than ritual impurity—a deduction that gains credence from the way the evangelists employ "unclean spirit" and "evil spirit" interchangeably.

Yet this only begs the question of the circumstances resulting in possession, as well as the impact of a possessing "unclean spirit" on the possessed. Unlike ritual impurity, which was considered contagious, moral impurity was not—presumably because it presupposed intentionality and, by implication, accountability for its debasing and disordering effects.[26] So, unless the possessed in the gospel accounts were judged to be complicit with their possessors (and there is no evidence to suggest they were), it seems probable that possession was envisaged as a form of bodily invasion carried out against the will of the possessed, incarcerating the victim yet conveying no moral stain or imputation of guilt or culpability—in a comparable manner, perhaps, to Rome's military conquest of Israel, the body politic or covenantal body, and subjugation of its citizens.

We shall return to this comparison between possession and invasion in a moment, but before doing so we must further clarify the impact of possession by an unclean or evil spirit on the victim. Significantly, the possessed in the gospel accounts are not portrayed as sinners who had become corrupted through wrongdoing, but as victims of factors beyond their control. In contrast to passages where transgression and sickness appear to be linked,[27] no such moral correlation is made with respect to possession. Consequently, forgiveness of sins is never a prerequisite to or component of exorcism in the New Testament, which is portrayed more in terms of the vanquishing of enemy forces. This is nowhere clearer than in the miniparable cum similitude of the binding of the strong man, which formed part of Jesus' response to the accusation of being demon-possessed and so to the implication that he drew on demonic powers to exorcise: "But no one can enter a strong man's house and plunder his property without first tying up the strong man; then indeed the house can be plundered" (Mark 3:27). Although not all details readily correlate with the practice of Jesus' deliverance ministry,[28] there can be little doubt

---

26. Klawans, *Impurity*, 41–42.

27. E.g., Mark 2:1–12; John 5:14; Pap. Eg. 2; these texts, together with those challenging the link between illness and sin, were discussed in chapter 4.

28. For example, in cases of possession, the "strong man" is portrayed as invading somebody else's "property"; although it could be argued that, through executing such an invasion successfully, the "strong man" had in effect laid claim to it, and, through doing so, now considered it to be his own. Graham Twelftree offers an alternative

that the likening of exorcism to the overpowering and binding of a potent force was intended.[29]

Further support for this deduction is supplied by the longest of the gospel exorcism narratives, where we encounter not only the overpowering of an alien, invading force, but also its subsequent expulsion. It can be no coincidence that the "unclean spirit"[30] of Mark 5:1–20 is named Legion (vv. 9, 15)—a Latin loanword coterminous in first-century Palestine and its environs with the emperor's tenth legion, Fretensis, stationed in Syria, whose military standards and seals displayed, among other symbols, the image of a boar.[31] Although the tradition history of this Decapolis-based narrative is debated, by the time of its inclusion in Mark and quite probably a good deal earlier, two interconnected correlations were pronounced:[32] first, between Roman occupation of the land and the unclean spirit's possession of the man; second, between the exorcism of the unclean spirit and the expulsion of Roman forces. The dynamics of these correlations are not spelled out—perhaps intentionally,

---

interpretation: "Thus, in conclusion, what we have here is a *parable of an exorcism*. Satan, the Strong Man, is bound and his house, the possessed person, is taken from him." (*Jesus the Exorcist*, 112).

29. For a discussion of the tradition-history (Q 11:21–22 [Luke 11:21–22//Matt 12:29//Gos. Thom. 35; Mark 3:27) and interpretation of this verse, see Meier, *Marginal Jew*, 2:418–22: Meier argues persuasively for attributing this miniparable/similitude to the historical Jesus.

30. In fact, within Mark's version, the "intruder" is variously described as "unclean spirit" (vv. 2, 8); "unclean spirits" (vv. 12–13); "demon" (vv. 15, 16, 18). In contrast, Matthew exclusively (8:28–34) and Luke with one exception (8:26–39; v. 29, "unclean spirit") only speak of demons. It is possible, therefore, that the original version contained the ambiguous "unclean spirit/s" which was replaced or supplemented in later iterations by the more explicit "demon/s."

31. Caesar's tenth legion had been stationed at Cyrrhus in northwestern Syria since 6 CE where it remained until relocating to Judea to prosecute the first Jewish War (66–70 CE), including the siege of Jerusalem. For further details and sources, see Collins, *Mark*, 268–70; and Theissen, *Gospels in Context*, 110–11.

32. On the tradition-history of this pericope, see Twelftree, *Jesus the Exorcist*, 72–87, and Meier, *Marginal Jew*, 2:650–53; a variant, involving a possessed woman, can be found in the (Arab.) Gos. Inf. 14. With respect to the pre-Markan genesis of the two interconnected correlations, it is generally recognized that the evangelist entertained pro-Roman sympathies (e.g., Mark 15:1–15, 39) and, consequently, is unlikely to have forged the link between Jesus' exorcisms and political emancipation. That said, the swine incident (vv. 11–14) may well be secondary to the original narrative, constituting an interpretative gloss highlighting the sociopolitical dimension of possession and exorcism.

thereby underlining the subversive nature of the text;[33] but the inference favors causation: military invasion and occupation manifesting itself as spiritual invasion and occupation; conversely, spiritual emancipation in the form of exorcism signaling political emancipation in the form of liberation from Roman rule.[34] Why else would the spiritual legion of unclean spirits become subsumed within a herd of unclean creatures (cf. the tenth Legion's porcine insignia; Lev 11:7; Deut 14:8), both of which were subsequently driven from the land (Mark 5:10–13)?[35] Recognition of the sociopolitical, even insurrectionist, consequences of Jesus' exorcistic activity would also account for why local inhabitants, recognizing a potential troublemaker in their midst, urged him to move on before incurring the wrath of Rome (Mark 5:17).[36]

The revolutionary significance of Jesus' exorcisms is further underlined within those texts that locate them within his broader struggle against forces, cosmic or terrestrial, that frustrate the emergence of Yahweh's reign. For example, those traditions where Jesus is accused of being possessed by Beelzebul, the ruler of demons, by whose authority he was judged able to control lesser demons.[37] Significantly, Jesus' ability

33. See James Scott's insightful exposition of the subversive role of what he describes as "hidden transcripts" within oppressed communities, *Domination*, and Richard Horsley's application of his insights to Mark and other early Christian documents in *Hidden Transcripts*, and *Jesus in Context*, 169–204.

34. On the sociopolitical interpretation of this exorcism, as well as others, see Hollenbach, "Demoniacs," 567–88, Guijarro, "Politics," 159–74, and Myers, *Binding*, 190–94.

35. Duncan Derrett highlights the military terminology employed within the narrative (e.g., *agelē*, "herd/band [of troops]," *epitrepō*, "to permit/to dismiss," *hormaō*, "to rush/to charge"), lending further support to the interpretation offered here ("Contributions," 2–17).

36. "By interpreting the casting out of demons as a sign of the coming of the kingdom of God, and by making his exorcisms part of a strategy for restoring Israelite integrity, Jesus threatened the stability of the social order . . . By casting out the demons and restoring people to society, Jesus threatened a social order in which demonic possession was an escape-valve. The puzzling reaction to his exorcisms from his family, as well as from the people, the scribes, and Herod Antipas, suggests that the social reintegration of demoniacs had societal and political connotations for Jesus and for his contemporaries that are opaque to us . . . The sign of the coming of God's reign was the restoration to society of those who were at the margins. Jesus called them to be part of a new family, together with him and his followers (Mark 3:31–35; 10:28–30), and this was highly disruptive" (Guijarro, "Politics," 166, 172).

37. As previously discussed, there appear to have been versions of this controversy, including the parable of the house divided, in both Mark (3:22–25) and Q (11:14–20

to exorcise is not in question here; what is challenged is the source of his authority and, by implication, the basis for his success. He is accused not simply of being spirit-possessed but of being possessed by a malevolent presence.[38] Evidentially, for Jesus, as well as for his opponents, his exorcisms were neither inexplicable nor morally neutral; rather, they constituted instantiations of an overarching spiritual conflict being played out on a human stage.

We encounter a comparable scenario in which real-time skirmishes were thought to make visible or embody an all-encompassing spiritual struggle between Yahweh and evil in the book of Daniel. Chapters 10–12 lay out a vision relating, with varying degrees of specificity, to a period in Israelite history from king Cyrus of Persia (550–530 BCE) through to Antiochus Epiphanes IV (175–163 BCE), concluding with the emergence of Israel's guardian angel, Michael, to administer Yahweh's justice (12:1–3). Underpinning this scenario is the conviction that "a celestial battle between opposing angelic forces was thought to correspond to the terrestrial conflict experienced by God's people"[39] in which their vindication would ultimately be secured through Yahweh's mediated initiative in the form of angelic intervention.

Admittedly, the Beelzebul controversy was not precipitated by military conflict prosecuted in the land of Israel, but was occasioned by spiritual conflict executed in the lives of Israelites who had in some way internalized the attrition characterizing an oppressed people (see below). And just as that oppression-manifested-as-possession, mediated by Roman hegemony, was ultimately malevolent in origin, so its overthrow, mediated by Jesus, was ultimately a demonstration of Yahweh's presence and sovereign rule: "And if I by Beelzebul cast out demons, your sons, by whom do they cast «them» out? This is why they will be your judges. But if it is by the finger (Matthew: "spirit") of God that I cast out demons, then there has come upon you God's reign." (Q 11:19–20 [*CEQ*; Luke

---

[Luke 11:14–20//Matt 11:22–28]), with Matthew expanding the material further (10:24–25). Allied to these is the parable of the return of an unclean spirit to a house swept clean (Q 11:24–26 [Luke 11:24–26//Matt 12:43–45]; Matt 9:43–45) which, in its original context, presumably referred to the state of those who had been exorcised by Jesus, but who had yet to decide whether to embrace his message and way—see Davies and Allison, *Matthew*, 2:359–62, who review the interpretative options and map out a tradition history.

38. Interestingly, the charge that Jesus was demon-possessed is recorded three times in the Fourth Gospel (John 7:20; 8:48–52; 10:20–21).

39. Webb, *John the Baptizer*, 239; see also Wink, *Unmasking the Powers*, 88–91.

11:19–20//Matt 12:27–28])[40] The challenge of Jesus' deliverance ministry for existing sociopolitical authorities is also stressed in another saying attributed to him, which is only recorded in Luke and takes the form of a pronouncement or, possibly, a warning:

> At that very hour some Pharisees came and said to [Jesus], "Get away from here, for Herod wants to kill you." He said to them, "Go and tell that fox for me, 'Listen, I am casting out demons and performing cures today and tomorrow, and on the third day I finish my work. Yet today, tomorrow, and the next day I must be on my way, because it is impossible for a prophet to be killed outside of Jerusalem.'"[41]

The narrative context suggests that at least some members of the pharisaic movement viewed Jesus in a positive light.[42] More importantly for our purposes, the saying presents Jesus' healing and deliverance ministry as integral to his prophetic role.[43] As such, these actions may well have constituted the basis for Antipas's resolve to kill him, as well as the grounds for Jesus' anticipation of his own demise. We know from Josephus's account of John the Baptist's death that Herod Antipas felt threatened by popular unrisings of a potentially subversive bent (*Ant.* 18.116–19). In light of this, especially as Jesus' healings and exorcisms supply the most plausible basis for his own popularity—such activity, when interpreted as manifestations of the emergence of Yahweh's reign (cf. Q 7:18–23 [Luke 7:18–23//Matt 11:2–6]; Q 11:19–20 [Luke 11:19–20//Matt 12:27–28])—would surely have set alarm bells ringing in Antipas's ears. And, if in his, then in any other ruler responsible for maintaining the *Pax Romana* in Palestine at that time.

By now it will have become apparent that however alien they may appear to the modern mind, exorcisms were considered a characteristic and defining component of Jesus' kingdom ministry to the extent that most of the synoptic evangelists' summaries of that ministry make mention of

---

40. Twelftree, *Jesus the Exorcist*, 166–71; and Witmer, *Galilean Exorcist*, 125–29.

41. Luke 13:31–33.

42. On Luke's more sympathetic stance towards the Pharisees, see Brawley, "Pharisees"; Gowler, *Host*; Steele, "Table-Fellowship"; and Ziesler, "Luke," 146–57.

43. The link between healing/exorcism and the prophetic vocation can be traced back to Moses (Num 21:1–9) and is particularly pronounced within the traditions relating to Elijah and Elisha (e.g., 1 Kgs 17:17–24; 2 Kgs 4:8–37; 5:1–19); see, especially, Kolenkow, "Relationships," 1470–506.

them.[44] As you would expect, various contemporary *etic* theories have been propounded to account for the phenomenon of spirit-possession. In an influential article, Paul Hollenbach summarizes three of these approaches:[45]

1. Internalization of social tension or conflict, where people suffering the effects of economic, military, or political upheaval involuntarily internalize that unrest, which is subsequently played out in their lives.[46]

2. Escape from or protest against oppression—an intentional strategy, often ritually induced, by which those experiencing external oppression place themselves beyond the reach of their oppressors.[47]

3. A strategy by which oppressors stigmatize, disempower, and thereby neutralize their oppressed—silencing their legitimate protest by undermining their status and significance.[48]

To which can be added a fourth:

4. A culturally conditioned role within a dramatic performance of transformation through which demonic, oppressive capacities within a community are identified and expunged.[49]

Of these, option 1 resembles most closely the first-century understanding reconstructed above where, as we have sought to demonstrate, correspondence between external disorder and internal disorder was already recognized. As ailments within the personal body reflected ailments in the covenantal or societal body caused by disordering behavior, so oppression of the covenantal body by military invasion or occupation, which itself could be acknowledged as a manifestation of an overarching spiritual conflict, caused oppression within the personal body.

---

44. Mark 1:32–34//Matt 8:16–17//Luke 4:40–41; Mark 3:7–12//Luke 6:17–19; Luke 7:21; also Acts 2:22; 10:38. Furthermore, Graham Twelftree has made a strong case for maintaining that such "deeds of power" (*dynameis*) were embraced by the apostle Paul and other leaders of the early Jesus movement as part of his enduring legacy (see Twelftree, *Name of Jesus*; and Twelftree, *Paul and the Miraculous*).

45. Hollenbach, "Demoniacs," 567–88.

46. E.g., Fanon, *Wretched*.

47. E.g., Bourguignon, *Possession*.

48. E.g., Lewis, *Ecstatic Religion*.

49. E.g., Strecker, "Jesus and the Demoniacs," 117–33.

All this needs to be placed on a broader canvas where spirit-possession or endowment was not always interpreted pejoratively. Certainly, within Israelite faith there was a long tradition of Yahweh's leaders, prophets, and other ministers being imbued with divine spirit to empower and inspire.[50] In light of this, it is significant that the Beelzebul controversy revolves around the provenance of Jesus' spiritual endowment, rather than whether or not he was endowed per se. Equally, it can be no coincidence that all four Gospels commence Jesus' ministry with his spiritual anointing at baptism by Yahweh (Mark 1:9–11//Matt 3:13–17// Luke 3:21–22),[51] which serves as a source for all that ensues, whether in terms of preaching and teaching, healings and exorcisms, or the intimacy of Jesus' relationship with God.[52] What is more, it is Jesus' exorcisms that make explicit what is implicit throughout, namely, that Jesus conceived of his ministry as, on the one hand, exercised in space and time, yet, on another, contributing decisively to a cosmic struggle between Yahweh and the forces of evil. In Jesus' ministry, demons, evil, and unclean spirits are manifestations of dissonance and destruction that, left unchecked, possess the capacity to pervert, at least temporarily, the sacred ordering of creation, as well as to frustrate the fulfilment of Yahweh's covenantal promises.

It is for this reason that visions and images of Yahweh's longed-for return and favor often depict a dispensation of abundance and joy following the vanquishing of oppression and death.[53] For example, Isaiah envisages a time when God will host a great banquet for his people on Mount Zion:

50. E.g., Gen 41:38; Exod 31:3; 35:31; Num 11:29; 24:2; Judg 3:10; 8:34; 11:29; 1 Sam 10:6, 10; 11:6; 16:13–16; 2 Sam 23:2; 1 Kgs 18:12; 2 Kgs 2:16; Ps 51:11; Isa 11:2; 61:1; Ezek 36:26–27; 37:1. There was also the expectation of a wholesale spiritual anointing of Israel at the eschatological consummation of their covenant with Yahweh (e.g., Ezek 39:29; Joel 2:29).

51. Although the Fourth Gospel doesn't record Jesus' baptism explicitly, the evangelist nonetheless alludes to it: "And John testified, 'I saw the Spirit descending from heaven like a dove, and it remained on him. I myself did not know him, but the one who sent me to baptize with water said to me, "He on whom you see the Spirit descend and remain is the one who baptizes with the Holy Spirit"'" (John 1:32–33).

52. For a thorough analysis of the gospel evidence, see Dunn, *Jesus and the Spirit*, 11–92; and Borg, *New Vision*, 23–75.

53. See the discussion in Priest, "Messianic Banquet," 222–38.

On this mountain the Lord of hosts will make for all peoples
a feast of rich food, a feast of well-aged wines,
of rich food filled with marrow, of well-aged wines strained clear.

And he will destroy on this mountain
the shroud that is cast over all peoples,
the sheet that is spread over all nations;
he will swallow up death forever.
Then the Lord God will wipe away the tears from all faces,
and the disgrace of his people he will take away from all the earth,
for the Lord has spoken. (Isa 25:6–8)

The author of 1 Enoch anticipates God's righteous and elect ones being robed in "garments of glory" as they share in the victory feast following the vanquishing of their enemies when "[t]he Lord of the Spirits will abide over them; they shall eat and rest and rise with that Son of Man forever and ever" (62:14 [OTP]). Or, again, the author of 2 Baruch (from the second century CE) captures a vision of the world transformed into a cornucopia of divine munificence:

> The earth will also yield fruits of ten thousandfold. And on one vine will be a thousand branches, and one branch will produce a thousand clusters, and one cluster will produce a thousand grapes, and one grape will produce a cur of wine. And those who are hungry will enjoy themselves and they will, moreover, see marvels every day. For winds will go out in front of me every morning to bring the fragrance of aromatic fruits and clouds at the end of the day to distil the dew of health. And it will happen at that time that the treasury of manna will come down again from on high, and they will eat of it in those years because these are they who will have arrived at the consummation of time. (2 Bar. 29:5–8 [OTP])

Returning to the recognition that Jesus was acknowledged as being, to borrow Marcus Borg's preferred epithet, a "spirit person,"[54] as noted above with reference to demon possession, attempts have been made to account for this phenomenon in terms of contemporary interpretative models. For example, drawing on the pioneering work of Erika Bourguignon and others, Stevan Davies advocates that Jesus was able to enter, and to enable others to do similarly, a trancelike state of altered consciousness:

54. Introduced, I think, in Borg, *Conflict*, 88, then subsequently developed in publications such as Borg, *New Vision*, 23–75; and Borg, *Religious Revolutionary*, 109–36.

If Jesus brought about, induced, dissociative religious trance experience called "kingdom of God," and also announced the imminent arrival of an objectively observable kingdom of God (for which the induced experience of kingdom served as foretaste and supporting evidence) then Jesus combined in his own discourse both idealist and realist perspectives, indeed, New Testament evidence tells us he did.[55]

Whether one needs to resort to altered states of consciousness for a satisfactory etiology depends on what is implied by the phrase.[56] If the gospel records can be trusted, the emergence of Yahweh's dynamic reign, informed by Israel's story and the hopes it engendered, so pervaded Jesus' consciousness that it became his reality. It was his worldview, his norm, his social imaginary (Charles Taylor)—one he inhabited wholeheartedly and so effectively that it became not only visible but also accessible. There is little evidence to suggest this was a state Jesus needed to induce in himself; rather, once awakened—presumably on the occasion of his baptism—it became all-pervading, which accounts for the confidence with which he conducted himself, as well as the authority and allegiance he engendered in some of those whom he encountered. Davies would appear to be correct, therefore, when he claims that those able to participate in Jesus' "subjective," enhanced reality experienced profound and enduring transformation.[57] That said, this "enhanced reality" was not infinitely malleable, which helps to explain the relatively limited range of symptoms and conditions where Jesus is remembered for making therapeutically beneficial interventions.

With this in mind, it will be insightful to identify in the relevant gospel material which characteristics and behaviors were associated with the presence of, on the one hand, Yahweh's spirit and, on the other hand, a demon or an unclean or evil spirit. At least three contrasting sets can be identified:

55. Davies, *Jesus the Healer*, 206; also Pilch, "Altered States," 103–15.

56. See the overview of alternatives supplied by Pierluigi Piovanelli in "Jesus' Charismatic Authority," 395–427.

57. A partial analogy, perhaps, is supplied by those who claim to have experienced some form of paranormal event (e.g., out-of-body experiences [OBEs], near-death experiences [NDEs], extrasensory perception [ESP]). However fleeting it may have been, participants regularly attest its transformational effect upon their lives. See, for example, Hardy, *Spiritual Nature*, 81–103; and the work of the Alister Hardy Religious Experience Research Centre, https://www.uwtsd.ac.uk/library/alister-hardy-religious-experience-research-centre/.

Collaboration—Coercion

As the baptism narratives affirm, Jesus' spiritual anointing was associated with the moment when he embraced the Baptist's message and underwent a ritual of repentance and renewal. Interestingly, Mark doesn't clarify the provenance of the spirit (*to pneuma*),[58] which must be deduced from the context of John's baptism program and the content of the accompanying divine voice, "You are my Son, the Beloved; with you I am well pleased." (1:11) Although the evangelist notes that Jesus' animating spirit immediately compels (*ekballō*)[59] him into the wilderness to be tempted by Satan (1:12–13), the tenor throughout his gospel, as well as the other Gospels, is one of collaboration[60] as Jesus inhabits his vocation wholeheartedly to the point of death.[61] By contrast, those possessed by unclean spirits or demons lose control of their lives to the extent that their personalities all but disappear. In the four narrative exorcisms found in Mark, Jesus only engages with the "host" on one occasion, and then only after the exorcism had taken place;[62] elsewhere, Jesus dialogues with and confronts the occupying malevolent presence with a view to securing its departure

58. Matthew ("the spirit of God," *to pneuma tou theou*; 3:16) and Luke ("the holy spirit," *to pneuma to hagion*; 3:22)—both clarify the provenance of Jesus' anointing spirit.

59. *Ekballō* is frequently used by Mark, as well as by the other synoptic evangelists, to denote the casting out of demons or unclean spirits (e.g., 1:34, 39; 3:15, 22; 6:13; 7:36; 9:18, 28, 38). Its use in the present context reinforces the involuntary basis of Jesus' wilderness temptation, in contrast to his baptism, suggesting it was an inevitable consequence of his spiritual anointing/awakening. For a similar use of *ekballō* in Mark, see 1:43; 5:40; 11:15.

60. This collaboration is epitomized in the Gethsemane declaration, "Abba, Father, for you all things are possible; remove this cup from me; yet, not what I want, but what you want" (Mark 14:36).

61. Dominic Crossan has coined the phrase "collaborative eschatology," to describe Jesus' kingdom program in which, again to quote Crossan, "the Great Divine Clean-Up of the World" takes the form of peacemaking through nonviolent justice as like-minded human beings draw inspiration, and vision from God, thereby offering themselves to be the "means" by which Yahweh's "ends" are furthered (Crossan, "Collaborative Eschatology," 105–32).

62. "As he was getting into the boat, the man who had been possessed by demons begged him that he might be with him. But Jesus refused, and said to him, "Go home to your friends, and tell them how much the Lord has done for you, and what mercy he has shown you." And he went away and began to proclaim in the Decapolis how much Jesus had done for him; and everyone was amazed" (Mark 5:18–20). The four narrative exorcisms are Mark 1:21–28//Luke 4:31–37; Mark 5:1–20//Matt 8:28–34// Luke 8:26–39; Mark 7:24–30//Matt 15:21–28; Mark 9:14–19.

in a manner as enforced as, one assumes, was the initial invasion and possession.

Empowering—Debilitating

Again, as the baptism narratives affirm, Jesus' spiritual anointing was considered to be the wellspring from which his ministry flowed—a conviction made explicit in the Baptist's testimony to him: "The one who is more powerful than I (*ho ischyroteros*) is coming after me; I am not worthy to stoop down and untie the thong of his sandals. I have baptized you with water; but he will baptize you with the Holy Spirit" (Mark 1:7–8). We noted in chapter 4, how Jesus was remembered as someone who possessed charismatic authority that both inspired his teaching and preaching as well as empowered his healings and exorcisms—acts often described as "deeds of power" (*dynameis*).[63] In this respect, Luke makes explicit what is implied in all the Synoptics when he comments, "Then Jesus, filled with the power of the Spirit, returned to Galilee" (4:14). This emphasis upon the empowering resourcefulness of Yahweh's spirit becomes even more pronounced when viewed in light of the debilitating effects of demon-possession where victims are portrayed as being disempowered by their alien tormentors, suffering convulsions (Mark 1:26), derangement (Mark 5:3–5), and seizures (Mark 9:17–20), as well as dumbness (Mark 9:17; Matt 9:32–33; 12:22) and blindness (Matt 12:22).

Flourishing—Diminishing

As mentioned earlier in this chapter, Jesus' exorcisms engendered controversy, especially in relation to the source of his powers. Significantly, the effectiveness of his deliverance ministry was not called into question, but only its provenance. In response, Jesus uses a permutation of his *fruitfulness argument* employed elsewhere,[64] maintaining that spiritual forces are self-serving and transparent in the sense that they are incapable of yielding outcomes at variance to their character and purpose: "How can Satan

---

63. Mark 6:2, 5; Q 10:13 [Luke 10:13//Matt 11:21]; Matt 7:22; 11:20, 23; Mark 9:39; Luke 19:37; cf. Acts 2:22; 1 Cor 12:28.

64. Cf. "No healthy tree bears rotten fruit, nor [on the other hand] does a decayed tree bear healthy fruit. For from their fruit the tree is known. Are figs picked from thorns, or grape[s] from thistles?" (Q 6:43–44 [*CEQ*; Luke 6:43–44//Matt 7:16–18]).

cast out Satan? If a kingdom is divided against itself, that kingdom cannot stand. And if a house is divided against itself, that house will not be able to stand. And if Satan has risen up against himself and is divided, he cannot stand, but his end has come" (Mark 3:23–26). Exorcisms, then, as acts of emancipation from the grip of evil, disclose their "means" as well as their "ends": "But if it is by the finger [Matthew: "spirit"] of God that I cast out demons, then there has come upon you God's reign" (Q 11:20 [CEQ; Luke 11:20//Matt 12:28]). Although they are implicit elsewhere, both the detrimental consequences of demon-possession and the beneficial effects of exorcism are highlighted in Mark 5, where dementia, self-harm, and ostracism are portrayed as a living death[65] from which the man possessed by Legion is liberated by Jesus: he regains sanity and self-respect (he is "clothed and in his right mind," 5:15), and can participate once more in communal living ("Go home to your friends," 5:19), with all that entailed.

These three interrelated pairs of what we might call symptoms (and there may well be others) seem to be the basis upon which "diagnoses" were reached with respect to the provenance of both the originating spiritual source and the subsequent intervention. There is a partial parallel here to the testing of spirits, which became a pressing issue in certain early communities of Christ followers. For example, 1 Cor and 1 John include material on spiritual discernment, advocating a confessional touchstone:[66]

---

65. "And when he had stepped out of the boat, immediately a man out of the tombs with an unclean spirit met him. He lived among the tombs; and no one could restrain him any more, even with a chain; for he had often been restrained with shackles and chains, but the chains he wrenched apart, and the shackles he broke in pieces; and no one had the strength to subdue him. Night and day among the tombs and on the mountains he was always howling and bruising himself with stones" (Mark 5:2–5).

66. Another issue encountered in early Christian communities related to the invoking of Jesus' name by itinerant exorcists who were neither trained disciples nor professing believers: "John said to him [Jesus], 'Teacher, we saw someone casting out demons in your name, and we tried to stop him, because he was not following us.' But Jesus said, 'Do not stop him; for no one who does a deed of power in my name will be able soon afterward to speak evil of me. Whoever is not against us is for us'" (Mark 9:38–40). In fact, this and other texts may well confirm the historicity of Jesus' reputation for exorcism on the basis that other exorcists were attempting to invoke his power within their own practices (cf. Acts 8:14–24; 19:13–16). On these and other texts, see Evans, "Jesus and the Spirits," 146–61. Evans concludes, "Long before Easter and the Christian movement's proclamation of the resurrection and heavenly enthronement of its Lord and Master, professional healers and exorcists of all stripes had begun to invoke the name of Jesus" (157).

Therefore I want you to understand that no one speaking by the Spirit of God ever says "Let Jesus be cursed!" and no one can say "Jesus is Lord" except by the Holy Spirit. (1 Cor 12:3; cf. 12:10)

Beloved, do not believe every spirit, but test the spirits to see whether they are from God; for many false prophets have gone out into the world. By this you know the Spirit of God: every spirit that confesses that Jesus Christ has come in the flesh is from God, and every spirit that does not confess Jesus is not from God. And this is the spirit of the antichrist, of which you have heard that it is coming; and now it is already in the world. (1 John 4:1–3)

Judging from the gospel exorcisms, however, this criterion would have proved ineffective as at least some of the demons, unlike their human counterparts, were endowed with a clear understanding of Jesus' theological identity and ready to articulate as much:

What have you to do with us, Jesus of Nazareth? Have you come to destroy us? I know who you are, the Holy One of God. (Mark 1:24)

What have you to do with me, Jesus, Son of the Most High God? I adjure you by God, do not torment me. (Mark 5:7)

Whenever the unclean spirits saw him, they fell down before him and shouted, "You are the Son of God!" But he sternly ordered them not to make him known. (Mark 3:11–12; cf. "And he cured many who were sick with various diseases, and cast out many demons; and he would not permit the demons to speak, because they knew him." Mark 1:34)[67]

---

67. The christological articulacy of demons in Mark's Gospel, and their corresponding silencing by Jesus, are often accounted for in terms of the evangelist's "messianic secret" literary device whereby Jesus' true identity remains at best ambiguous, if not completely obscure, until after the resurrection (cf. Chris Tuckett's helpful review article, "Messianic Secret," 797–800). This may be the case; although, as an aside, it is questionable whether such an explanation adequately accounts for the phenomenon of precognition and clairvoyance identified in contemporary analyses of possession syndrome (see Perry, *Deliverance*, 118–26; and Richards, *Deliver Us from Evil*, 150–54). Significantly, William Wrede, the architect of the "messianic secret" hypothesis, recognized it was not entirely a literary invention: "First of all the story was told of how the demons where afraid at the approach of Jesus, their enemy. This was an accepted idea. But as the idea existed that Jesus' messiahship was unknown, it attracted attention that the demons constituted an exception. This idea then became important and

A more robust assessment, however, and one that resonates with Jesus' orthopraxy over orthodoxy emphasis (cf. "You will know them by their fruits," Matt 7:16, 20), can be found in the early Christian work known as the Didache (c 100 CE): "Do not test or condemn a prophet speaking in the Spirit. For every sin will be forgiven, but not this sin. Not everyone who speaks in the Spirit is a prophet, but only one who conducts himself like the Lord. Thus the false prophet and the prophet will both be known by their conduct (*apo tōn tropōn*)" (11.7–8 [LCL 24]).[68]

No review of exorcism in the ministry of Jesus would be complete without acknowledging that certain of the so-called nature miracles, especially the stilling of the storm (Mark 4:35–41//Matt 8:23–27//Luke 8:22–25), may well have been understood in this light.[69] Certainly the use of *epitimaō* ("to rebuke"), a word closely associated with exorcisms, is suggestive in this respect: "He [Jesus] woke up and rebuked (*epetimēsen*) the wind, and said to the sea, 'Peace! Be still!' Then the wind ceased, and there was a dead calm."[70] The rationale for this resides in the way certain natural phenomena were believed to be animated by forces of disorder and destruction. For example, the primordial struggle through which creation emerged from the dark, watery chaos (cf. Gen 1) was rehearsed in Yahweh's combat with the archetypal sea-monsters of the deep:

---

acquired a definite character" (Wrede, *Messianic Secret*, 34).

68. Also "'How, then, Lord,' I asked, 'is a person to know which of these is a prophet and which a false prophet?' 'Listen,' he said, 'concerning both kinds of prophet. For you will discern the prophet and the false prophet in the way I am about to tell you. You must discern the person with the divine spirit by his way of life'" (Herm. Mand. 11.7 [c 110–40 CE; LCL 25]). On these and other texts, see Brown, *Epistles of John*, 504–6.

69. "'The reason why the wind and sea are treated like demons is that demons or evil spirits were thought to be responsible for inclement weather" (Collins, *Mark*, 260–62): In addition to the texts cited there, see van der Loos, *Miracles of Jesus*, 641–46.

70. Mark 4:39//Matt 8:26//Luke 8:24. Within the context of exorcisms, see "But Jesus *rebuked* him, saying, 'Be silent, and come out of him!'" (Mark 1:25//Luke 4:35); "When Jesus saw that a crowd came running together, he *rebuked* the unclean spirit, saying to it, 'You spirit that keeps this boy from speaking and hearing, I command you, come out of him, and never enter him again!'" (Mark 9:25//Matt 17:18//Luke 9:42); "Demons also came out of many, shouting, 'You are the Son of God!' But he *rebuked* them and would not allow them to speak, because they knew that he was the Messiah." (Luke 4:41). It should also be noted that Luke uses *epitimaō* in the context of healing (4:49), while all three synoptic evangelists employ it in nonexorcism/nonhealing settings (e.g., Mark 8:32–33//Matt 16:22; Luke 9:55; 17:3; 23:40). Howard Kee maintains that the gospel usage of *epitimaō* needs to be understood in the light of its employment in Second Temple Judaism, where it occurs in the context of Yahweh's struggle with demonic forces, for example 1QapGen 20.29 ("Terminology," 232–46).

Yet God my King is from of old,
> working salvation in the earth.

You divided the sea by your might;
> you broke the heads of the dragons in the waters.

You crushed the heads of Leviathan;
> you gave him as food for the creatures of the wilderness.
> (Ps 74:12–14; also 89:9–10)

By his power he stilled the Sea;
> by his understanding he struck down Rahab.

By his wind the heavens were made fair;
> his hand pierced the fleeing serpent. (Job 26:12–13)

Awake, awake, put on strength,
> O arm of the Lord!

Awake, as in days of old,
> the generations of long ago!

Was it not you who cut Rahab in pieces,
> who pierced the dragon?

Was it not you who dried up the sea,
> the waters of the great deep;

who made the depths of the sea a way
> for the redeemed to cross over? (Isa 51:9–10; also 27:1)

Other texts claim that Yahweh created from the outset not only the elements but also their animating spirits:

> For on the first day he [Yahweh] created the heavens, which are above, and the earth, and the waters and all of the spirits which minister before him: the angels of the presence, and the angels of sanctification, and the angels of the spirit of fire, and the angels of the spirit of the winds, and the angels of the spirit of the clouds and darkness and snow and hail and frost, and the angels of resounding years and thunder and lightning, and the angels of the spirits of cold and heat in winter and springtime and harvest and summer, and all of the spirits of his creatures which are in heaven and on earth.[71]

71. Jub. 2:2 (second century BCE); also "Again, on the second day, you created the spirit of the firmament, and commanded him to divide and separate the waters, but one part might move upward and the other part remain beneath" (4 Ezra 6:41 [late

In the light of these associations, it is not surprising that the Psalmist celebrates Yahweh's rebuking of the Red Sea on the occasion of the exodus: "He rebuked (LXX, *epetimēsen*) the Red Sea, and it became dry; he led them through the deep as through a desert. So he saved them from the hand of the foe, and delivered them from the hand of the enemy" (Ps 105:9-10, MT 106). Nor is it surprising in the Testament of Solomon [from the first through the third century CE], to find Israel's king with a reputation for exorcism confronting a demon of the sea: "King Solomon, I am a cruel spirit of the sea. I rise up and come on the open seas with the sea and I trip up the greater number of men (who sail) on it. I raise myself up like a wave and, being transformed, I come in against the ships, for this is my activity: to receive beneath the sea treasures and men. For I raise myself up, take men, and hurl them under the sea."[72] Solomon finds an unlikely accomplice in the form of Beelzeboul, "the ruler of the spirits of the air and the earth and beneath the earth," who delivers this maritime menace into his hands for incarceration within a suitable vessel, reinforced and sealed—exorcism complete.[73]

This infusion of the stuff of creation, whether natural elements or children of clay, with spiritual forces also finds expression in the way Yahweh's final vindication is conceived in apocalyptic literature of the Second Temple period. Divine judgment administered on the stage of human history, either directly by Yahweh or through an intermediary, is a recurring theme, resulting in punishment for the wicked and vindication for the righteous.[74] Although the language is often consummatory in tone, this does not necessarily signal the end of history, but rather the inauguration of an eschatological age where the kingdom of Israel would be restored and populated by righteous Israelites resurrected from

---

first century CE]; cf. 1 En. 60:15-22; 61:10; 66:2; 69:16-17; 82:7-20 [second century BCE—first century CE], *OTP*).

72. T. Sol. 16:1-2: On the evidence for Solomon as an exorcist, see Duling, "Solomon," 235-52.

73. Interestingly, in the gospel accounts of the exorcism of the spirited weather, as with those of possessed persons such as Legion or the boy suffering from convulsions, the emphasis rests upon the return of peace, order and balance or right-relating (e.g., "He [Jesus] woke up and rebuked the wind, and said to the sea, 'Peace! Be still!' Then the wind ceased, and there was a dead calm." "They came to Jesus and saw the demoniac sitting there, clothed and in his right mind, the very man who had had the legion; and they were afraid" [Mark 4:39; 5:15]).

74. See the survey in Webb, *John the Baptizer*, 219-60.

ignominious death.[75] In some texts, this final cataclysm is correlated with the overthrow of the spiritual forces of evil that transcend human agency and yet are manifested through it. We have already drawn attention to the book of Daniel where the archangel Michael "intervenes" in human history to prosecute Yahweh's cause (chapters 10–12). We find a comparable conviction espoused in the War Scroll found at Qumran[76] where the priestly battle against the Kittim (columns 2–9), almost certainly an alias for the Romans, is correlated with the celestial overthrow of the prince of darkness by Yahweh's angelic enforcer (columns 15–19):

> On the day when the Kittim fall, there shall be battle and terrible carnage before the God of Israel, for that shall be the day appointed from ancient times for the battle of the destruction of the sons of darkness. At that time, the assembly of gods and the hosts of men shall battle, causing great carnage; on the day of calamity, the sons of light shall battle with the company of darkness amid the shouts of a mighty multitude and the clamor of gods and men to (make manifest) the might of God . . . This is the day appointed by Him (Yahweh) for the defeat and overthrow of the prince of the kingdom of darkness, and He will send eternal succor to the company of His redeemed by the might of the princely Angel of the kingdom of Michael. With everlasting light He will enlighten with joy [the children] of Israel; peace and blessing shall be with the company of God. He will raise up the kingdom of Michael in the midst of the gods, and the realm of Israel in the midst of all flesh. Righteousness shall rejoice on high, and all the children of His truth shall jubilate in eternal knowledge.[77]

Again, we encounter a similar correlation between the establishing of Yahweh's reign on earth and the celestial victory against the forces of evil articulated in other texts of the Second Temple period, suggesting a sophisticated or at least nuanced appreciation of the causes behind Israel's beleaguered history. Although there is no attempt to obfuscate

75. Especially, Horsley, *Revolt of the Scribes*; and Horsley, *Prophet Jesus*, 9–64.

76. The War Scroll is usually dated to from around late first century BCE to the early first century CE. Versions have been found in Caves 1 and 4, with material from the latter helping to reconstruct lacunae in the former. It is a composite work in which the earthly victory of Yahweh's sacerdotal army against the Kittim, and Yahweh's celestial victory over the powers of darkness are juxtaposed. See Davies, *War Scroll*; and Davies, "War Rule," 875–76.

77. 1QM 1.9–11; 17.5–8 [*CDSSE*].

the identity of their conquerors, there is a growing recognition that such perpetrators were no more than intermediaries within a spiritual or cosmic conflict between good and evil, God and the devil—angels either who had remained loyal to their creator or who had rebelled, and whose rebellion visited disorder upon the earth, thereby threatening to frustrate Yahweh's creative purposes to be fulfilled through servant Israel. What is more, the source of such disruption could take the form not only of foreign armies, but also of malevolent Israelites and "sinners" of other nations, whose evil intentions constituted nothing short of rebellion. And with this recognition came another, namely, that Yahweh's sovereign rule of earth would not come about without a concomitant vanquishing of evil in the spiritual or celestial realm:

> And the Lord will raise up a new priest to whom all the words of the Lord will be revealed. He shall effect the judgment of truth over the earth for many days . . . In his priesthood sin shall cease and lawless men shall rest from their evil deeds and righteous men shall find rest in him. And he shall open the gates of paradise; he shall remove the sword that has threatened since Adam, and he will grant to the saints to eat of the tree of life. The spirit of holiness shall be upon them. And Beliar shall be bound by him. And he shall grant to his children the authority to trample on wicked spirits. (T. Levi 18:1–2, 9–12 [OTP])

> Sinners shall be destroyed from before the face of the Lord of the Spirits—they shall perish eternally, standing before the face of his earth . . . They [angels of plague] are preparing these [chains] for the kings and potentates of this earth in order that they may be destroyed thereby . . . These [chains] are being prepared for the armies of Azaz'el, in order that they may take them and cast them into the abyss of complete condemnation . . . (1 En. 53:2, 5; 54:5 [OTP])

Such texts help to sketch the canvas against which Jesus' kingdom vision, including his practice of healing and exorcism, must be interpreted and understood.

6

Healing, Exorcism, and the Kingdom of God

AT SEVERAL JUNCTURES IN our examination of Jesus' healings and exorcisms, we have proposed that their meanings and significance should be sought in Jesus' understanding of *hē basileia tou theou* which has been variously translated along the lines of "the kingdom of God," "the reign/rule of God," "God's imperial rule" and so forth. If the Synoptic Gospels are a reliable guide, even after allowance has been made for the evangelists' reworking of inherited material, the "kingdom of God" supplies the overarching hermeneutical key for unlocking the rationale for why Jesus invested so much time and energy in attempting to transform the lives of ailing, incapacitated, and oppressed compatriots through personal interventions.[1]

As we have seen, it is almost beyond doubt that Jesus earned a reputation for being an effective healer and exorcist. It is also self-evident that this reputation was appropriated by the early Christian movement to establish his theological credentials in terms of divine authorization or, in some cases, divine identity.[2] However, it is equally apparent, especially

1. "Jesus healings and exorcisms served both . . . and as a symbolic enactment of the eschatological kingdom of God he proclaimed, a kingdom that would replace existing power structures . . . To be sure, Jesus proclaimed the kingdom more as a promise to the poor than as a threat to the powerful . . . and within the context of that promise healings and exorcisms would have demonstrated God's liberating power in action. The combination of eschatological proclamation with healings and exorcisms performed in the context of that proclamation best explains how Jesus came to make the impact he did" (Eve, *Healer from Nazareth*, 144).

2. As noted previously, this approach is strongly represented from the Fourth

from the Synoptics, that an earlier interpretative stratum can be identified in which healings and exorcisms served not primarily as confirma-
tions of Jesus' status, but as demonstrations of Yahweh's presence as a
source of blessing and favor.

We will review the pertinent evidence shortly. Before doing so, it will
be helpful to clarify whether healings, exorcisms, or both, formed part of
hope-filled expectation inspiring Israelite faith in the first century CE,
expectation that was far from homogenous—some (messianic) revolving
around the emergence of a divinely authorized mediator or mediators,
others envisaging Yahweh's direct intervention either to restore Israel's
fortunes in this world (eschatological) or to bring this age to an abrupt,
cataclysmic end before inaugurating a new dispensation of salvation
(apocalyptic). Our concern is not so much how these three emphases
relate to one another as whether healing and/or exorcism feature within
them and, if they do, how they would come about.

In chapter 2, we noted how the language of disease and health could
be deployed with reference not only to the bodies of individual Israelites,
but also to the covenantal body of Israel, where it was applied to the condition of relationships between Israelites and Yahweh or between Israelites and Israelites. Especially within the prophetic literature, we identified
how healing could denote restoration of these relationships deemed to
have been disrupted through disobedience or transgression (e.g., Jer
3:22; 14:19; 30:17; see also Hos 6:1–2). It may be misleading to describe
such usage as metaphorical or symbolic[3] because of the perceived correlation between personal well-being and communal well-being, which,
in turn, informed a rationale that can be expressed thus: if the former
(i.e., personal well-being) became diseased, it was because the latter (i.e.,
communal well-being) had been compromised; if the latter was restored,
so also would the former be. This mind-set was not beyond challenge
(cf. Job), but equally it does feature, implicitly and explicitly, in much of
the extant literature, including the Gospels, and appears to represent the
prevailing consensus.

Gospel onwards: "Now Jesus did many other signs in the presence of his disciples,
which are not written in this book. But these are written so that you may come to
believe that Jesus is the Messiah, the Son of God, and that through believing you may
have life in his name" (John 20:30–31); also "how God anointed Jesus of Nazareth with
the Holy Spirit and with power; how he went about doing good and healing all who
were oppressed by the devil, for God was with him" (Acts 10:38).

3. E.g., Kvalbein, "Wonders," 87–110.

For this reason, it can be difficult to interpret texts that envisage the restoration of Israel's fortunes in terms of healing and wholeness—whether they relate exclusively to the mending of covenantal relationships or extend to embrace their outworking in the lives of Israelites. Consider, for example, the following texts, which fall between the second century BCE and second century CE:

> And as for the visitation of all who walk in this spirit, it shall be healing, great peace in a long life, and fruitfulness, together with every everlasting blessing and eternal joy in life without end, the crown of glory and a garment of majesty in an unending light.[4]

> And there (will be) no old men and none who is full of days. Because all of them will be infants and children. And all of their days will be complete and live in peace and rejoicing and there will be no Satan and no evil (one) who will destroy, because all of those days will be days of blessing and healing. And then the Lord will heal his servants, and they will rise up and see great peace.[5]

> Be hopeful, you righteous ones, for the sinners shall soon perish from before your presence . . . But you, who have experienced pain, fear not, for there shall be a healing medicine for you, a light shall enlighten you, and a voice of rest you shall hear from heaven.[6]

> And what good is it that an everlasting hope has been promised us, but we have miserably failed? Or that safe and healthy habitations have been reserved for us, but we have lived wickedly? . . . Or that paradise shall be revealed, whose fruit remains unspoiled and in which are abundance and healing, but we shall not enter it, because we have lived in unseemly places?[7]

> For winds will go out in front of me every morning to bring the fragrance of aromatic fruits and clouds at the end of the day to distil the dew of health. And it will happen at that time that the treasury of manna will come down again from on high, and they

4. 1QS 4.6–8 [CDSSE].
5. Jub. 23:28–30 [OTP].
6. 1 En. 96:1, 3 [OTP].
7. 4 Ezra 7:121, 123 [OTP].

will eat of it in those years because these are they who will have
arrived at the consummation of time.[8]

In each case, healing characterizes the dispensation of salvation associated with Yahweh's presence and, equally importantly, with the absence
of those disruptive forces believed to compromise the emergence of the
blessings of covenantal promises fulfilled—land and self-determination,
peace and well-being, abundance and fruitfulness. It is quite possible,
even likely, that the eradication of disease would have been anticipated
within these scenarios as a defining feature of Israel restored, but what is
less clear is whether specific acts of healing were envisaged and, if so, how
they would have come about.

A second reference to healing in 2 Baruch is associated with the
emergence of Yahweh's "Anointed One," although it remains uncertain
whether healing in this context constitutes the messiah's prerogative in
particular or accompanies his campaign more generically:

> After the signs have come of which I have spoken to you be-
> fore, when the nations are moved and the time of my Anointed
> One comes, he will call all nations, and some of them he will
> spare, and others he will kill . . . And it will happen that after
> he has brought down everything which is in the world, and has
> sat down in eternal peace on the throne of the kingdom, then
> joy will be revealed, and rest will appear. And then health will
> descend in dew, and illness will vanish, and fear and tribulation
> and lamentation will pass away from among men, and joy will
> encompass the earth. And nobody will again die untimely, nor
> will any adversity take place suddenly.[9]

One of the strongest pieces of evidence for healing within Israelite
expectation around the time of Jesus is supplied by the Eighteen Benedictions, also known as the *Tefillah* or *Shemoneh Esreh*. A robust case can

8. 2 Bar. 29:7–8 [*OTP*]. Manuscript evidence from Qumran and Masada favors a
Hebrew autograph for the book of Jubilees which can now only be accessed via Ethiopic translations in its entirety; a Palestinian provenance in the second century BCE is
favored by scholars. First Enoch is a composite work with marked Galilean resonances,
dated to between the second century BCE and the first century CE. It was probably
written in Hebrew and Aramaic originally; that said, the entire text is preserved only
in Ethiopic. Fourth Ezra may also be a Semitic work of Palestinian provenance, dating
from the first century CE; the *OTP* translation is based on Latin manuscripts. Dated a
little later (from the second century CE), the text of 2 Baruch comes to us via a Syriac
translation of what was probably a Hebrew/Aramaic original with a possible Greek
intermediary; once again, Palestine is the most likely origin.

9. 2 Bar. 72:2; 73:1–3.

be made for much of the contents of the Benedictions being current in first-century Palestine before the fall of Jerusalem,[10] raising the possibility that whether or not Jesus and his contemporaries recited it verbatim, they would have been familiar with a good deal of its substance and may well have shared its sentiments. Here are the relevant petitions from an early Palestinian recension:

(6) Forgive us, our Father, for we have sinned against You. Blot out and remove our transgressions from before Your sight, for Your mercies are manifold . . .

(7) Look at our affliction, and champion our cause, and redeem us for the sake of Your Name . . .

(8) Heal us, O Lord our God, of the pain of our hearts. Remove from us grief and sighing, and bring healing for our wounds. You are praised, O Lord, who heals the sick of His people Israel . . .

(10) Sound the great horn for our freedom, and lift up a banner to gather in our exiles.[11]

Unlike the passage from 2 Baruch 72, there is no reference here to a messianic agent, and once again healing is spoken of in generalized terms. Interestingly, though, its close association with forgiveness of sins and liberation from oppression underlines the conviction highlighted previously, namely, that disease results from disordered or fractured relationships. From this perspective, healing may represent a consequence or outworking of Yahweh's restorative interventions—whether in the form of emancipation from the thrall of sin or the yoke of hegemony—rather than an initiative in its own right.

We concluded chapter 2 with what is perhaps the most promising text for our investigation, formulated during the Babylonian exile of sixth century BCE:

The wilderness and the dry land shall be glad,
    the desert shall rejoice and blossom;
like the crocus it shall blossom abundantly,
    and rejoice with joy and singing.
The glory of Lebanon shall be given to it,
    the majesty of Carmel and Sharon.

10. See, for example, Instone-Brewer, "Eighteen Benedictions," 25–44.

11. *Eighteen Benedications* 6–10; we have used the translation by Petuchowski and Brocke in *Lord's Prayer*, 27–30.

They shall see the glory of the LORD,
the majesty of our God.

Strengthen the weak hands,
and make firm the feeble knees.
Say to those who are of a fearful heart,
"Be strong, do not fear!
Here is your God.
He will come with vengeance,
with terrible recompense.
He will come and save you."

Then the eyes of the blind shall be opened,
and the ears of the deaf unstopped;
then the lame shall leap like a deer,
and the tongue of the speechless sing for joy.[12]

As with previous texts, healing in this passage is a consequence of Yahweh's saving presence. What is different, however, is that specific symptoms are detailed, which has the effect of grounding the generic expectation of Israel's restoration in the concrete suffering of individual Israelites.[13] But was this and similar Isaianic passages interpreted in this light around the turn of the eras? According to the Isaiah Targum (Targum Jonathan),

---

12 Isa 35:1–6; see also Isa 19:19–25; 26:19; 29:18; 61:1–2.

13 Hans Kvalbein challenges this approach, favoring a metaphorical interpretation of the original passage on the basis that "Isaiah 35 is a poetical description of Israel's return from the exile. The text describes the procession way for the people through a blossoming desert and exhorts the people to strengthen their weak hands and their feeble knees (v. 3). These phrases are metaphors for anxiety and fear . . . From this context a metaphorical reading of the following lines is probable . . . The blind and the deaf are then those who lack understanding and who cannot hear and accept the message of salvation" ("Wonders," 94–95). As we have already noted, this may be an artificial dichotomy in that restoration of Israel's relationship with Yahweh, signaled through the return from Babylonian exile, may imply restoration of health within Israelites as well. Unless Kvalbein wishes to maintain the prophet's language of return is also metaphorical, then there is little reason to conclude that restoration of sight is any less in mind then restoration of homeland, etc. Kvalbein seems to acknowledge as much when commenting on Isa 33:24 ("And no inhabitant will say, 'I am sick'; the people who live there will be forgiven their iniquity."), a passage affirming the link between reordering the relationship with Yahweh through forgiveness and reordering the relationship within the body through healing: "There existed an expectation of a full physical restitution of the people of Israel. But the text does not mention any individual healings like those of Elijah, Elisha or of Jesus" (96). This looks like special pleading, not least because when the prophet does specify particular healings, Kvalbein explains them away (cf. Isa 35).

an Aramaic rendering of the prophetic book, which bears witness to a Palestinian interpretative tradition possibly reaching back to the time of Jesus, the answer is emphatically no:[14]

> Then the eyes of *the house of Israel, that were as blind to the law,* shall be opened, and *their* ears, which *were as* deaf *to listen to the sayings of the prophets, shall listen*; then, *when they see the exiles of Israel who are gathered and going up to their land, even as swift* harts, *and not to be checked, their* tongue *which was* dumb shall sing for joy. For waters have broken out of the wilderness, and streams in the deserts; and the parched ground shall become pools *of water,* and the thirsty area springs of water; *the place where* jackals *dwell, there* reeds and rushes *will increase.*[15]

As Bruce Chilton's translation demonstrates, symptoms such as blindness, deafness, and dumbness have been spiritualized and applied to Israel's blossoming obedience to the Torah and the Prophets, precipitated by Yahweh's powerful presence.[16] However, this interpretation is likely to reflect a period following the fall of Jerusalem in 70 CE when rabbinic Judaism, with its focus upon Tanak (i.e., Scripture: Torah, Prophets, Writings) over temple (now destroyed), was emerging as the dominant voice within Israelite faith. What is more, we know that Isaiah 35 was cited in the early church as an example of scriptural prophecy finding fulfilment in Jesus' healing ministry. For instance, after quoting the relevant Isaianic verses, the second-century Christian apologist Justin Martyr (100–165 CE) claims:

---

14. It is difficult to date the Isaiah Targum with any precision. What seems probable is that it bears witness to an interpretive tradition that was originally oral in form, reflecting the role of *meturgeman* (translators/interpreters of the Hebrew Scriptures into the Aramaic vernacular) in the synagogue worship of Palestine and beyond. At some point, probably during the so-called *Amoraim* generations of Rabbis (commencing 219 CE), these oral traditions were codified. For an authoritative introduction see Alexander, "Targum," 320–31: On the Isaiah Targum, in particular, see Chilton, *Isaiah Targum*, whose translation we have used—words in *italics* reflect Targumic revisions to the Hebrew text (MT).

15. Tg. Isa. 35:5–7 [ArBib]; cf. Jub. 23:23–31.

16. Schrage discusses many texts from the Hebrew Bible and later Jewish literature where blindness is employed with a "transferred sense," to borrow his phrase. Interestingly, however, he maintains that Isa 35:5 "does not merely refer to figurative healing but also to the end of physical defects" ("*typhlos*," 281; for references to a transferred sense, see Schrage, "*typhlos*," 270–86).

The spring of living water which gushed forth from God in the land destitute of the knowledge of God, namely the land of the Gentiles, was this Christ, who also appeared in your nation, and healed those who were maimed, and deaf, and lame in body from their birth, causing them to leap, to hear, and to see, by His word. And having raised the dead, and causing them to live, by His deeds He compelled the men who lived at that time to recognize Him.[17]

Another witness has been uncovered recently that affords valuable insight into end-time expectation in Palestine around the time of Jesus. The handwriting can be dated to the first century CE or a little earlier. It was found in what has been designated Cave 4, close to the Qumran community, although not necessarily produced by it. This fragmentary document was titled *A Messianic Apocalypse* by its original editor,[18] although a description along the lines of *An Eschatological Psalm* is probably more accurate.[19] Fragment 2 anticipates the emergence of the Lord's messiah in the following terms:[20]

. . . heaven and earth will obey his messiah, (2) [and all th]at is in them will not turn away from the commandments of the holy ones. (3) You who seek the Lord, strengthen your souls in his service. (4) Is it not in this that you will find the Lord, all who hope in their hearts. (5) For the Lord will seek out the pious and call the righteous by name, (6) and his spirit will hover over the poor and he will renew the faithful by his might. (7) For he will glorify the pious on the throne of an eternal kingdom, (8) releasing captives, giving sight to the blind and raising up those who are bo[wed down]. (9) Forever I will cleave to [those who]

17. Justin, *Dial.* 69 [*ANF*]; also Justin, *1 Apol.* 1.48: See too: "And now he [Celsus] represents us as saying that 'we deemed Jesus to be the Son of God, because he healed the lame and the blind.' And he adds: 'Moreover, as you assert, he raised the dead.' That He healed the lame and the blind, and that therefore we hold Him to be the Christ and the Son of God, is manifest to us from what is contained in the prophecies: 'Then the eyes of the blind shall be opened, and the ears of the deaf shall hear; then shall the lame man leap as an hart'" (Origen, *Cels.* 2.48 [*ANF*]).

18. Cf. Puech, "Apocalypse," 1–38.

19. See, for example, Collins, *Scepter*, 131–41. We have followed Collins's English translation; also Collins, "Works," 98–112.

20. Most scholars maintain that the lines following the "messiah" reference relate to this figure, directly or indirectly; however, a minority view holds that the messiah material precedes it and is now largely lost, ending with the extant line 2. See the discussion of Strathearn, "4Q521," 402–3.

hope, and in his kindness . . . (10) The fru[it of a] good [wor]k will not be delayed for anyone (11) and the glorious things that have not taken place the Lord will do as he s[aid] (12) for he will heal the wounded, give life to the dead and preach good news to the poor (13) and he will [sat]isfy the [weak] ones and lead those who have been cast out and enrich the hungry . . . (14) . . . and all of them . . .[21]

As is apparent, even this brief text is incomplete and raises a number of interpretative issues, not least the subject of the saving activity adumbrated in lines 7–8 and 12–13. Grammatically, this is most likely to be the "Lord" (*adonay*; lines 3, 4, 5, 11), although this would require God to be responsible for preaching "good news to the poor" (line 12), an undertaking usually delegated to an anointed intercessor of some guise as in Isa 61:1–2. However, given the poetic nature of this text, attempting to distinguish between actions undertaken by Yahweh directly and those undertaken by Yahweh's intermediary may well be artificial, for, as we have seen, Israelite faith was more than capable of recognizing different levels of causality and, as a consequence, saw no incompatibility between affirming God as the ultimate source of salvation while looking to a messianic figure for its implementation.[22]

For obvious reasons, 4Q521 has received considerable scholarly attention since its publication in the early 1990s. Most commentators identify Ps 146:7b–8 as a likely source for the salvific actions mentioned in lines 7–8 and 12–13. However, other texts have been proposed, yet none includes all the components, as the following table illustrates:[23]

21 4Q521, fr. 2, 2–14.

22. "But this means this text is not a systematically constructed theological treatise but a poetic evocation of God's imminent saving act; it is highly allusive in nature, making frequent use of psalms and prophecy and weaving them into a tapestry designed more with evocative than with didactic goals in mind . . . This does not mean that he will have been content to write any old nonsense. But it allows the possibility that he was prepared to slip a little carelessly between one subject and another. In particular, he may not have been greatly concerned to distinguish between what God was going to bring about directly and what God was going to effect through the person of his Messiah" (Eve, *Jewish Context*, 195). Also, Collins "Works," 100; and Collins, *Scepter*, 132–33, as well as Strathearn, "4Q521," 404–5.

23. The abbreviation 18 Ben denotes the Eighteen Benedictions introduced earlier. The scroll 11Q13, also known as 11QMelchizedek, can be dated to the first century BCE and takes the form of an eschatological midrash in which texts such as Lev 25, Deut 15 and Isa 61 are applied to an endtime scenario in which Melchizedek serves as Yahweh's implementer of the Jubilee of forgiveness, liberty, and restoration. (Brackets)

4Q521	Ps 146:7-8	Isa 26:19	Isa 61:1	11Q13	18 Ben
Glorifying the pious (7)	(x)				
Releasing the captives (8)	x		x	x	(x)
Giving sight to the blind (8)	x		x		
Raising up . . . bo[wed down] (8)	x				
Healing the wounded (12)					x
Giving life to the dead (12)		x			x
Preaching good news to the poor (12)			x	x	
[Sat]isfying the weak ones (13)	(x)				
Leading those . . . cast out (13)					(x)
Enriching the hungry (13)					(x)

As with Isa 35 and other prophetic texts previously mentioned, Hans Kvalbein advocates that 4Q521 should also be understood metaphorically. He identifies two lists of recipients of Yahweh's salvific initiatives:

> List 1 (lines 5-8): "You who seek the Lord . . . all who hope in their hearts . . . the pious . . . the righteous . . . the poor/meek (*anawim*) . . . the faithful . . . the pious . . . captives . . . the blind . . . bo[wed down]."

> List 2 (lines 12-13): ". . . the wounded . . . the dead . . . the poor/meek (*anawim*) . . . the weak ones . . . cast out . . . the hungry."

Kvalbein claims that just as the first list of largely positive attributes doesn't refer to different groups within Israel, but to different descriptions of the same body of people, so the second list of predominantly debilitating conditions should be understood in the same way. What is more, the *anawim* ("poor, meek"), who feature in both, provide a control for interpreting the nature of Yahweh's anticipated intervention, which takes the form of renewed hope and reassurance rather than changing the material circumstances of sufferers. Kvalbein deduces:

---

denote a thematic correspondence, for example, Psalm 146 celebrates how Yahweh "loves the righteous" (v. 8), which is similar to how God will "glorify the pious." Also, Isa 61:1 in the Septuagint includes the phrase, "and recovery of sight to the blind (*kai typhlois anablepsin*)."

In the first list the *anawim* referred to Israel. If the reference is the same in the second list, we may ask if the other expressions in the second list also may point to the people of Israel as a whole. This would imply a metaphorical meaning of the descriptions of the receivers in the second list, too. Then they do not point to distinct groups with specific needs, but are poetical designations of the one and same suffering people, expecting God to bring a new time of salvation.[24]

After a detailed investigation of the relevant material, Eric Eve is persuaded by Kvalbein's "metaphorical reading" of these texts. With reference to 4Q521, he writes:

Moreover, it is not even clear that the text looks forward to the performing of actual individual miracles of healing and raising the dead . . . the language may be rather the traditional language of salvation. What may be in view is not so much a literal revival of the dead or healing of the mortally wounded as the revival of God's hard-pressed people (Ezek 37:1–14; Hos 6:2). This may well be the language of eschatological salvation, but it is not necessarily a prediction of individual healing miracles.[25]

Clearly, a case can be made along these lines. But is it a strong one? A number of considerations cause us to sound a note of caution. First, for obvious reasons, hope of future salvation tended to be shaped by what was perceived to be lacking or lost and, as a consequence, longed for in the present. The plight of the sick, plus the parlous state of medical provision in Palestine throughout the period of Israelite occupation, made the restoration of health a likely candidate for hope-filled expectation. What is more, Israelite faith unanimously recognized Yahweh as the ultimate source of healing, and given the correlation between the restoration of health within the covenantal body of Israel and the restoration of health within the physical bodies of Israelites, the former could imply the latter. For this reason, longevity was often a defining characteristic of future salvation (e.g., Isa 65:20; Zech 8:4; 2 Bar. 73:3; Jub. 23:27–29), likely finding its ultimate expression in eternal life or resurrection.

Along with Kvalbein and Eve, we could argue that such sentiments inform an expectation of healing as a general characteristic rather than as particular occurrences in the lives of ailing Israelites. This is difficult to call, not least because their position begs the question of how a climate

24 Kvalbein, "Wonders," 91.

25. Eve, *Jewish Context*, 196.

of health could be established without individual acts of healing. Further, certain symptoms were considered, at least by some, to render the body blemished, disordered, or ritually impure and, as a consequence, barred sufferers from full participation in Yahweh's blessings, whether in the present or the future.[26] The blind and the lame were particularly singled out in this respect, being excluded from participation in Temple worship,[27] as well as from the sacred meal at the heart of the Qumran "messianic" community.[28] Whether these bans were implemented and over what period remain open questions, although Matthew's location of Jesus' final healing of the blind and the lame within the Temple precincts at the conclusion of his ministry to cries of "Hosanna to the Son of David" is suggestive that the evangelist was at least aware of this prohibition when writing towards the end of first century CE (Matt 21:14–15).[29]

We asked earlier whether healing from disease or deliverance from demonic possession characterized Israelite end-time expectation in first century CE Palestine. Since then, various texts have been reviewed which refer to the former and, in some cases, possibly the latter by implication.[30] Whether the language of healing and deliverance was being used

26. "The dominating picture portrayed in fragment 2 column II is that God, through his messiah, will not only vindicate the righteous (lines 5–6), but he will also heal those who would have otherwise been denied access to any office in the community because of their physical deformities (1Q28a II, 3–9)" (Strathearn, "4Q521," 408).

27. "Speak to Aaron and say: No one of your offspring throughout their generations who has a blemish may approach to offer the food of his God. For no one who has a blemish shall draw near, one who is blind or lame, or one who has a mutilated face or a limb too long, or one who has a broken foot or a broken hand, or a hunchback, or a dwarf, or a man with a blemish in his eyes or an itching disease or scabs or crushed testicles" (Lev 21:17–20; cf. Deut 28:28–29; 2 Sam 5:8).

28. "And no man smitten with any human uncleanness shall enter the assembly of God; no man smitten with any of them shall be confirmed in his office in the congregation. No man smitten in his flesh, or paralyzed in his feet or hands, or lame, or blind, or deaf, or dumb, or smitten in the flesh with an invisible blemish; no old and tottery man unable to stay still in the midst of the congregation; none of these shall come to hold office among the congregation of the men of renown, for the Angels of Holiness are [with] their [congregation]" (1 QSa 2.3–9; cf. 4Q394.3–4).

29. Schrage points out that "cultic discrimination does not imply rejection" of the blind (280) before commenting: "According to M Ex 4:9 on 20:18 the end time corresponds to that of Moses, for there were no blind at the receiving of the Torah. Nor were there any blind, lame or deaf among the Israelites at the exodus. Because the Law was perfect, God did not will to give to a defective people and hence He healed them, Pesikt 106b" ("typhlos," 284).

30. E.g., "releasing captives" in line 8 could be interpreted in this way; cf. Meadows,

metaphorically in such instances to denote the restoration of Israel and its covenantal relationship with Yahweh or whether it gave expression to a hope that sick and oppressed members of Israelite society would be restored to health and liberated from their oppressors remains unclear. That said, the language of healing and deliverance unquestionably belonged to the vocabulary of salvation when Jesus was alive and perhaps, like much messianic, eschatological or apocalyptic speculation, was intentionally vague, thereby remaining open to multiple interpretations, applications, and layers of meaning.

For this reason, it seems more likely that when Jesus was remembered for responding to the question over his identity by tapping into this language, he was less locating this aspect of his ministry within a clearly defined profile for either Yahweh's sovereign rule or Yahweh's harbinger of salvation and was much more reinterpreting such expectations in the light of his healings and exorcisms.

> Go and tell John what you have seen and heard: the blind receive
> their sight, the lame walk, the lepers are cleansed, the deaf hear,
> the dead are raised, the poor have good news brought to them.
> And blessed is anyone who takes no offense at me.[31]

These verses resonate with the language of restoration found repeatedly in Isaiah and elsewhere. Significantly, though, as the comparative table below illustrates,[32] no one passage includes all or even most of these components.[33] With respect to provenance, it seems plausible that this Q tradition reflects an early attempt to make sense theologically of Jesus'

"'Messianic," 262–63.

31. Q 7:22–23 (Luke 7:22–23//Matt 11:4–6).

32. This text from the Sibylline Oracles is another possible source, although this document (including the relevant section) shows signs of Christian interpolation: "There will be a resurrection of the dead and most swift racing of the lame, and the deaf will hear and the blind will see, those who cannot speak will speak, and life and wealth will be common to all" (8.205–208 [OTP]). For this reason, it has been discounted.

33. It should be noted that the cleansing or healing of lepers is not mentioned in any of these or similar texts. Cf. "The basic list [minus lepers] is therefore taken from scripture, which means that this response is a piece of Christian apologetic, designed to demonstrate that these activities fulfil ancient prophecies" (Funk et al., Five Gospels, 177–78). The impetus to make theological/scriptural sense of Jesus' healings and exorcisms surely reaches beyond early Christian apologetics to Jesus himself. As we shall see, it seems more plausible that Jesus reinterpreted end-time expectation in the light of his ministry than that his ministry or its presentation by the evangelists was shaped by such expectation.

healings and exorcisms by interpreting them in the light of the hope of salvation to which the texts surveyed above bear witness.

Q 7:22–23 (Luke 7:22–23/ Matt 11:4–6)	Isa 26:19	Isa 29:18	Isa 35:5–6	Isa 61:1	4Q521	18 Ben
Blind receive sight		x	x		x	
Lame walk			x			
Lepers cleansed						
Deaf hear		x	x			
Dead raised	x				x	x
Poor receive good news				x	x	

Although Jesus' response is precipitated by a question from John relating to his identity, it is framed in such nonspecific language as could be accommodated within many, if not all, strands of messianic, eschatological, or apocalyptic expectation fueling hope in first-century Palestine. From what we can gather, "the coming one (*ho erchomenos*)" was not a recognized title in that period for any of the profiles for Yahweh's intermediaries. That said, the construction does occur in prophetic passages and was interpreted christologically by the early church, where it becomes imbued with messianic connotations.[34] On the lips of John's disciples, however, it is best viewed in the light of his teaching recorded earlier in the Gospels where the Baptist anticipates one coming after him who will administer Yahweh's justice:[35]

---

34. E.g., "Blessed is the one who comes (*ho erchomenos*) in the name of the Lord. We bless you from the house of the Lord" (Ps 117:26 [LXX/NETS]; cf. "Then those who went ahead and those who followed were shouting, 'Hosanna! Blessed is the one who comes in the name of the Lord! Blessed is the coming kingdom of our ancestor David! Hosanna in the highest heaven!'" (Mark 11:9–10//Matt 21:9//John 12:23; also Matt 23:39; Luke 13:35; 19:37–38). Although Ps 118 comes to be interpreted messianically in post-70-CE Judaism (Jeremias, *Eucharistic Words*, 256–62, and Lohse, "Hosanna," 113–19), there is little if any evidence of this development beforehand. See also, "I was watching in the night visions, and lo, as it were a son of man coming (*hōs huios anthrōpou erchomenos*) with the clouds of heaven. And he came as far as the ancient of days and was presented to him" (Dan 7:13 [Theodotion]) and "For there is still a vision for an appointed time, and it will rise up at the end and not in vain. If it should tarry, wait for it, for when it comes (*erchomenos*) it will come and not delay" (Hab 2:3 [LXX/NETS]).

35. *Ho opisō mou erchomenos*, Matt 3:11; John 1:27; cf. *opisō mou*, Mark 1:7;

I baptize you with water; but one who is more powerful than I is coming; I am not worthy to untie the thong of his sandals. He will baptize you with the Holy Spirit and fire. His winnowing fork is in his hand, to clear his threshing floor and to gather the wheat into his granary; but the chaff he will burn with unquenchable fire.[36]

From this perspective, by drawing attention to acts of restorative healing and forgiveness, Jesus' response must have seemed at best inconclusive, which may well account for his closing makarism, "Blessed is anyone who takes no offense at me." Significantly, by using the third person throughout (i.e. "the blind receive their sight" rather than "I healed the blind"), Jesus establishes an indirect link between himself and these happenings—presenting them not so much as proof of his identity as evidence of the kind of salvific acts associated with his ministry. While acknowledging a correlation by amplifying resonances with texts from the Hebrew Scriptures, Jesus stresses the emergence of Yahweh's kingdom over his exclusive role within it. As such, his response to the Baptist is not so much an unequivocal answer in the affirmative as a challenge to reconceive the question and, with it, expectations of the nature and means of Yahweh's relation to the present and its consummation.[37]

If Q 7:22–23 (Luke 7:22–23//Matt 11:4–6) represents an attempt to interpret Jesus' healings in light of the blessings associated with the fulfilment of Yahweh's covenantal promises to Israel, then another Q tradition makes that link more explicit, this time with reference to exorcism: "And if I by Beelzebul cast out demons, yours sons, by whom do they cast «them» out? This is why they will be your judges. But if it is by the finger (Matthew: "spirit") of God that I cast out demons, then there has come

erchetai, Luke 3:16: The Gospels bear witness to three different versions of John's preaching about the "coming one": (i) Mark 1:7–8; (ii) Q 3:16–18 (Luke 3:16–18// Matt 3:11–12); (iii) John 1:26–34; see Webb, *John the Baptizer*, 261–306. Although "the coming one" has been variously interpreted (e.g., Yahweh, the son of man, Elijah, the messiah, a disciple of John the Baptist; see Davies and Allison, *Matthew*, 1:312–14), John Nolland is probably on the correct lines when he comments, "'The Coming One' is deliberately nonspecific, bringing to expression the essence of all the strands of Jewish eschatological hope which expected God to act by means of an agent" (*Matthew*, 450; also Fitzmyer, *Luke*, 1:328–39).

36. Q 3:16–17 (Luke 3:16–17//Matt 3:11–12).

37. This may help to explain the otherwise difficult saying, "I tell you, among those born of women no one is greater than John; yet the least in the kingdom of God is greater than he" (Q 7:28 [Luke 7:28//Matt 11:11]). Participation in Yahweh's reign of salvation is not mediated through accomplishment, but perception.

upon you God's reign."[38] Few scholars doubt that this kingdom saying belongs among our earliest memories of Jesus.[39] What is less is clear is the origin of the previous verse and its relationship to this one. That said, their juxtaposition brings into focus a substantive issue that quite conceivably could have arisen during Jesus' ministry, namely, the provenance of his exorcistic abilities. Significantly, he is not accused of being a charlatan any more than he levels such a charge against the exorcists of his antagonists (Pharisees?); instead, he is condemned for being a Satanist who invokes malevolent powers to cast out demons. Jesus' "kingdom divided" discourse (Mark 3:23-26//Matt 12:25-26//Luke 11:17-18) challenges the rationale behind this charge; but this, in turn, begs the question of the grounds on which Jesus distinguishes his own deliverance ministry from those of others. It could be that he simply turns the tables and deflects the demon-possession accusation upon his adversaries, yet this seems implausible given his criticism just outlined. This leaves two options: Jesus stresses either his own agency within ("that I cast out . . .") or the effects of his exorcisms (". . . there has come upon you God's reign").

The first may well reflect the redactional predilections of one or more of the evangelists,[40] but is unlikely to mirror Jesus' own attitude given those traditions stressing an unwillingness to perform wonders as a means of establishing his theological identity or significance, as well as those highlighting the expectation that his disciples would also be exorcists.[41] This latter observation favors the view that in line with what

38. Q 11:19-20 (CEQ; Luke 11:19-20//Matt 12:27-28).

39. See the exhaustive analysis and qualified endorsement of Meier, *Marginal Jew*, 2:404-30. Again, most scholars conclude that Luke's "finger of God" (cf. Exod 8:19) is more primitive than Matthew's "spirit of God" (see Davies and Allison, *Matthew*, 2:339-41).

40. For example, Matthew, who emphasizes the christological significance of Jesus' healings and exorcisms (e.g., 8:17; also "Son of David" in 12:22-23 and 9:27; 15:22; 20:30-31). See Duling, "Therapeutic," 392-410, and Held, "Miracle Stories," 165-299. A similar redactional motivation may lie behind the inclusion of the emphatic personal pronoun *egō* in Matt 12:28: "But if it is by the Spirit of God that I (*egō*) cast out demons, then the kingdom of God has come to you."

41. On Jesus' refusal to perform signs, see Mark 8:11-12//Matt 12:38-39//Matt 16:1-4//Luke 11:29-30; Mark 13:21-23//Matt 24:23-25; Luke 11:16. This appears to be one area where at least some members of the early Christian movement adopted a different approach to Jesus (e.g., Mark 16:17, 20; John 2:11, 18-23; 6:14; 20:30-31 [cf. John 4:48; 6:26, 30-36; 12:37]; Acts 2:22). On the disciples as exorcists, see: Mark 3:14-15//Matt 10:1-2; Mark 6:7-13//Matt 10:1-16//Luke 9:1-6; cf. Mark 9:14-29// Matt 17:14-21//Luke 9:37-43; Mark 9:38//Luke 9:49; Matt 7:22.

has been said about Q 7:22–23 (Luke 7:22–23//Matt 11:4–6), Jesus considered exorcisms to be emblematic of Yahweh's sovereign presence, the kingdom of God, rather than demonstrative of his exclusive role within its emergence or realization.

As a consequence, this early memory of Jesus' exorcistic activity (Q 11:20 [Luke 11:20//Matt 12:28]) distinguishes his wonders from those attributed to prophetic figures such as Moses, Elijah, and Elisha, as indeed from later Christian depictions of the Christ, where wondrous acts of thaumaturgy or philanthropy were performed to establish or confirm the theological credentials of the perpetrator:

> *Moses* ("signs" associated with the exodus; Exod 4:1–17, 28–31): "If they will not believe you or heed the first sign, they may believe the second sign."

> *Elijah* (resuscitation of the widow of Zarephath's son; 1 Kgs 17:17–24): "So the woman said to Elijah, 'Now I know that you are a man of God, and that the word of the LORD in your mouth is truth.'"

> *Elisha* (cleansing of the leprosy of Namaan, army commander in Aram; 2 Kgs 5:1–19): "Then he returned to the man of God, he and all his company; he came and stood before him and said, 'Now I know that there is no God in all the earth except in Israel; please accept a present from your servant.'"

> Also *Theudas* (claims to be able to part the River Jordan; Josephus, *Ant.* 20.97–99 [LCL 456]; cf. Acts 5:36): "He stated that he was a prophet and that at his command the river would be parted and would provide them an easy passage."

> *Eleazer* (exorcism in the presence of Emperor Vespasian; Josephus, *Ant.* 8.45–49 [LCL 281]): "Then, wishing to convince the bystanders and prove to them that he had this power, Eleazer placed a cup or foot-basin full of water a little way off and commanded the demon, as it went out of the man, to overturn it and make known to the spectators that he had left the man."

> *Vespasian* (healing of a blind man and one suffering from paralysis; Tacitus, *Hist.*, 4.81 [LCL 249]): "Such perhaps was the wish of the gods, and it might be that the Emperor had been chosen for this divine service; in any case, if a cure were obtained, the

glory would be Caesar's, but in the event of failure, ridicule
would fall only on the poor suppliants."[42]

It would be overstating the case to claim that Q 11:20 (Luke 11:20//Matt
12:28) originally served no such confirmatory function with respect
to Jesus, but the emphasis rests upon the emergent reign of Yahweh of
which these phenomena bear witness, rather than upon Jesus' identity
per se. In this way, the saying under review, together with Q 7:22–23
(Luke 7:22–23//Matt 11:4–6), locate Jesus' healings and exorcisms within
an interpretative frame informed by expectation concerning Yahweh's
eagerly anticipated salvation—grounding characteristics of that expectation within the lives of debilitated Israelites manifesting telltale signs of
oppression.

What has hopefully become clear by now is that there were no
sharply prescribed profiles for the shape of future salvation or the means
of its realization that Jesus adopted to define this aspect of his ministry.
Instead, he appears to have drawn on characteristics articulated in the extant eschatological and apocalyptic literature, or their oral counterparts,
to interpret his healings and exorcisms theologically. That is to say, Jesus
didn't depart from the Baptist's program of repentance and moral refor-
mation in the face of impending judgment in order to fulfil outstanding
expectations unaccommodated within this schema; rather, a charismatic
gifting for healing and exorcism shaped his understanding of Yahweh's
orientation towards the present and involvement in the lives of ordinary
Israelites—convictions that gained significance and poignancy when
interpreted in light of allusions to liberation and restoration within current end-time expectation, as well as in light of his own preaching about
Yahweh's sovereign presence or reign.

From this perspective, Jesus' healings and exorcisms become mi-
crocosms of Israel's restoration, while highlighting the constituents and
scope of its macro realization. This insight throws light on many aspects
of the gospel accounts that otherwise appear superfluous or opaque. For
example:

---

42. See Eve's discussion of "sign-prophets" in Eve, *Jewish Context*, 296–325 as well
as Evans, *Contemporaries*, 53–81, 213–50.

Healing and Divine Reconciliation

We have already drawn attention to the links within Israelite faith between, on the one hand, sin and disease and, on the other, healing and
forgiveness. We have also proposed that such associations reflect a conviction concerning how the disordering of relationship with Yahweh
through transgression resulted in either a disordering within the body or
an imbalance between bodily members manifested as sickness, even unto
death. These correlations, reflecting a disease etiology foreign to modern
Western medicine, may appear arbitrary and, for this reason, have been
judged secondary in some cases;[43] however, in first-century Palestine,
they would have been commonplace, underlining the theological dimension to both sickness and healing, while celebrating the reconciling and
restorative function of the latter. Put simply, healing within the material
body of an Israelite makes manifest and is occasioned by healing within
the covenantal body between Israelites and Yahweh, their God. For this
reason, healing is not only a potent metaphor for salvation, but also a
powerful realization of Yahweh's promise to bless and renew the fortunes
of an alienated people. Little wonder Jesus is remembered for grounding his proclamation about the immanence of Yahweh's reign within the
experience of those around him through such profound acts of bodily
restoration. Through doing so, he created strong resonances with those
prophetic and priestly voices shaping Israelite faith which amplified Yahweh's presence by means of performatory actions which both embodied
and reinforced the accompanying message.[44]

Healing and Economic Empowerment

One or two of the gospel healing narratives emphasize what is implied
throughout, namely, the economic implications of illness or possession.
Many of the presenting symptoms of those who approached Jesus were
debilitating to the extent of rendering sufferers incapable of earning a
living or of contributing productively within a family or community
context. Richard Horsley goes so far as to say that people seeking Jesus'

43. Cf. "The story [Mark 2:1–12] itself has two points: 1, the miracle; 2, the saying
about forgiveness, and obviously the second is somewhat extraneously inserted into
the first: vv. 5b-10 are a secondary interpolation" (Bultmann, *History*, 14–15).

44. On the function of "prophetic drama" in Israelite faith traditions, see Stacey,
Prophetic Drama; on Jesus' use of prophetic actions, see Hooker, *Signs*, 35–54.

healing were "fundamentally debilitating in the social-economic as well as the personal sense . . . Blindness, deafness, paralyzed legs, withered hands, and demon possession are all long-term disablings of the most fundamental functions of personal and social life, without which a person cannot function in social-economic life and without which a society cannot long survive."[45] Bartimaeus is a case in point whose blindness, Mark informs us, had reduced him to penury and a life of begging.[46] In the absence of any charitable or state-sponsored welfare provision, sufferers were abandoned to the mercy of others for survival, and even where supporting relationships existed, income levels for many were so modest that the demands of providing for "unproductive members" would have proved unsustainable. As a consequence, bodily restoration meant not only symptom relief and rescue from premature death, but also a return to economic productiveness and self-determination. This underlying reality is occasionally stressed by the evangelists, as in the case of Peter's mother-in-law, who, once recovered, sets about her household tasks once more (Mark 1:30–31), and Mary Magdalene, who becomes a benefactor of Jesus once freed from her oppressors (Luke 8:1–3).

Healing and Social Integration

Following on from this, many of the presenting symptoms in the gospel wonder stories will have severely compromised the social interactions of sufferers. The most obvious of these are the skin conditions referred to as "leprosy" (*lepra*), which, if judged by the local priest to meet the criteria specified in Lev 13, would have rendered sufferers ritually unclean and in all probability condemned them to quarantine—presumably, in order to limit contagion.[47] Social exclusion would have extended

45. Horsley, *Jesus and the Politics*, 97–98.

46. "As he and his disciples and a large crowd were leaving Jericho, Bartimaeus son of Timaeus, a blind beggar, was sitting by the roadside (*typhlos prosaitēs ekathēto para tēn hodon*) . . . So throwing off his cloak (*to himation*), he sprang up and came to Jesus" (Mark 10:46, 50). Cotter emphasizes how beggars tended to be reviled and treated with disdain in ancient Middle Eastern cultures, which may explain Matthew's omission of this detail (Matt 20:29–34; cf Luke 18:35–43). She also suggests, quite plausibly, that when Bartimaeus petitions Jesus for mercy, he was seeking alms (Cotter, *Christ*, 42–75).

47. It is difficult to be confident over the grounds for quarantine in these cases. As noted previously, within the context of a rudimentary disease etiology, it seems unlikely that skin conditions per se were considered infectious, given there was little

to embrace many, if not all, aspects of life, including family, community, employment, and worship, although it is likely that sufferers sought out each other's company to alleviate loneliness and increase the chances of survival.[48] Jesus' cleansing of lepers, therefore, extended well beyond the amelioration of symptoms and the lifting of a curse to facilitate nothing short of a return from exile and restoration of relationships.

A similar point is emphasized in the narrative about the person oppressed by Legion, especially in Mark's version where the contrast between the socially excluding effects of possession ("He lived among the tombs; and no one could restrain him any more . . . Night and day among the tombs and on the mountains he was always howling and bruising himself with stones." Mark 5:3, 5) and the socially integrating impact of deliverance ("Go home to your friends, and tell them how much the Lord has done for you, and what mercy he has shown you." Mark 5:19) are made explicit. A different communal dimension comes to the fore within the account about the woman suffering from chronic blood loss (Mark 5:25–34//Matt 9:20–22//Luke 8:43–48), a condition which would have rendered her ritually unclean (Lev 15:19–30; cf. Num 5:1–4). Despite little scholarly consensus over the extent of her resultant contagiousness,[49] there can be little doubt about the impact of the hemorrhage upon her capacity to conceive and thereby fulfil a maternal role within the family and community. Given the importance of motherhood within Israelite faith,[50] this healing celebrated the restoration of her integrity as a woman

---

understanding of how diseases were "caught" or "spread." What we do know is that ritual impurity was deemed to be contagious and could be transferred though contact. Be that as it may, in cases of "leprosy," this distinction all but disappears because, whatever the cause, the consequences were the same—social exclusion.

48. Luke 17:12 is suggestive of a rudimentary form of a "leper colony," as is 2 Kgs 7:3–10 (cf. Josephus, *Ant.* 9.74–76). See also this insightful comment found in a variant of the synoptic narrative about the healing of a leper (Mark 1:40–44//Matt 8:2–4// Luke 5:12–16): "And behold, a leper approached him and said, 'Teacher Jesus, while I was traveling with some lepers and eating with them at the inn, I myself contracted leprosy'" (Pap. Eg. 2, frag 1.11–14).

49. We are inclined to follow Susan Haber in concluding that while the narrative is principally about the woman's healing, the ritual impact of her symptoms is also in view (Haber, "Woman's Touch," 171–92). Haber points out that although the source of the woman's hemorrhage is not made explicit, the balance of probability favours a genital discharge which would have carried purity implications.

50. "For a couple to be childless in Judaism was a misfortune, even a disgrace or a punishment for sin (see Gen 16:4, 11; 29:32; 30:1; Lev 20:20–21; 1 Sam 1:5–6; 2 Sam 6:23). But Elizabeth's barrenness [cf. Luke 1:7] is intended by Luke in a class with that

and, with that, her role within the community of promise in which blessing and progeny were conterminous.

Healing and Political Emancipation

If, as we have sought to demonstrate, the disruption and disordering of relationships within the economic, social and theological spheres were thought to result in or at least become manifest in disease within the bodies of those suffering these breakdowns, then any form of healing—especially when interpreted in light of the emergence of Yahweh's saving presence—would carry political connotations. This is reflected in the way Herod Antipas recognizes Jesus' threat to the so-called *Pax Romana* when he learns of the healings and exorcisms being performed among the populace (Mark 6:12-16)—a link made explicit in the following saying: "Go and tell that fox [Herod] for me, 'Listen, I am casting out demons and performing cures today and tomorrow, and on the third day I finish my work.'"[51] Evidently, Jesus' healings could be interpreted as demonstrations of emancipation, giving grounds for expecting a further act of liberation. We have already drawn attention to the political significance of Jesus' exorcisms as adumbrated in Mark 5, where expulsion of a demonic force possessing Legion is linked with the expulsion of the occupying forces of Rome, represented by the herd of swine. Finally, the use of "Son of David," an epithet imbued with messianic connotations in the first century CE,[52] within a petition for healing underlines the conviction

---

of Sarah (Gen 16:1), Rebecca (Gen 25:21), Rachel (Gen 30:1), the mother of Samson (Judg 13:2), and Hannah (1 Sam 1-2), i.e. the mothers of famous Old Testament patriarchs or leaders" (Fitzmyer, *Luke*, 1:323).

51. Luke 13:32. Further support may be supplied by the taunt directed at Jesus on the cross, condemned for political insurrection (cf. "King of the Jews"), "He saved others; he cannot save himself" (Mark 15:31). The Greek word, *sōzō*, translated here as "save" can also mean "heal" and is used frequently with this sense in the gospel (e.g., Matt 9:21, 22; Mark 3:4; 5:23, 28, 34; 6:56; 10:52; Luke 6:9; 8:36, 48, 50; 17:19; 18:42). See BAGD, 798-99.

52. "See, Lord, and raise up for them their king, the son of David (*huion David*), to rule over your servant Israel . . . And he will be a righteous king over them, taught by God. There will be no unrighteousness among them in his days, for all shall be holy, and their king shall be the Lord Messiah (*christos kyrion*)." (Pss. Sol. 17:21, 32 [*OTP*]). "This [Son of David] was a standard messianic title for the rabbis (see e.g., b Sanh. 97a–98a), and a titular use *may* already be attested in the first century BC, in Ps Sol 17. Developing out of older expressions such as 'sprout of Jesse' (Isa 11:10) and 'shoot (of David)' (Jer 23:5; 33:15; Zech 3:8; 6:12; 4QPatrBless 3; 4QFlor1.11–12; 4QpIsa frags

that restoration of sight was considered to fall within the salvific program of Yahweh's anointed one, who would liberate Israel from thralldom.[53]

These, then, are some of the broader consequences of Jesus' healings and exorcisms, suggesting this aspect of his ministry was far from peripheral. In fact, the proportion of gospel material dedicated to such practices,[54] when considered in light of their close association with his preaching and teaching,[55] favors the view that they were remembered as constituting an integral component of Jesus' ministry[56]—not in the sense of attracting an audience (although they certainly did that) or of authenticating his identity (another beneficial consequence) but of embodying his message. In this respect, we may well be on the right lines were we to identify a capacity for healing and deliverance as one of the reasons why Jesus revised the Baptist's conviction that judgment would define Yahweh's immanent intervention in the present order,[57] to embrace a gospel of restoration through liberation, enabling the excluded and incapacitated to participate in a community of blessing reconstituting the covenant people of God.[58] Within Jesus' kingdom program, healing and exorcism, like forgiveness (another form of deliverance), become manifestations of Yahweh's saving presence and readiness to bless. They didn't accompany Jesus' kingdom message; they were instantiations of that

7-10, 11–17), 'Son of David' became the focus of a rich tradition; and, by the time of Jesus, the dominant, although not exclusive, Jewish expectation" (Davies and Allison, *Matthew*, 1:156).

53. See Duling, "Solomon," 235–52; and Chilton, "Jesus ben David," 88–112.

54. Cf. John Wilkinson's statistics cited in chapter 1 (based on the Authorized Version): Mark: 20 percent; Matt: 9 percent; Luke: 12 percent; John: 13 percent. These percentages increase considerably when restricted to narrative verses: Mark: 40 percent; Matt: 40 percent; Luke: 35 percent; John: 33 percent.

55. Many of the healings and exorcisms occur concurrently with Jesus' preaching/teaching (e.g., Mark 1:21–28, 39; 2:1–12; 3:7–12; 6:1–6) or en route between preaching venues/occasions (e.g., Mark 5:1–20, 21–43; 6:53–56; 7:24–30, 31–37; 8:22–26; 9:14–29; 10:46–52).

56. Certainly, this is the impression gained from the evangelists' summaries (e.g., Mark 1:32–34, 39; Matt 8:16–17; Acts 10:38).

57. On Jesus' experience of Yahweh's Spirit and capacity for healing/exorcism as the basis for his revising of or departure from John the Baptist's repentance program, see Hollenbach, "Conversion," 196–219.

58. In this respect, we agree with scholars such as Richard Horsley and Bruce Chilton, who maintain that Jesus was leading a village-based restoration movement within Israel (e.g., Horsley, *Prophet Jesus*, 111–49; and Chilton, *Jesus' Baptism*, 58–97).

message, grounding it in human experience with transforming effect.[59] For this reason, those whom he commissioned to share in this collaborative enterprise were also expected to heal and exorcise (e.g., Mark 3:14–15; 6:7–13; cf. Mark 9:14–29; 9:38).[60]

Before drawing this chapter to a close, it is worth underlining one of its principal findings, namely that the impetus behind Jesus' healings and exorcisms should not be sought in profiles of Yahweh's eschatological or messianic rule current in the first century CE, which he subsequently sought to emulate. Rather, an extraordinary capacity for releasing, or at least relieving, sufferers from the debilitating effects of illness and oppression becomes associated with his charismatic anointing at baptism by John and is interpreted theologically in the light of texts that draw on the language of healing and liberation to express hope of Israel's restoration. In this earliest phase, which quite plausibly originated in Jesus, healing and deliverance become manifestations of Yahweh's powerful presence and authoritative reign. As such, their performance, while intimately associated with his ministry, were not judged by him to be exclusive to it, but rather to characterize the realization of the kingdom vision he sought to embody and to engender in those whom he recruited and commissioned for that purpose.

---

59. "In the casting out of demons, the mission of Jesus itself is taking place, being actualized or fulfilled. In short, in themselves the exorcisms of Jesus are the kingdom of God in operation" (Twelftree, *Jesus the Exorcist*, 170), and "The saying does then, in my view, tell us something important: that Jesus linked his exorcisms in some fundamental way with the coming of God's reign; that is, he saw his exorcisms as evidence that God's reign had broken through in his exorcisms, even if incompletely" (Witmer, *Galilean Exorcist*, 129).

60. "From such a cursory examination of the evidence in the canonical New Testament, it is clear that mighty acts were a part of the Christian traditions from the earliest stages, that not only was Jesus remembered to have done them, but that such acts were done, indeed expected, by those who followed Jesus" (Achtemeier, "Miracle Workers," 151–52).

7

Overview and Conclusions

IT IS TIME TO return to our opening dilemma: on the one hand, Jesus' reputation for healing and exorcism is as well established in our earliest sources as pretty much any other claim made about him; on the other hand, the challenges posed to that reputation are real in the light of twenty centuries of intellectual inquiry, scientific discovery, and advances in the Western medical paradigm that have rendered the interpretative category of miracle both unnecessary and incoherent for many.

In making a fresh inquiry into the origins of that reputation, we began by examining how illness and healing were perceived within the Israelite faith tradition to which Jesus and his contemporaries belonged. We confirmed what others have concluded previously, namely that they tended to be viewed theologically, not least because there was little alternative in terms of disease etiology. However, we were able to bring into focus a number of corollaries that have not always been recognized:

1. The relational nature of sickness and health. The link between sin and sickness is often noted, but what tends to be missed is that this reflects or correlates with the state of relations between sufferers and Yahweh or between Israelites themselves. On the whole, illness was not viewed as a punishment for transgression in some sort of forensic way, but the consequence for it in an organic sense. Dis-ease occurred when an Israelite compromised right-relating; healing occurred when right-relating was restored through repentance and return to God's way.

147

2. One of the assumptions underpinning this understanding is a reciprocal relationship between an Israelite's body and the covenantal
body to which he or she belonged—if one became dis-eased, the
other also became dis-eased. Although there were dissenting voices
challenging this conviction (e.g., Job), the majority view was that if
your physical body was disordered in some way, it was because you
had disordered the covenantal body through transgression. Equally,
remedying covenantal relations would yield bodily restoration as a
consequence.

3. Again, following on, the language of dis-ease and restoration could
be used, especially within the prophetic tradition, to describe the
state of relations between Yahweh and the Israelite people in general
or a particular grouping within. We also noted how the language
of healing was deployed in eschatological discourse to express the
restoration of right-relating with its associated blessings. That said,
it is debatable whether such language carried metaphorical or literal
force, although we pointed out that given the reciprocal dynamics
between personal and covenantal health, restoration of the latter
implied restoration of the former.

4. Despite universal recognition within Israelite faith traditions that
Yahweh was the ultimate source of all healing, this did not preclude
what we might describe as secondary or proximal causation. That is
to say, Yahweh's healing, like much of the divine prerogative, could
be mediated through Yahweh's creatures whether in the form of
people or therapeutically beneficial plants or substances. What is
more, given the almost complete lack of disease etiology, all healing was inexplicably wondrous and served as evidence of Yahweh's
covenantal faithfulness.

5. Yet it does not follow from this that healing was considered miraculous in a Humean sense, not least because the distinction between
nature and supernature had yet to be drawn. But more importantly,
as Ps 19 perceptively celebrates, there were laws ordering the realm
of creation as much as there were laws ordering the human domain;
but they were all Yahweh's laws, beyond creaturely comprehension.
As a consequence, no one would have been in a position to judge
whether Yahweh had contravened the sacred taxonomy that was
Yahweh's prerogative alone and that remained inscrutable to the human mind—even Job ultimately refrained from doing so.

On turning to the evidence for Jesus' reputation for healing and exorcism, we drew attention to two phenomena that our evaluation could not ignore. First, why it was that Jesus, who initially embraced the Baptist's theological convictions and ensuing reform program, at some juncture came to understand Yahweh's relation to the present in a more favorable light, characterized by emergent blessing rather than immanent judgment. Second, how it was that Jesus managed to generate such a popular following to the extent that, even if he had never attempted to perform cures of any kind, such newsworthy and crowd-drawing wonders were attributed to him.

We then engaged with the evidence itself and noted that, with the exception of demon-possession, the gospel records do not supply diagnoses of sufferers' conditions, but only their symptoms. Furthermore, putting to one side the reference to Jesus' restoring of a severed ear, which is poorly attested and looks secondary,[1] none of the symptoms viewed from an etic perspective necessarily indicates the presence of an underlying biochemical malfunction of the body but could reflect psychosocial disorders emerging from the circumstances defining first-century Galilee and its environs.

This is important for at least two reasons. For one thing, if Jesus had restored missing limbs, conjured up eyeballs for empty sockets, or mended fractured bones, we would surely have known about it; but we don't, and as a consequence it seems reasonable to conclude that his healing was restricted to certain conditions and their presenting symptoms. For another, given the link between personal well-being and social wellbeing, Jesus' healings and (especially) exorcisms possessed a pronounced sociopolitical message, engendering a quality of life characterizing a new dispensation—the kingdom of God.

While acknowledging that from the Fourth Gospel onwards, Jesus' wonderworking supplied evidence for his theological credentials, we nonetheless identified in the Synoptics, especially Mark and Q, healings and exorcisms serving a different function, namely, instantiating his message about the emergence of Yahweh's sovereign presence. Within this

1. "Judging from the Marcan source, which seems to be the only extended source Luke had for his Passion Narrative, we are justified in concluding that the whole incident of the healing of the ear is a Lucan creation. In addition to the Lucan vocabulary and style that pervade the pericope, such a redactional touch fits in perfectly with Luke's theological tendencies which highlight Jesus the merciful healer, Jesus the defender of the marginalized of society, and Jesus the compassionate teacher of forgiveness" (Meier, *Marginal Jew*, 2:716).

context, they characterize what it means in practice to pray "let your reign come," (Q 11:2 [*CEQ*; Luke 11:2//Matt 6:10]) and, as a consequence, are not the exclusive prerogative of Jesus; rather, this prerogative belongs to all who share his convictions and are willing to invest wholeheartedly in their realization.

On looking at the healing dynamic as portrayed in the relevant synoptic narratives, we were struck by the almost total lack of reference to prayer or invocation of Yahweh's spirit; instead, emphasis falls upon the horizontal axis between Jesus, sufferers, and their petitioners, where qualities exercised by all parties are stressed. For example, the intensity of personal encounter, the character and motivation of participants, the employment of bodily contact or therapeutically beneficial substances are all highlighted. Two ingredients in particular receive greater coverage. First, Jesus' exercising of *consensual or permissive authority* through performatory utterance, expressed as a healing command or pronouncement of forgiveness, or through declarations of transformation, enabling sufferers to break free from dis-eased modes of life and inhabit a new identity. Second, the presence of a particular *species of faith* precipitated, on the one hand, by an unwillingness to be constrained by debilitating symptoms or, on the other, by the conviction that opportunity for healing was at hand—a trusting, risk-taking, boundary-crossing faith that invests itself wholeheartedly in a particular outcome and finds expression in purposeful action or tenacious speech. One that Jesus engendered in others and, in all probability, embodied himself.

With respect to exorcisms, we noted that spirit-possession was not necessarily viewed pejoratively within the Israelite faith tradition. In fact, belief in the existence of malevolent spirits locked in cosmic combat with Yahweh's forces, which could be played out on the stage of human history, was a relatively late development. As the baptism narratives affirm, Jesus was celebrated for being a charismatic within whom Yahweh's spirit was at work; and as the Beelzebul controversy demonstrates, that charismatic status was not challenged by his adversaries, but only its provenance. We identified within the relevant gospel traditions three contrasting pairs of interrelated characteristics (one associated with sacred blessing, the other with malevolent affliction) which constitute the effects of spirit-endowment/possession, enabling the creators and custodians of those traditions to distinguish between Jesus and those whom he purportedly exorcised: (1) the collaborative resourcing of Jesus versus the coercive manipulation of the oppressed; (2) the empowerment of Jesus versus the

debilitation of the oppressed; (3) the flourishing of others as a consequence of Jesus versus the resulting diminishment of the oppressed and
those associated with them.

We also noted that demon-possession constituted one of the earliest
"germ" etiologies where disease was deemed to result from a form of alien
invasion. Furthermore, given the reciprocal relationship within the Israelite faith tradition between bodily health and covenantal health, it would
be surprising had the cause of the personal invasion of an Israelite by an
evil spirit not been linked to the geopolitical invasion of Israel by the
Roman Empire, an Empire which had been framed as an earthly manifestation of evil within a cosmic struggle. This link between Rome and
evil becomes all but explicit in Mark 5, where the force possessing the
man bears the name of the force occupying the land, Legion—and where
the expulsion of the unclean spirit not only points toward the expulsion
of the Roman forces, but by implication identifies the occupation as the
source of the man's oppression.

Jesus' authority is once again emphasized in the context of exorcism,
although unlike in the healings where it was exercised consensually, here
it is coercive in the sense that oppressive forces are vanquished. Whether
the oppressor should be conceived as an evil spirit from beyond or as an
estranged identity adopted consciously or unconsciously from within (as
some modern approaches suggest) is perhaps to mix up emic and etic
approaches. Yet without wishing to encourage such confusion, our investigations do suggest that external repression was recognized as a source
of internal oppression with the corollary that liberation within required
emancipation without. What is more, we noted that different levels of
causation could be recognized, enabling the source of oppression manifested as possession to be identified as both the Roman occupying forces
and the source of evil animating their hegemony.

This also required us to sketch in the vertical axis to Jesus' exorcisms, which appears only faintly in the healing narratives. As at least
one Q tradition confirms, "But if it is by the finger (Matthew: "spirit") of
God that I cast out demons, then there has come upon you God's reign"
(Q 11:20 [CEQ; Luke 11:20//Matt 12:28]), Jesus understood himself to be
an agent or mediator through whom Yahweh's will could be instantiated
on the human stage. But more than that, as the Beelzebul controversy[2]
demonstrates, he located each exorcism within an overarching struggle

2. Mark 3:22–25; Q 11:14–20 [Luke 11:14–20//Matt 11:22–28]; Matt 10:24–25; cf.
Q 11:24–26 [Luke 11:24–26//Matt 12:43–45]; Matt 9:43–45.

between God and Satan, good and evil, where every earthly skirmish successfully prosecuted pointed towards the ultimate vanquishing or transformation of all that is contrary to Yahweh's creative purposes.

This, in turn, alerted us to the theological context in which Jesus locates his healing ministry as a whole, and which supplies its kerygmatic significance. As we have observed previously, there may be few if any references to Jesus praying or invoking God's spirit in relation to healing or deliverance, but the rationale for such activity is his message about the proximity of Yahweh's sovereign presence and how it is becomes manifest. It would be incorrect to claim that Jesus departed entirely from his mentor John's convictions about divine judgment—far from, it;[3] yet he did embrace a more nuanced understanding of what it means to pray and strive for the coming of God's kingdom. In particular, he appears to have inhabited a more expansive experience of reality than was commonplace—one that was sensitive to the possibilities and potentialities implicit within each moment or situation. Strictly speaking, it was neither alternative nor delusional, for he did not deny, for example, that Israel lived under Roman rule, or that some of his compatriots were struggling with the debilitating effects of disease, spiritual oppression, or the consequences of sinful behavior—or that others were hungry, ostracized or without hope. He did not deny any of this, but neither was he willing to live within such constraints. Instead, inspired by his own experience of God, which, in turn, was shaped by the Israelite faith tradition to which he belonged, Jesus responded accordingly—not in a contrived manner that sought to manipulate through magic or to perform the impossible through naïve self-belief, but through discerning what was realizable within each relational dynamic and committing to it wholeheartedly.

In certain respects, this capacity is not so unfamiliar as might first appear. As I implied in an earlier chapter, the placebo response supplies a partial correlate in which sources of healing become both accessible and effective within a particular set of personal interactions characterized by trust between participants, confidence in the prescribed course of action, and openness to—if not expectation of—therapeutic benefit resulting as a consequence.[4] Within such 'chemistry,' outcomes emerge that appear

3. N. T. Wright helpfully collects the relevant material together in *Jesus*, 182–86.

4. In suggesting a correspondence between Jesus' healings and the placebo response, no attempt is being made to offer a scientific explanation for the former. We are simply drawing attention to a comparable phenomenon which is increasingly being recognized within medical circles, where factors characterizing the relational

to transcend inputs. Or, from a rather different angle, the loss of one or more senses is often compensated for by an increased capacity in the remaining ones, to the extent that they supply at least some of the lost capacity. For example, some blind people are able to construct mental images of aspects of the outside world through touch and sound. Such phenomena are not miraculous, but they do alert us to aspects of human potential that are neither fully understood nor, in most circumstances, effectively harnessed.

There are, no doubt, limits to what can be accomplished through the deployment of the placebo response or sensory compensation. Significantly, there were also limits to what Jesus was able to bring about. Unsurprisingly, this is not an aspect that is highlighted in the Gospels, but it is at least implied in Mark 6 when the evangelist comments, "And he [i.e., Jesus] could do no deed of power there [i.e. his hometown], except that he laid his hands on a few sick people and cured them. And he was amazed at their unbelief" (vv. 5–6). This episode is doubly insightful because, like the one involving the spiritually oppressed boy in Mark 9 (vv. 14–29), it also suggests that a therapeutically beneficial outcome was not dependent upon Jesus alone but required the cooperation of other interested parties.

We explored various attempts to account for Jesus' reputation for healing and deliverance. In particular, we found recourse to the language of miracle anachronistic within a worldview where all creation was deemed to be the work of God and where Yahweh was considered to be no less operative in causing the sun to rise each day than in performing the equally incomprehensible feat of parting the Red Sea. We also found equally unsatisfactory any attempts to deny that Jesus effected any material change in his patients' debilitating symptoms, altering instead the manner in which such symptoms were experienced personally and responded to more broadly. How would an itinerant preacher go about this, especially when most of the presenting symptoms (minus possibly "leprosy" and "blood loss") would not have rendered sufferers ritually unclean or proved to be particularly socially isolating? The paralytic of

---

dynamics between participants, such as trust, are identified as therapeutically significant. It should also be noted that while the placebo response is acknowledged by at least some of its practitioners, Western medicine to date has proved incapable of formulating a satisfactory account for it within its own paradigm. On the limits of the placebo response as an explanatory model for Jesus' healings, see Henriksen and Sandnes, *Jesus as Healer*, 147–51; and Porterfield, *Healing*, 13–18, along with the literature cited in these works.

Mark 2, for instance, was clearly well supported, otherwise he would never have made it into Jesus' presence (Mark 2:1–12)! But perhaps more importantly, it is highly questionable whether claiming that Jesus healed illness without curing disease, a distinctly modern distinction, would adequately account for his popularity and appeal, especially when most, if not all, the healing and exorcism narratives bear witness to the latter.

In light of this, our investigations have led us to conclude that the most plausible source for Jesus' reputation for healing and deliverance is transformational encounters engendering, among other outcomes, the alleviation of debilitating symptoms or the experience of liberation from oppressive forces. If further evidence for this conclusion was required, we need look no further than the practice of the early Christian movement following the first Easter. If the Acts of the Apostles is any indication in this respect, then healing, exorcism, and resuscitation should be listed among the wonderworking activities accompanying Paul's preaching of the gospel,[5] with healings and a resuscitation also attributed to Peter, as well as healings to other apostles.[6] All these occurred in missional contexts where extraordinary acts not only added persuasive force to the gospel message, but also—as with Jesus' ministry—instantiated that message in human experience. None of this would make any sense unless precedented by Jesus himself.

We may be able to deduce further support for the continuation of healing and exorcism from the Gospels themselves, which, as we have noted, devote a sizeable proportion of their presentations of Jesus to this aspect of his ministry—an allocation that would be difficult to explain if the evangelists didn't recognize its ongoing significance. Further, there are other clues in the texts themselves. For example, Mark's editorial comment following Jesus' commissioning of the Twelve[7] or the post-mortem" with his disciples following their failure as exorcists,[8] where we find practices (anointing, prayer, and fasting) that didn't feature in Jesus'

5. Healing (Acts 14:8–11; 19:11–20; 28:8–9); exorcism (Acts 16:16–18); resuscitation (Acts 20:9–12); cf. Rom 15:18–19; 2 Cor 12:12; Gal 3:5.

6. Peter: healing (Acts 3:1–10; 5:15–16; 9:32–35); resuscitation (Acts 9:36–43); Ananias: healing (Acts 9:17–19); Philip: healing (Acts 8:6–7).

7. "So they went out and proclaimed that all should repent. They cast out many demons and anointed with oil many who were sick and cured them" (Mark 6:12–13).

8. "When he had entered the house, his disciples asked him privately, 'Why could we not cast it out?' He said to them, 'This kind can come out only through prayer [and fasting]'" (Mark 9:28–29).

own ministry. Reference to other Christian exorcists in Mark 9 may also be pertinent in this respect (vv. 38–40), as is the secondary "longer" ending to the gospel: "And these signs will accompany those who believe: by using my name they will cast out demons . . . they will lay their hands on the sick, and they will recover" (Mark 16:17–18).

Some scholars have seen in Matthew's depiction of the disciples as possessed of "little faith" (*oligopistos/oligopistia*), almost always in relation to wonderworking, as insightful to how this aspect of Jesus' legacy was being appropriated by the community reflected in that gospel.[9] Equally, Luke's inclusion of Jesus' commissioning of a further seventy or seventy-two disciples to preach and heal quite plausibly reflects a post-Easter scenario, supplying dominical authorization for a mission to the Gentile world already underway (10:1–12).[10] Nor should we overlook John's prediction that the disciples "will do greater works" (14:12) than those performed by Jesus himself, which, according to the Fourth Gospel, included healings and a resuscitation, although interestingly not exorcisms (e.g., 4:46–5:9; 9:1–12; 11:1–44).[11]

The practice of healing *within* early Christian communities, in contrast to missionary initiatives, is evidenced from 1 Corinthians and the Epistle of James:

> To one is given through the Spirit the utterance of wisdom, and to another the utterance of knowledge according to the same Spirit, to another faith by the same Spirit, to another gifts of healing (*charismata iamatōn*) by the one Spirit, to another the working of miracles (*energēmata dynameōn*), to another prophecy, to another the discernment of spirits, to another various kinds of tongues, to another the interpretation of tongues.[12]

---

9. Matt 8:26; 14:31; 16:8; 17:20; cf. 6:30. See Held, "Miracle Stories," 291–96: Also, Matthew's reworking of Jesus' mission charge: "'These twelve Jesus sent out with the following instructions: 'Go nowhere among the Gentiles, and enter no town of the Samaritans, but go rather to the lost sheep of the house of Israel. As you go, proclaim the good news, "the kingdom of heaven has come near." Cure the sick, raise the dead, cleanse the lepers, cast out demons. You received without payment; give without payment'" (10:5–8).

10. E.g., Fitzmyer, *Luke*, 2:841–50.

11. This raises the question of how this silence should be interpreted. For example, does it indicate that exorcisms did not take place within the sphere of Johannine Christianity? See the discussion in Twelftree, *Name of Jesus*,183–208, and the insightful comments of Edwin Broadhead on John 6:66–71: Broadhead, "Echoes," 111–19.

12 1 Cor 12:8–10; also 12:28–30.

Are any among you sick (*asthenei*)? They should call for the
elders of the church (*tous presbyterous tēs ekklēsias*) and have
them pray over them, anointing them with oil in the name of
the Lord. The prayer of faith will save the sick, and the Lord will
raise them up (*hē euchē tēs pisteōs sōsei ton kamnonta kai egerei
auton ho kyrios*); and anyone who has committed sins will be
forgiven. Therefore confess your sins to one another, and pray
for one another, so that you may be healed (*iathēte*). The prayer
of the righteous is powerful and effective.[13]

In the case of the former, healing continues to be seen as a charismatic
spirit-gifting bestowed, in this case, upon certain Christ-followers to be
exercised on behalf of, and for the benefit of, the community as a whole.
It is distinguished from "the working of miracles" (NRSV; *energēmata
dynameōn*), which can be translated more literally as "powerful works"
or "deeds of power," and which may, in turn, include exorcism.[14] What
is interesting is that Paul's list of charismata falls within his exposition of
the Corinthian church as the body of Christ (*sōma christou*; 1 Cor 12:12,
27)—a rich metaphor overflowing with meaning, including the obvious
correspondence between the earthly body of Jesus, which, animated
by God's spirit, embodied the gospel through word and deed, and his
ecclesial body, which, animated by his spirit, continued to do so, possessing corporately those gifts that Jesus possessed personally. Although
the apostle encouraged his audience to strive for the higher gifts (1 Cor
12:31; 14:1), there is nonetheless a democratization of spiritual anointing
that appears to be independent of social status, gender, or any kind of
institutional control.

By contrast, healing in the Epistle of James no longer appears to be a
charismatic gifting but has become the responsibility of leadership, to be
undertaken by church elders through prayer and anointing. That said, the
exhortation to pray is not restricted to office-bearers, but is encouraged

13 Jas 5:14–16.

14. Graham Twelftree thinks this is unlikely given that Paul indicates these gifts are
for use within the Christian community, whereas exorcism is more typically associated with conversion (Twelftree, *Name of Jesus*, 73–76). Historically, this proved to be
the case, not least with exorcism becoming incorporated within baptismal initiation
(see later in this chapter), but whether this was the practice when Paul ministered is
another matter. Certainly, he refers to believers' ongoing struggle against Satan (1 Cor
7:5; 2 Cor 2:11; 11:14; 1 Thess 2:18), instructs that an errant Christian wrongdoer
should be handed over to Satan to secure his ultimate salvation (1 Cor 5:5), and refers
to his own "thorn in the flesh" as a "messenger from Satan" (2 Cor 12:7). Further, according to Luke, Paul performed exorcisms (Acts 16:16–18).

in all participants—reflecting, perhaps, the central role of faith in Jesus' healing ministry. Interestingly, the syntactic structure of "the prayer of faith will save the sick (*hē euchē tēs pisteōs sōsei ton kamnonta*)" is similar to that of "Your faith has saved/healed you (*hē pistis sou sesōken se*)," with faith serving as the subject of the saving action in both cases. We also find in James the correspondence between disease within the personal body manifesting as sickness and disease within the covenantal body manifesting as sin, with the sin in the covenantal body needing to be remedied in order for the sickness in the personal body to be resolved.

Although a detailed survey of what became of Jesus' legacy for healing and exorcism beyond the apostolic area would require a further book,[15] we can offer a number of observations, while acknowledging considerable variation geographically, as well as through time.

Conventional Medicine

First, with a few possible exceptions,[16] conventional medicine soon became recognized by leading Christian thinkers, sometimes with qualifications,[17] as a source of divine healing or at least as compatible

15. A number of surveys exist that come to significantly different conclusions from Evelyn Frost's continuation to the Council of Nicaea and beyond (Frost, *Christian Healing*) through Benjamin Warfield's apostolic dispensationalism (Warfield, *Counterfeit Miracles*) to Gary Ferngren's healing and exorcism giving way to conventional medicine (Ferngren, *Health Care*, chapters 4–5). Probably the most comprehensive and nuanced study currently available in English is that of Andrew Daunton-Fear which not only takes a diachronic perspective but also a geographical one, drawing attention to how the practice of healing and exorcism varied not only through time, but also regionally (Daunton-Fear, *Healing*).

16. The Syrian biblical scholar Tatian (120–173 CE) is usually cited in this respect. However, Darrel Amundsen has made a strong case for him not rejecting conventional medicine in total, but only the use of *pharmaka* or drugs, which Tatian understood as the means by which demons gained access to the body. (Amundsen, "Tatian's 'Rejection,'" 158–74). It should be pointed out, however, that in places Tatian seems unwilling to recognize levels of causation and, as a consequence, came to view medicine as being in conflict with a believer's allegiance to God: "Why is he who trusts in the system of matter not willing to trust in God? For what reason do you not approach the more powerful Lord, but rather seek to cure yourself, like the dog with grass, or the stag with a viper, or the hog with river-crabs, or the lion with apes? Why you deify the objects of nature? And why, when you cure your neighbour, are you called a benefactor? Yield to the power of the Logos!" (Tatian, *Or. Graec.* 18 [*ANF*]).

17. E.g., "For since the science of medicine is useful and necessary to the human race, and many are the points of dispute in it respecting the manner of curing bodies,

with Christian faith, constituting an expression of God's providential care woven within the fabric of the created order.[18] The Alexandrian theologian Clement (150–215 CE) articulates a reasonable approach adopted by many:

> Now, then, many things in life take their rise in some exercise of human reason, having received the kindling spark from God. For instance, health by medicine, and soundness of body through gymnastics, and wealth by trade, have their origin and existence in consequence of Divine Providence indeed, but in consequence, too, of human co-operation. Understanding also is from God.[19]

Caring for the Sick

Second, charitable caring for the sick and needy became a defining characteristic of Christian practice and was not only exercised within church communities, but offered more broadly.[20] In fact, according to Rodney Stark and others, there was little by way of charitable care provision within the Roman Empire prior to Christianity.[21] As a consequence, when mass fatalities followed the epidemics of 165 CE (smallpox?) and 251 CE (measles?), wiping out up to one-third of the population of the Roman Empire and disrupting all social networks from the family upwards, not only were survival rates higher within Christian communities where pastoral care was practiced, but also offering charitable care to others who had suffered bereavement and loss proved to be an effective means of church growth. What is more, such charitable care was not simply offered

---

there are found, for this reason, numerous heresies confessedly prevailing in the science of medicine among the Greeks, and also, I suppose, among those barbarous nations who profess to employ medicine . . . And yet no one would act rationally in avoiding medicine because of its heresies; nor would he who aimed at that which is seemly entertain a hatred of philosophy and adduce its many heresies as a pretext for his antipathy. And so neither are the sacred books of Moses and the prophets to be condemned on account of the heresies in Judaism" (Origen, *Cels.* 3.12 [*ANF*]).

18. See, especially, Amundsen, "Medicine and Faith," 127–57; also Risse, *Mending Bodies*, 76–79.

19. Clement of Alexandria, *Strom.* 6.17; also *Paed.* 1.2; Ign. *Pol.* 2; Tertullian, *Cor.* 8.

20. For overviews and analysis of pastoral care in the early church, see Vonhoff, *People Who Care*; and Hanawalt and Lindberg, eds., *Eye of a Needle*.

21. Stark, *Rise of Christianity*, 73–94; also Ferngren, *Health Care*, 86–139.

on an ad hoc basis but came to be organized by bishops, funded by con-
gregations, and undertaken by officers authorized for this purpose.[22]
Although there are a number of accounts highlighting Christian philanthropy penned by Christians,[23] none highlights the impact of it throughout the Roman Empire more eloquently than the letter of Emperor Julian
(361–63 CE), a sworn enemy of the faith, to Arsacius, a pagan high-priest
of Galatia in 362 CE, in which he criticizes the lack of public service offered in the name of the Hellenic gods before going on to write, "For it is
disgraceful that, when no Jew ever has to beg, and the impious Galilaeans
support not only their own poor but ours as well, all men see that our

22. Whether this was the role of deacons in the early church is difficult to assess.
Luke seems to suggest as much, but then those appointed in Acts 6, who are not actually called *diakonoi* in this context, appear to undertake other duties. In the *Apostolic
Tradition*, deacons are commissioned for this purpose ("Over the deacon, then, [the
bishop] shall say thus: God, who created all things and ordered them by your Word,
Father of our Lord Jesus Christ, whom you sent to serve your will and make known
to us your desire, give the holy Spirit of grace and caring and diligence to this your
servant whom you have chosen to serve your Church." Hippolytus, *Trad. ap.* 8 [*ApT*]),
whereas in Bishop Polycarp's letter to the Philippians, pastoral care seems to be the
responsibility of Presbyters ("The presbyters also should be compassionate, merciful to
all, turning back those who have gone astray, caring for all who are sick, not neglecting
the widow, the orphan, or the poor." Pol. *Phil.* 6 [LCL 24]). For a thorough re-appraisal
of the role of deacons in the early church, see Collins, *Diakonia*; and Collins, *Deacons*.

23. Few are more eloquent (and possibly hyperbolic) than Bishop Dionysius of
Alexandra's festal letter following the measles epidemic of the third century recorded
by the church historian Eusebius: "Most of our brother-Christians showed unbounded
love and loyalty, never sparing themselves and thinking only of one another. Heedless
of the danger, they took charge of the sick, attending to their every need and ministering to them in Christ, and with them departed this life serenely happy; for they
were infected by others with the disease, drawing on themselves the sickness of their
neighbors and cheerfully accepting their pains. Many, in nursing and curing others,
transferred the death to themselves and died in their stead, turning the common for-
mula that is normally an empty courtesy into a reality: 'Your humble servant bids you
goodbye.' The best of our brothers lost their lives in this manner, a number of presbyters, deacons, and laymen winning high commendation, so that death in this form,
the result of great piety and strong faith, seems in every way the equal of martyrdom.
With willing hands they raised the bodies of the saints to their bosoms; they closed
their eyes and mouths, carried them on their shoulders, and laid them out; they clung
to them, embraced them, washed them, and wrapped them in grave clothes. Very soon
the same services were done for them, since those left behind were constantly following those gone before. The heathen behaved in the very opposite way. At the first onset
of the disease, they pushed the sufferers away and fled from their dearest, throwing
them into the roads before they were dead and treating unburied corpses as dirt, hoping thereby to avert the spread and contagion of the fatal disease; but do what they
might, they found it difficult to escape" (*Hist. eccl.* 7.22 [EHC]).

people lack aid from us." (*Letter* 22 [LCL 157]. That said, the following excerpt from Tertullian (160–220 CE), over 150 years earlier, is insightful for how Christian charitable care was viewed both within and beyond the church:

> Every man once a month brings some modest coin—or whenever he wishes, and only if he does wish, and if he can; for nobody is compelled; it is a voluntary offering. You might call them the trust funds of piety. For they are not spent upon banquets nor drinking-parties nor thankless eating-houses; but to feed the poor and to bury them, for boys and girls who lack property and parents, and then for slaves grown old and shipwrecked mariners; and any who may be in mines islands or prisons, provided that it is for the sake of God's school, become the pensioners of their confession. Such work of love (for so it is) puts a mark upon us, in the eyes of some. "Look," they say, "how they love one another" (for themselves hate one another); "and how they are ready to die for each other" (for themselves will be readier to kill each other).[24]

In all probability, the early Christian movement practiced compassionate care of the sick and needy precisely because it was exemplified by Jesus and was deemed to constitute a nonnegotiable part of his legacy. Significantly, although the Gospels record him commissioning the first disciples to preach, heal, and exorcise, they are not similarly authorized to care. Dominical precedent for such activity is supplied by the marrying of love of God with love of neighbor (Mark 12:28–34; cf. Deut 6:5; Lev 19:18) and, even, of one's enemies (Q 6:27–28 [Luke 6:27–28//Matt 5:44; cf. Luke 6:35]) where, as John Meier has convincing demonstrated, love means "to will good and do good"[25]—a link underlined in Luke's Gospel where the double commandment is illustrated by the parable of the good Samaritan (Luke 10:25–37). The Johannine depiction of Jesus as the good shepherd (John 10:11, 14) also becomes a defining image within early Christian iconography where it could serve to emphasize

24. Tertullian, *Apol.* 39 [LCL 250].

25. "To love this 'neighbor' means to will good and do good to him, even if one feels some personal enmity toward him. More specifically, in the immediate context, loving one's fellow Israelite means promoting, protecting, and, if need be, restoring that person's rights, honor, status in the community . . . Jesus is commanding his disciples to will good and do good to their enemies, no matter how the disciples may feel about them, and no matter whether the enemies remain enemies despite the goodness shown to them" (Meier, *Marginal Jew*, 4:492, 530).

Jesus' care for his own, even to the point of securing their salvation at the cost of his own life.[26] No doubt, in the absence of any form of state-run welfare or healthcare provision, the cries of the needy could not always be met (cf. Acts 6:1–6); but, it is equally the case that by the fourth century, the Christian commitment to supplying charitable care to the sick and impoverished had given rise to the first medical hospitals, which existed to serve the general public and not just a closed group such as soldiers or slaves (cf. *Valetudinaria*).[27]

Spiritualizing Sickness and Healing

Third, as we noted within the Israelite prophetic tradition, the language of disease and healing is spiritualized—a further development with dominical precedent. For example, when the disciples were challenged about his practice of sharing table-fellowship with sinners and tax-gatherers, Jesus is remembered for responding, "Those who are well have no need of a physician (*iatrou*), but those who are sick (*kakōs*); I have come to call not the righteous but sinners" (Mark 2:17). Or consider the way the language of sight and blindness is deployed metaphorically to express the mystery of faith, where those physically blind appear to be spiritually sighted while, by contrast, those able to see are portrayed as spiritually blind.[28] Or, again, this time in the Pastoral Epistles, note how the language of health or soundness (*hygiainō, hygiēs*), which frequently denotes physical well-being in the Gospels,[29] is employed with respect to the soundness of teaching or of faith itself.[30]

26. Jensen, *Understanding*, 37–41.

27. See, especially, the exhaustive study Risse, *Mending Bodies*, chapters 2–4; also Ferngren, *Health Care*, chapter 6; and Avalos, *Health Care*.

28. E.g., "And [Jesus] said to them, 'To you has been given the secret of the kingdom of God, but for those outside, everything comes in parables; in order that "they may indeed look, but not perceive, and may indeed listen, but not understand; so that they may not turn again and be forgiven"'" (Mark 4:11–12). "They came to Jericho. As he and his disciples and a large crowd were leaving Jericho, Bartimaeus son of Timaeus, a blind beggar, was sitting by the roadside. When he heard that it was Jesus of Nazareth, he began to shout out and say, 'Jesus, Son of David, have mercy on me!'" (Mark 10:46–47). "Jesus said, 'I came into this world for judgment so that those who do not see may see, and those who do see may become blind'" (John 9:39).

29. E.g., Matt 12:13; 15:31; Mark 5:34; Luke 5:31; 7:10; 15:27; John 5:6, 9, 11, 14–15; 7:43; also Acts 4:10.

30. E.g., *hygiainousa didaskalia* (1 Tim 1:10; 2 Tim 4:3; Titus 1:9; 2:1); *hygiainontes*

Each of these applications features in the ensuing literature. The image of Christ the physician becomes particularly compelling from the writings of Ignatius of Antioch (35–108 CE) onwards, where it appears in a protocreedal formulation: "For there is one physician (*heis iatros estin*), both fleshly and spiritual, born and unborn, God come in the flesh, true life in death, from both Mary and God, first subject to suffering and then beyond suffering, Jesus Christ our Lord" (*Eph* 7:2 [LCL 24]).[31] The metaphorical use of medical language also receives further attention as, for instance, in this allegorical flurry from Origen:

> I would say, moreover, that, agreeably to the promise of Jesus, His disciples performed even greater works than these miracles of Jesus, which were perceptible only to the senses. For the eyes of those who are blind in soul are ever opened; and the ears of those who were deaf to virtuous words, listen readily to the doctrine of God, and of the blessed life with Him; and many, too, who were lame in the feet of the "inner man," as Scripture calls it, having now been healed by the word, do not simply leap, but leap as the hart, which is an animal hostile to serpents, and stronger than all the poison of vipers. And these lame who have been healed, receive from Jesus power to trample, with those feet in which they were formerly lame, upon the serpents and scorpions of wickedness, and generally upon all the power of the enemy; and though they tread upon it, they sustain no injury, for they also have become stronger than the poison of all evil and of demons.[32]

And perhaps most influential of all is the growing importance of right belief or sound doctrine, which finds expression in the emergence

---

logoi / *logos hygiēs* (1 Tim 6:3; 2 Tim 1:13; Titus 2:8); *hygiainein tē pistei* (Titus 1:13; 2:2).

31. Also Ep. Apos. 21; Clement of Alexandria, *Paed.* 1.2. For further references, see Ferngren, *Health Care*, 29–31 and the literature cited there. We have already drawn attention to the comparisons made between Jesus and the Greco-Roman healing god Asclepius/Asclepius (e.g., Justin, *1 Apol.* 22–23, 54; Origen, *Cels.* 3.24; Tertullian, *Apol.* 23; *Cor.* 8). Often they are portrayed in the secondary literature as competitors, but Ferngren offers an alternative interpretation: "Yet in Christian apologetics Jesus became not an alternative healer whose miracles of healing could compete with those of Asclepius but rather the healer of sinners" (Ferngren, *Health Care*, 31). He quotes from Clement of Alexandria in support (*Paed.* 1.2); however, the passage goes on to claim: "But the good Instructor, the Wisdom, the Word of the Father, who made man, cares for the whole nature of His creature; the all-sufficient Physician of humanity, the Saviour, heals both body and soul" [ANF].

32. Origen, *Cels.* 2.48 [ANF].

of rudimentary rules of faith and then full-fledged creeds,[33] Among the earliest nonbiblical *rules of faith* (*regula fidei*; also *regula veritatis*; *kanōn tēs pisteōs*; *kanōn tēs alētheias*) is the following from Tertullian:

> The rule of faith, indeed, is altogether one, alone immoveable and irreformable; the rule, to wit, of believing in one only God omnipotent, the Creator of the universe, and His Son Jesus Christ, born of the Virgin Mary, crucified under Pontius Pilate, raised again the third day from the dead, received in the heavens, sitting now at the right (hand) of the Father, destined to come to judge quick and dead through the resurrection of the flesh as well (as of the spirit).[34]

Alongside the evolution of creedal statements of belief, probably as a distillation of Christian faith to be taught to catechumens and professed by them at baptism, we find a growing body of polemical tractates that attempt to refute what is judged to be inadvertently mistaken or intentionally misleading—unwholesome doctrine.[35]

There are many other examples of the spiritualizing of the language of sickness and healing in the early centuries. Bishop Ignatius describes the eucharistic bread as "medicine that brings immortality (*pharmakon athanasies*), an antidote that allows us not to die but to live at all times in Jesus Christ" (*Eph.*, 20.2 [LCL 24]). Eusebius of Caesarea (c 260–340 CE) echoes this medicinal application when he describes Luke the Evangelist's two books as "medicine for souls" (*psychōn therapeutikēs*) (*Hist. eccl.* 3.4 [LCL 153]), while in the early Christian apocalypse, the Shepherd of

---

33. For a collection of texts and commentary, see Kelly, *Early Christian Creeds*. Frances Young makes in interesting observation: "Christianity is the only major religion to set such store by creeds and doctrines. Other religions have scriptures, others have their characteristic ways of worship, others have their own peculiar ethics and lifestyle; other religions also have philosophical, intellectual or mystical forms as well as more popular manifestations. But except in response to Christianity, they have not developed creeds, statements of standard belief to which the orthodox are supposed to adhere" (Young, *Making*, 1).

34. Tertullian, *Virg.* 1 [*ANF*].

35. E.g., Irenaeus (130–202 CE), *Haer.*; Origen (184–253 CE), *Cels.*; Athanasius (296–373 CE), *C. Ar.* This is a highly controversial area revolving around whether the person and gospel of Jesus Christ can be prescribed in terms of right belief, at the exclusion of other expressions, and, if so, what are the criteria for and who is qualified to make such judgments. Among many, see the discussions of Ehrman, *Lost Christianities*; and Lüdemann, *Heretics*. Orthodoxy also raises important questions about the nature and status of doctrinal belief; see, especially, Lindbeck, *Nature of Doctrine*; and McGrath, *Genesis of Doctrine*.

Hermas (110–40 CE), readers are repeatedly reassured that if they truly repent, God will heal (*iaomai*) their former transgressions.[36]

Attitudes to Suffering

Fourth, attitudes to suffering resulting from disease changed, at least in parts of the Christian world. As we have seen, in Israelite faith and at least some strands of the nascent Jesus movement, illness tended to be viewed as a consequence of wrongdoing or as divine punishment for the same. Within this scenario, the ensuing suffering was unlikely to engender a generous response; quite the opposite, it elicited revulsion and rejection or, at best, an exhortation to repentance. With time, this link between suffering and sin eased, bringing sick people into focus as persons worthy of compassion, rather than as deserving of disdain.[37] This is nowhere more apparent than in attitudes towards those suffering from serious skin conditions such as elephantiasis, often described under the general category of leprosy. In addition to causing revulsion and constituting a source of religious and ritual impurity, physicians such as Aretaeus of Cappadocia (from the first century CE?) maintained this disease was contagious, adding further support to the widespread practice of excluding "lepers" from all forms of society apart from their own company.[38] In the fourth century, the three Cappadocian Fathers—Basil the Great (330–79 CE), Gregory of Nazianzus (329–90 CE), and Gregory of Nyssa (335–94 CE)—changed attitudes to the poor in general and to "lepers" in particular, providing sanctuaries where they could be cared for and treated with dignity.[39] Gregory of Nyssa in particular challenged whether leprosy could be contracted through contact with or being in the vicinity of sufferers, seeing this as an excuse for hardness of heart.[40] The Grego-

36. E.g., Herm. Vis. 1.3; Mand. 12.6; Sim. 5.7; 7.1–7; 8.11; 9.23, 28, 31–32.

37. See Ferngren, *Health Care*, 140–45.

38. "[T]here is a danger of the disease being communicated" (Aretaeus, quoted in Holman, "Social Leper," 294).

39. See, for example, Gregory of Nazianzus, *On the Love of the Poor* (oration 14) and Gregory of Nyssa, *On the Love of the Poor* (sermons 1 and 2). For a detailed discussion of their contribution, see Holman, "Social Leper," 283–309; Risse, *Mending Bodies*, 69–87; and Ferngren, *Health Care*, 140–45.

40. Gregory of Nyssa, *On the Love of the Poor*, sermon 2. One theory of contagion held that disease was airborne and could be contracted if one was in the vicinity of a sufferer even if there was no physical contact.

ries, in their sermons on the poor, spoke of the divine sanctity possessed by those set apart from society—even going so far as to describe leprosy as a "sacred disease" (*hē hiera nosos*)[41]—a sanctity that was contagious when sufferers were welcomed and cared for as Christ's own rather than rejected and forced into penury. Susan Holman describes this remarkable transformation in the following terms, quoting from the Cappadocians:

> The sick bodies of the destitute poor are imbued with a very particular importance that is somehow rooted precisely in the state of their poverty and is related to their identification with Christ. From its identification as the prototype of all religions pollution, physical leprosy is transformed into sanctity, and its identification with pollution is reversed for "spiritual" leprosy, the diseased soul. The physical leper becomes the essential means by which the spiritual leper may find a mediator to wipe away his own polluting spots of greed and passion. Here the leper, once set apart for his pollution, becomes a symbol of all that is now "set apart" for God. For both Gregories, as with Chrysostom, the ill beggars lying on the ground are holy coins that "bear the image of the Savior" . . . To regard these people who share our own nature as unrelated strangers is to tear apart "the unity of the spirit." They ought to be touched physically, without repulsion, since "the Lord of the angels put on this stinking and unclean flesh, with the soul thus enclosed, in order to affect a total cure of your ills by his touch."[42]

Exorcism

Fifth, despite the silence of the Apostolic Fathers, there are many references to the continuing practice of exorcism within the literature of the second, third, and fourth centuries, as the following sample demonstrates:

> For numberless demoniacs throughout the whole world, and in your city, many of our Christian men exorcising them in the name of Jesus Christ, who was crucified under Pontius Pilate, have healed and do heal, rendering helpless and driving the possessing devils out of the men, though they could not be cured by all the other exorcists, and those who used incantations and drugs.[43]

41. Gregory of Nazianzus, *Or. Bas.* 14.6.

42. Holman, "Social Leper," 298.

43. Justin [100–65 CE], *2 Apol. 6* [*ANF*]; also Justin, *Dial.* 30; 76; 85.

The clerk of one of them who was liable to be thrown upon the ground by an evil spirit, was set free from his affliction; as was also the relative of another, and the little boy of a third. How many men of rank (to say nothing of common people) have been delivered from devils and healed of diseases![44]

And the name of Jesus can still remove distractions from the minds of men, and expel demons, and also take away diseases; and produce a marvelous meekness of spirit and complete change of character, and a humanity, and goodness, and gentleness in those individuals who do not feign themselves to be Christians for the sake of subsistence or the supply of any mortal wants, but who have honestly accepted the doctrine concerning God and Christ, and the judgment to come.[45]

And as He Himself before His passion put to confusion demons by His word and command, so now, by the name and sign of the same passion, unclean spirits, having insinuated themselves into the bodies of men, are driven out, when racked and tormented, and confessing themselves to be demons, they yield themselves to God, who harasses them.[46]

In fact, the oppressive effects of evil, usually attributed to demons, came to be recognized as ubiquitous, characterizing the pre-Christian condition of humanity. As a consequence, exorcism increasingly became ritualized and incorporated within Christian initiation. Although not mentioned in our earliest extant church order, the Didache (c 100 CE), exorcism appears to be a daily undertaking for catechumens in the Apostolic Tradition, as well as featuring in their actual baptisms where it is administered by bishops:

From the time that they were set apart, let hands be laid on them daily while they are exorcized. And when the day of their baptism approaches, the bishop shall exorcise each one of them, in order that he may know whether he [i.e. the initiate] is pure . . . And he [i.e. the bishop] shall lay his hand on them and exorcize all alien spirits, that they may flee out of them and never return

44. Tertullian [160–220 CE], *Scap.* 4 [*ANF*]; also Tertullian, *Apol.* 23; 37; *Test.* 3.

45. Origen [184–253 CE], *Cels.* 1.67 [*ANF*]; also 1.6, 24; 3.36; 7.67.

46. Lactantius [240–320 CE], *Epit.* 51 [*ANF*]; also Lactantius, *Inst.* 2.16; 5.22; Irenaeus [130–202 CE], *Haer.* 2.6.2; Theophilus of Antioch [died c 180 CE], *Autol.* 2.8; Minucius Felix [died c 260 CE], *Oct.* 27; Eusebius, *Hist. eccl.* 2.3.2; 7.17; Acts Andr. 2–10, 25–26.

into them. And when he has finished exorcizing them, he shall breathe on their faces; and when he has signed their foreheads, ears, and noses, he shall raise them up.[47]

In addition, by the fourth century and quite possibly earlier, as ecclesial structure and leadership continued to develop with the definition of particular roles and functions, the ongoing need for exorcism among the initiated[48] as well as the unbaptized gave rise to the office of exorcist. It is quite possible that Cyprian, bishop of Carthage (210–58 CE), alludes to this when he describes an exorcist as "a man approved and always of good conversation in respect of religious discipline" who was "inspired by God's grace" or, again, when he writes, "Lucianus wrote this, there being present of the clergy, both an exorcist and a reader."[49] The following reference from Eusebius's *Ecclesiastical History* seems unambiguous:

> This avenger of the Gospel [Novatian?] then did not know that there should be one bishop in a catholic church; yet he was not ignorant (for how could he be?) that in it there were forty-six presbyters, seven deacons, seven sub-deacons, forty-two acolyths, fifty-two exorcists (*exorkistas*), readers, and janitors,

47. Hippolytus, *Trad. ap.* 20 [*ApT*]); also 21. Scholarly consensus has moved away from the view that this work was composed by Hippolytus of Rome around the beginning of the third century. In its current form, it may well be a composite text reflecting a number of hands compiled considerably later, but incorporating earlier material. See the discussion in Bradshaw, *Origins*, 80–83. Other early references to exorcism within baptism include: Tertullian (160–220 CE), *Cor.* 3; Acts Thom. (early third century CE), 49–50; Cyril of Jerusalem (315–86 CE), *Pro.* 9; *Cat.* 1.2–9; 2.3; *Pilgrimage of Egeria* (c. 380s), 46; Apos. Con. (c 380s), 7.40–41. These and other texts have been conveniently gathered together in Whitaker, *Baptismal Liturgy*.

48. Cf. "This, finally, in very fact also we experience, that those who are baptized by urgent necessity in sickness, and obtain grace, are free from the unclean spirit wherewith they were previously moved, and live in the Church in praise and honour, and day by day make more and more advance in the increase of heavenly grace by the growth of their faith. And, on the other hand, some of those who are baptized in health, if subsequently they begin to sin, are shaken by the return of the unclean spirit, so that it is manifest that the devil is driven out in baptism by the faith of the believer, and returns if the faith afterwards shall fail" (Cyprian, *Ep.* 75.16 [*ANF*]).

49. Cyprian, *Ep.* 74.10, 16; also 75.15; cf. "In parting with Cornelius, it is useful to note that he represents his diocese in his day as numbering 'forty-six presbyters, seven deacons and the same number of sub-deacons, with forty-two acolytes and exorcists, readers and sacristans in all fifty-two'" (*Elucidations*, 15). However, it is highly questionable whether Cyprian was the author of this work.

and over fifteen hundred widows and persons in distress, all of whom the grace and kindness of the Master nourish.[50]

As, indeed, this passage from the fourth-century composite church order, the Apostolic Constitutions, which seems to indicate that in this part of the church (Syrian Antioch?),[51] exorcism continued to be seen as a charismatic anointing rather than an ecclesial office; it may also bear witness to the continuing belief that illness more generally was caused by demons:

> I the same make a constitution in regard to an exorcist. An exorcist is not ordained. For it is a trial of voluntary goodness, and of the grace of God through Christ by the inspiration of the Holy Spirit. For he who has received the gift of healing is declared by revelation from God, the grace which is in him being manifest to all. But if there be occasion for him, he must be ordained a bishop, or a presbyter, or a deacon.[52]

Spiritual Healing

Sixth and finally, the practice of healing in Jesus' name also continued beyond the apostolic era, if the records are to be trusted. Unsurprisingly, we find multiple references during the literature of this period to the gospel healings, which are sometimes augmented with a sufferer's name or some other detail,[53] although as Paul Achtemeier has pointed out there are pre-

---

50. Eusebius, *Hist. eccl.* 6.43.11 [*ANF*]; also 6.43.14.

51. Again, see the assessment in Bradshaw, *Christian Worship*, 84–86.

52. Apos. Con. 8.26 [*ANF*]; see also, for example, Cyril of Jerusalem (c. 311–386 CE): "Let thy feet hasten to the catechisings; receive with earnestness the exorcisms: whether thou be breathed upon or exorcised, the act is to thee salvation . . . Even so without exorcisms the soul cannot be purified; and these exorcisms are divine, having been collected out of the divine Scriptures . . . even so when the exorcists inspire terror by the Spirit of God, and set the soul, as it were, on fire in the crucible of the body, the hostile demon flees away, and there abide salvation and the hope of eternal life, and the soul henceforth is cleansed from its sins and hath salvation" (*Pro.* 9 [*NPNF*[2]]; also *Cat.* 16.19).

53. E.g., Gospel of Nicodemus (Acts Pil.) forms A and B, with form A supplying the name of the woman with a flow of blood (Mark 5:24–34) as "Bernice" (7), and form B her location, "Paneas," a correspondence also attested by Eusebius in *Hist. eccl.* 7:17–18: Or, again, the Clementine Homilies which name the Syrophoenician woman of Mark 7:24–30 as "Justa" (2:19). We have already mentioned the version of Mark 1:40–44 contained in Papyrus Egerton 2, which includes various additional details,

cious few new accounts attributed to Jesus' adult ministry, unlike some of the Infancy Gospels where they proliferate.[54] We should probably sit lightly upon the so-called Apocryphal Acts, where exorcisms, healings, and even resuscitations attributed to the apostles abound, on the grounds that it is now impossible to identify the historical credibility of what are manifestly embellished, if not wholly fictional, narratives—although, on the principle that "there is no smoke without fire," they do, perhaps, in a similar manner to the Acts of the Apostles, bear witness to reputations certain figures earned for continuing the ministry Jesus entrusted to his disciples.[55]

An exception should be made for the Acts of Peter and the Twelve Apostles which survives at the beginning of the sixth Nag Hammadi codex and has been dated to the second century CE.[56] The book purports to relate the experiences of some of Jesus' disciples, who, postresurrection, "agreed to fulfil the ministry to which the Lord appointed" them (1.10–12). During their sojournings, they encounter the risen Christ incognito under the pseudonym of Lithargoel, who appears to them in the guise of a physician, carrying a pouch of medicine (8.10–20). Once his identity has been revealed, he duly commissions his followers in these terms:

> He gave them the pouch of medicine and said, "Heal the sick of the city who believe [in] my name." Peter was afraid [to] reply to him a second time. He signaled to the one who was beside him, who was John: "You talk this time." John answered and said, "Lord, before you we are afraid to say many words. But it is you who asks us to practice this skill. We have not been taught to be physicians. How then will we know how to heal bodies as you have told us?" He answered him, "Rightly you have spoken, John, for I know that the physicians of this world heal what belongs to the world. The physicians of souls, however, heal the heart. Heal the bodies first, therefore, so that through the real powers of healing for their bodies, without medicine of the

---

such as the words "and sin no more" to Jesus' instruction to the cleansed leper, while Jerome informs us that the man with a withered hand (cf. Matt 12:9–14) was a mason by trade (*Comm. Matt.* on 12:13).

54. Achtemeier, "Miracle Workers," 161.

55. Again, see Achtemeier, "Miracle Workers," 149–86.

56. See McRae and Parrott's introduction in *NHL*, 271, whose translation we have used.

world, they may believe in you, that you have power to heal the illnesses of the heart also."[57]

What is particularly striking here is that although the risen Christ bestows upon his disciples the trappings of a physician (i.e., a pouch of medicine), he does not expect them to use such therapeutic aids in healing the maladies of the body. Instead they are to employ the (spiritual?) powers that, presumably, he bestows. However one evaluates the historical plausibility of this encounter, the document does reflect a setting in life where Christian missionaries not only continue Jesus' ministry of healing, but do so in competition with conventional medical provision, which, by implication, is rejected.[58]

In *Healing in the Early Church*, Andrew Daunton-Fear makes the maximal case for the practice of healing (and exorcism) continuing in the life of the early church by including references where the language of "wonders" and "acts of power" is employed in an unspecified manner, as well as passages where healing can possibly be inferred. However, even with these removed, there remains a modest core which seems to reflect its continuation in parts of the growing Jesus movement throughout the second and third centuries after which, as Gary Ferngren and others have suggested, the evidence is more difficult to assess given the proliferation of accounts relating extraordinary happenings associated with the cults of the saints.[59] We should also restate that within a mind-set where evil is deemed to be one of the causes of disease, healing necessarily involves exorcism so the distinction between the two becomes blurred.

In his dialogue with the Jew Trypho, which took place during the Bar Kokhba revolt of 132–35 CE, Justin refers to the "mighty deeds (*dynameis*) even now wrought" in Jesus' name before, a little later, alluding to the apostle Paul's teaching on the charismata in 1 Cor 12. He describes the Christian community of his day in these terms, "For one receives the spirit of understanding, another of counsel, another of strength, another of healing, another of foreknowledge, another of teaching, and another of the fear of God."[60] Meanwhile, a little later, over in Gaul, Irenaeus, bishop

---

57. Acts. Pet. 12 Apos. 10.30–11.25 [*NHL*].

58. See the historical reconstruction of Giovanni B. Bazzana in "Early Christian Missionaries," 232–51.

59. Ferngren, *Health Care*, 64–85.

60. Justin, *Dial.* 35, 39 [*ANF*].

of Lyon, with similar allusions to Paul's teaching, unequivocally bears witness to Christ's continuing ministry of healing and exorcism:

> If, however, they maintain that the Lord, too, performed such works simply in appearance, we shall refer them to the prophetical writings, and prove from these both that all things were thus predicted regarding Him, and did take place undoubtedly, and that He is the only Son of God. Wherefore, also, those who are in truth His disciples, receiving grace from Him, do in His name perform [miracles], so as to promote the welfare of other men, according to the gift which each one has received from Him. For some do certainly and truly drive out devils, so that those who have thus been cleansed from evil spirits frequently both believe [in Christ], and join themselves to the Church. Others have foreknowledge of things to come: they see visions, and utter prophetic expressions. Others still, heal the sick by laying their hands upon them, and they are made whole. Yea, moreover, as I have said, the dead even have been raised up, and remained among us for many years.[61]

In the middle of the third century, when established in Caesarea and not many years before his death, the Alexandrian biblical scholar and theologian Origen composed his extensive rebuttal of Celsus's anti-Christian treatise, *The True Doctrine* (180 CE). Within this work, not only does he defend the historicity and credibility of Jesus' healings and exorcisms, but he also stresses the continuation of that ministry within the life of the church. We have already cited one passage discussing exorcism; here is another in which Origen likens belief in Jesus to believing in the Greco-Roman deity of healing, Asclepius, before going on to demonstrate the former's superiority:

> And some give evidence of their having received through this faith a marvelous power by the cures which they perform, revoking no other name over those who need their help than that of the God of all things, and of Jesus, along with a mention of

61. Irenaeus, *Haer.* 2.32.4 [*ANF*]; cited also by Eusebius, *Hist. eccl.* 5.7; a little earlier, Irenaeus claims that resuscitations were also taking place: "And so far are they from being able to raise the dead, as the Lord raised them, and the apostles did by means of prayer, and as has been frequently done in the brotherhood on account of some necessity—the entire Church in that particular locality entreating [the boon] with much fasting and prayer, the spirit of the dead man has returned, and he has been bestowed in answer to the prayers of the saints—that they do not even believe this can possibly be done, [and hold] that the resurrection from the dead is simply an acquaintance with that truth which they proclaim" (2.31.2 [*ANF*]).

His history. For by these means we too have seen many persons
freed from grievous calamities, and from distractions of mind,
and madness, and countless other ills, which could be cured
neither by men nor devils.[62]

As noted with respect to exorcism, the Apostolic Tradition also
bears witness to the ongoing practice of spiritual healing within the
life of the church: "If anyone says, 'I have received a gift of healing by a
revelation,' hands shall not be laid on him, for the facts themselves will
show whether he has spoken the truth" (14 [ApT]). Interestingly, the gift
of healing is not conferred by the laying on of hands, but by spiritual
anointing—a self-authenticating charisma independent of ecclesial office or, presumably, any medical training. In addition to these and other
texts, Daunton-Fear finds support for the continuation of spiritual healing beyond the apostolic era in an unlikely source, namely the Jewish
collection of supplementary oral teaching, roughly contemporaneous
with the Mishnah (200 CE), but containing earlier traditions, known as
the Tosefta (the "Addition").[63] In it, a rabbi is prohibited from receiving
healing from a follower of Jesus, with death ensuing as a consequence:

> R Eleazar b Dama was bitten by a snake. And Jacob of Kefar
> Sama came to heal him in the name of Jesus son of Pantera. And
> R Ishmael did not allow him [to accept healing]. They said to
> him, "You are not permitted [to accept the healing from him],
> Ben Dama." He said to him, "I shall bring you proof that he may
> heal me." But he did not have time to bring the [promised] proof
> before he dropped dead. Said R Ishmael, "Happy are you, Ben
> Dama. For you have expired in peace, but you did not break
> down the hedge erected by sages. For whoever breaks down the
> hedge erected by sages eventually suffers punishment, as it is
> said, 'He who breaks down a hedge is bitten by a snake.' [Eccl
> 10:8)"[64]

According to Daunton-Fear, this tradition can be traced back to the
first half of the second century and seems to reflect the condemnation
of *minim*, heretics, including Christians, which became enshrined in the
Eighteen Benedictions.[65] Significantly, as we saw with Jesus and the Beel-

62 Origen, *Cels.* 3.24 [*ANF*]; also 1.6, 67; 2.8; 3.28, 33.

63. Daunton-Fear, *Healing*, 44–46.

64 t. Hull. 2.22–23 [Neusner].

65. "For the apostates let there be no hope, and uproot the kingdom of arrogance,
speedily and in our days. May the Nazarenes and the sectarians perish as in a moment.

zebul controversy, no attempt is made to challenge Jacob's effectiveness of a spiritual healer, which is assumed; rather, it is the provenance of his healing powers that is deemed objectionable.

Whether these texts evidencing the continuation of exorcism and spiritual healing in the life of the early church are sufficient to substantiate Ramsay MacMullen's contention that it was by such means that Christianity distinguished itself from competing religious cults and thereby gained converts remains debatable.[66] Interestingly, Adolf Harnack made a similar claim almost one hundred years previously, captured succinctly in this oft-referenced passage from *The Mission and Expansion of Christianity*: "Deliberately and consciously [Christianity] assumed the form of 'the religion of salvation and healing,' or of 'the medicine of soul and body,' and at the same time it recognized that one of its cardinal duties was to care assiduously for the sick in body."[67] It is perhaps at this juncture that we should return to the distinction between curing a disease and healing an illness introduced in chapter 3, where "disease relates to the biological, mental or psychological malfunctioning of the body" and "illness denotes the personal and social responses to such malfunctioning."

Despite recognizing that these are modern categorizations, we concluded that in relation to his ministry, Jesus' reputation was rooted primarily in curing disease; however, increasingly those who continued to minister in his name invested themselves in healing illness through, as Harnack rightly acknowledged, exercising a duty of care towards those unfortunates who, for no fault of their own, found themselves suffering ailments no amount of exorcism, anointing or forgiveness could alleviate. By the fourth century this commitment had innovated charitable hospitals and hostels for the poor—arguably, applications more appropriate for a religion singled out to serve an empire than charismatic manifestations or even liturgical rituals of curing disease could ever prove to be. It was an inspired improvisation of Jesus' legacy for healing, and one which enabled him to become the physician of the sick (cf. Mark 2:17), not only for a relatively few ailing Israelites, but also for the needy of many nations. There is little reason to conclude that exorcism and spiritual

---

Let them be blotted out of the book of life, and not be written together with the righteous. You are praised, O Lord, who subdues the arrogant" (Petuchowski, trans., "Eighteen Benedictions," benediction 12).

66. In a number of publications: for example, in MacMullen, *Christianizing*.

67. Harnack, *Mission and Expansion*, 131–32, quoted in this instance in Ferngren, *Health Care*, 64.

healing in Christ's name ceased with this development; but, equally, it is demonstrably the case that they no longer played such a determinative role as they had done in Jesus' ministry and, quite possibly, those of his earliest followers.

Appendix

Did Jesus Raise the Dead?

THIS STUDY HAS FOCUSED on investigating the origins of Jesus' reputation for healing and exorcism. As we have seen, there is significant overlap between these two categories, which lends coherence to the project. Before drawing to a close, however, it seems apposite to account for why those gospel traditions depicting Jesus raising the dead were deemed to fall outside of this undertaking, before highlighting some of the interpretative challenges this material presents should a similar exercise be attempted.

Let us begin with the evidence. The canonical Gospels contain three narratives in which Jesus is remembered for raising the dead. The first relates to the daughter of a synagogue leader, Jairus, who approaches Jesus to plead on her behalf.[1] Significantly, Jesus is petitioned as someone with a reputation for healing who, on learning of her subsequent demise, is asked to stand down—presumably, on the grounds that resuscitations were beyond his powers or, expressed differently, his reputation for healing did not extend to raising the dead.[2] Of equal significance is

1. Mark 5:21–24a, 35–43//Matt 9:18–19, 23–26//Luke 8:40–42, 49–56. I have examined this pericope in detail in another context, where I concluded that there are persuasive grounds for concluding that a version of Mark is the principal source drawn on by Matthew and Luke with respect to the synagogue leader's daughter. The significant differences, especially in the Matthean version, are best accounted for in terms of the Evangelist's redactional predilections ("Redaction-Critical Analysis," 11–13, 297–99).

2. "While he [Jesus] was still speaking, some people came from the leader's house to say, 'Your daughter is dead. Why trouble the teacher any further?'" (Mark 5:35// Luke 8:49). Matthew's practice of deleting details from Mark's account deemed to be unnecessary or misleading is in evidence here, including the dialogue of Mark 5.35–36 in which the synagogue leader learns of his daughter's death. As a consequence, the

Jesus' subsequent declaration that the girl was in fact asleep rather than deceased: 'When he [Jesus] had entered, he said to them, "Why do you make a commotion and weep? The child is not dead but sleeping"' (*to paidion ouk apethanen alla katheudei*).[3] Clearly, this declaration is open to multiple interpretations, one of which is that Jesus intended for his words to be taken literally—a possibility which, as we shall explore shortly, becomes plausible in the light of how death was understood within Israelite faith at that time, as well as the difficulties in confirming whether or not it had taken place.

The second tradition is exclusive to Luke and concerns the only son, and presumably sole bread-winner, of a widow from a village located a few miles from Nazareth, entitled Nain (Luke 7:11–17). In its current form, the story exhibits a striking resemblance to the account of Elijah's reviving of the widow from Zarephath's son and, to a lesser extent, with Elisha's raising of the son of a Shunammite couple.[4] In this case, Jesus is not asked to intervene, but is moved by compassion (*esplanchnisthē*, v. 13) to take the initiative. Unlike Jairus' daughter, funeral arrangements were underway with the boy in an open (?) coffin (*tēs sorou*, v. 14) en route for burial. However, given that burials tended to take place shortly after death,[5] this does not necessarily imply a significant lapse of time. It also needs to be noted that the diagnosing of death was far from an exact science in the ancient world as the archaeologist, Shimon Gibson, explains:

> Unless the person died through mutilation or execution, Jews were hard-pressed to know if their family member had actually died or was still in some sleeplike repose (a form of "slumber")

---

girl is dead from the outset in Matthew's version (9:18), although this is almost certainly an editorial revision of the Evangelist (Davies and Allison, *Matthew*, 2:126)

3. Mark 5:39; also Matt 9:24 and Luke 8:52. *Katheudō* can be used euphemistically to denote death (e.g., 1 Thess 5:10; also Ps 87:6 [LXX]; Dan 12:2 [LXX]); however, given it is deployed here to distinguish the girl's condition from death this seems unlikely.

4. 1 Kgs 17:17–24 and 2 Kgs 4:8–37. Meier offers a thorough analysis of the similarities and differences in *Marginal Jew*, 2:790–97. Of particular note is the verbatim agreement between Luke 7:15 and 1 Kgs 17:23: "The dead man sat up and began to speak, and Jesus *gave him to his mother* (*edōken auton tē mētri autou*)."

5. Cf. "Furthermore, every one that suffers his dead to remain overnight transgresses a negative command; but if he had suffered it to remain by reason of the honour due to it, to bring for it in a coffin and burial clothes, he does not thereby commit transgression" (m. Sanh. 6.5 [MD]). See the discussion of McCane, *Roll Back the Stone*, 27–60, esp. 31–33.

between *Sheol* (the Jewish equivalent of the underworld Hades) and the waking world. This is why the dead were more likely to be placed on benches in burial caves than in trench-dug graves in the ground. Those that were placed in trench-graves—usually poor peasants and shepherds, not townspeople—were only buried, however, after their bodies had first lain within a mortuary chamber in a cemetery.[6]

The third tradition is found in the Fourth Gospel alone, the raising of Lazarus (John 11:1–45). It is an extended narrative in which a distinctly personal episode between Jesus and some of his friends serves the theological predilections of the Evangelist in ways that can appear contrived and, in places, morally suspect. For example, Jesus refuses to attend to an ailing Lazarus and prevent him from dying in order that his subsequent demise would occasion a greater manifestation of divine glory which, in turn, would engender belief in him and his theological credentials.[7] Given the passage is saturated with Johannine themes and imagery, it is difficult to be confident whether there is an underlying tradition that has been developed by the Evangelist or whether it is entirely a literary creation composed to supply a setting for one of the "I am" declarations.[8] Equally, details intended to heighten the wonder of this sign,[9] such as Lazarus being in the tomb for four days (vv. 17, 39), stretch credulity to the limits as the reader is left contemplating not simply a resuscitation, but also the reversal of bodily decomposition.[10] Of particular interest for

6. Gibson, *Final Days*, 29.

7. "But when Jesus heard it, he said, 'This illness does not lead to death; rather it is for God's glory, so that the Son of God may be glorified through it.' Accordingly, though Jesus loved Martha and her sister and Lazarus, after having heard that Lazarus was ill, he stayed two days longer in the place where he was . . . Then Jesus told them plainly, 'Lazarus is dead. For your sake I am glad I was not there, so that you may believe. But let us go to him' . . . Many of the Jews therefore, who had come with Mary and had seen what Jesus did, believed in him" (11:4–6, 14–15, 45).

8. "I am the resurrection and the life. Those who believe in me, even though they die, will live, and everyone who lives and believes in me will never die" (John 11:25–26; also 6:35; 8:12; 10:7; 10:11/17; 14:6; 15:1; cf. Exod 3:14). See Meier's exhaustive analysis and plausible tradition history in *Marginal Jew*, 2:798–832.

9. In the Fourth Gospel, Jesus' wonders are employed as signs (*sēmeia*) which confirm his theological credentials and engender belief (2:1–11; 4:46–54; 5:1–9; 6:5–13; 6:16–20; 9:1–9; 11:1–45 [12:18]): "Now Jesus did many other signs in the presence of his disciples, which are not written in this book. But these are written so that you may come to believe that Jesus is the Messiah, the Son of God, and that through believing you may have life in his name" (20:30–31).

10. Cf. "The fact that Lazarus' body was not rotting after having been in the tomb

our study is that while Jesus' reputation for healing had clearly reached the ears of Lazarus' sisters, Mary and Martha, it doesn't appear to have extended to embrace raising the dead (vv. 3, 21, 32), leaving them uncertain about the outcome: "Martha said to Jesus, 'Lord, if you had been here, my brother would not have died. But even now I know that God will give you whatever you ask of him.' Jesus said to her, 'Your brother will rise again.' Martha said to him, 'I know that he will rise again in the resurrection on the last day'" (vv. 21–24).

In addition to these three narratives, mention should also be made of the Q tradition relating Jesus' response to the followers of John the Baptist, which we discussed in chapter 6 where we proposed that it represents an early attempt to make theological sense of Jesus' wonderworking by locating it within current expectation about how Yahweh would fulfil covenantal promises to Israel: "Go report to John what you hear and see: The blind regain their sight and the lame walk around, the skin-deseased are cleansed and the deaf hear, and the dead are raised, and the poor are evangelized. And blessed is whoever is not offended by me."[11] To date, no single text has been found which contains all of these elements,[12] suggesting that its author was not quoting an existing source, but compiling a catena of evidence with scriptural precedent which reflected the extent of Jesus' ministry. In this respect, it is highly significant that mention is made of the dead being raised (*nekroi egeirontai*).

In brief, this is the extent of the canonical evidence for Jesus revivifying the dead, which could be augmented a little if the net were to be cast wider to embrace other early Christian literature, although most of these texts are based on the gospel accounts already cited.[13] Perhaps of more substance are the references to raisings attributed to Peter and Paul in the Acts of the Apostles (9:36–43; 20:9–12) and, more generally, in the life of the nascent Jesus movement according to one or two early church fathers, as well as some of the apocryphal Acts.[14] However, what is

---

for four days suggests he must have been in a trance or state of catalepsy" (Gibson, *Final Days*, 28).

11. Q 7:22–23 (*CEQ*; Luke 7:22–23//Matt 11:4–6).

12. E.g., Ps 146:7–8; Isa 26:19; 61:1. As we noted in chapter 6, the first century CE fragment found in Cave 4 at Qumran, 4Q521, comes closest—including all components with the exception of cleansing lepers.

13. E.g., Clement of Alexandria, *Paed.* 1.2; Irenaeus, *Haer.* 2.31.2; Justin, *1 Apol.* 48; 54; *Dial.* 69; Origen, *Cels.* 2.48; cf. Inf. Gos. Thom. 9.1–3; 17.1–3; 18.1–2.

14. E.g., Irenaeus, *Haer.* 2.31.2; 2.32.4; Tertullian, *Carn. Chr.* 4.4; Or. 29.2. Pud. 21.

conspicuous by its absence is any reference to Jesus resuscitating the dead in the editorial summaries of Jesus' ministry in the Synoptic Gospels or in the Acts of the Apostles[15] which suggests that he wasn't remembered as one who had earned a reputation for such activity in the same way as he had for performing healings and exorcisms—a conclusion borne out by the fact that there are no extant traditions in which Jesus is approached to perform a raising of the dead; the initiative always resides with him.[16]

Hopefully, sufficient has been offered to account for why the material relating to Jesus' raising the dead falls outside the remit of this book and, indeed, the approach it adopts. Before concluding, however, it is worth pausing briefly to outline some of the interpretative challenges presented by these texts. Putting to one side the substantial scientific and philosophical issues associated with the claim that Jesus raised the dead, we need to recall an observation reiterated throughout this book, namely that the Gospels supply us with *symptoms* associated with ill-health and not *diagnoses*. That is to say, we are not informed about the underlying medical conditions. As a result, it would be more accurate to maintain that the narratives introduced above bear witness to Jesus' response to patients manifesting symptoms of lifelessness which do not conclusively confirm that death had taken place. A number of ancient sources confirm what is obvious, namely that in the absence of the diagnostic aids available today, establishing whether death had occurred could be extremely difficult and that, as a consequence, errors inevitably ensued. The following tradition attributed to Jesus' contemporary, Apollonius of Tyana, which bears comparison with Luke 7:11–17, is a particularly insightful example:

> Apollonius performed another miracle (*thauma*). There was a girl who appeared to have died (*tethnanai edokei*) just at the time of her wedding. The betrothed followed the bier, with all the lamentations of an unconsummated marriage, and Rome mourned with him, since the girl belonged to a consular family. Meeting with this scene of sorrow, Apollonius said, 'Put the bier down, for I will end your crying over the girl.' At the same time

---

Acts John 19–25; 46–7; Acts Pet. 23–9; Acts Thom. 30–8; 51–56.

15. Mark 1:32–34//Matt 8:16–17//Luke 4:40–41; Mark 3:7–12//Luke 6:17–19; Mark 6:53–56// Matt 14:34–36; Luke 7:21; 8:2; Acts 10:38; cf. Acts 2:22.

16. In the case of both Jairus' daughter and Lazarus, Jesus is approached when they were still alive and their petitioners became, at best, less confident that Jesus would be able to help once death ensued (Mark 5:35–36; John 11:21–24, 32).

he asked her name, which made most people think he was going to declaim a speech of the kind delivered at funerals to raise lamentation. But Apollonius, after merely touching her and saying something secretly, woke the bride from her apparent death (*tou dokountos thanatou*). The girl spoke, and went back to her father's house like Alcestis revived by Heracles. Her kinsmen wanted to give Apollonius a hundred and fifty thousand drachmas, but he said he gave it as an extra dowry for the girl. He may have seen a spark of life (*spinthēra tēs psychēs*) in her which the doctors had not noticed, since apparently the sky was drizzling and steam was coming from her face, or he may have revived and restored her life when it was extinguished, but the explanation of this has proved unfathomable, not just to me but to the bystanders.[17]

Whether or not this event took place as reported is of secondary importance for our purposes to the insight it offers into the difficulty in diagnosing death. In the light of this, confusion over how to interpret symptoms of lifelessness may explain why in each of the three gospel

17. Philostratus, *Vit. Apoll.* 4.45 [LCL 16]. Also: "The famous Asclepiades, the greatest of physicians with the sole exception of Hippocrates, and superior to all the rest . . . he happened to be returning to the city from his suburban estate when he noticed a large funeral prepared outside the city boundary, and a huge crowd of people standing around to attend the last rites, all of them very downcast and in very shabby clothing. He came closer, either from a human curiosity to learn who it might be, since he had inquired and got no reply, or else to observe something in the man for himself by his expertise. Actually, though the man was laid out and almost buried, he canceled his doom. For after surveying all the poor man's body when it was already sprinkled with perfumes, his face already daubed with fragrant ointment, his body already washed, already all but prepared for the flames, and after carefully observing certain signs, he ran his hands several times over the man's body and found hidden life in it. Immediately he shouted, 'The man is alive, so throw away the torches, scatter the fire, dismantle the pyre, move the funeral banquet from the grave to the table.' Meanwhile mutterings arose: some said that a medical man deserved belief, some even mocked the art of medicine. Finally, though all the relatives objected too, either because they already had a legacy, or as yet had no trust in him, even so Asclepiades with painful difficulty obtained a brief delay for the deceased, and, having thus wrested him from the hands of the undertakers, brought him home like one restored from the underworld, and immediately used certain medicines to revive the life hiding in the recesses of the body" (Apuleius, *Flor.* 19 [LCL 534]). Both of these examples are quoted by Collins (*Mark*, 277–79), to which can be added the following rabbinic reference: "During three days before the interment, experts repair to the cemetery and examine the dead whether they are really dead; [and although this is the custom of other nations], there is no fear of the prohibition of the deeds of the Amorites. It happened that one of the dead was examined (and found alive), and he lived twenty-five years after that; and to another one, that he begat five children before he died" (Sem. 8.1).

narratives discussed above Jesus actually addresses the patient directly, which makes little sense if they were already dead.[18]

We should also note that death was deemed to be more of a process than an event. In particular, a number of pseudepigraphal and rabbinic texts reflect the belief that the soul of the deceased person remained associated with the body for a period of three days.[19] This, in turn, raises the question about whether physical death resulted in the annihilation of the person or whether some essence (soul/spirit) endured. From what we can gather, there was a good deal of speculation about this in the first century CE, but the point to note here is that assumptions informing current thinking about death in the Western medical paradigm were not shared by Jesus and his contemporaries. Death did not necessarily entail the extinguishing of personal existence, which could continue in one form or another.[20]

These, then, are just some of the considerations that complicate the task of interpreting the traditions bearing witness to Jesus as someone who could raise the dead and, more so, of assessing the most plausible source for this claim. In truth, it could be argued that such an undertaking lies beyond the reaches of historical inquiry.

18. "'Talitha cum,' which means, 'Little girl, get up!'" (Mark 5:41). "Young man, I say to you, rise!" (Luke 7:14). "Lazarus, come out!" (John 11:43).

19. "And as soon as they brought the body [of Job] to the tomb, all the widows and orphans circled about forbidding it to be brought into the tomb. But after three days they laid him in the tomb in a beautiful sleep, since he received a name renowned in all generations forever. Amen" (Test. Job 53.5–8 [OTP]). "And they tended the body of the righteous Abraham with divine ointments and perfumes until the third day after his death. And they buried him in the promised land at the oak of Mamre" (Test. Abr. [Rec. A] 20.11 [OTP]). Consider, also, the views of the rabbis: "R. Abba b. R. Pappai and R. Joshua of Siknin said in the name of R. Levi: For three days [after death] the soul hovers over the body, intending to re-enter it, but as soon as it sees its appearance change, it departs, as it is written, 'When his flesh that is on him is distorted, his soul will mourn over him (Job 14.22)'" (Lev. R. 18.1 [MR]; also Eccl. R. 12.6). "Evidence may not be given [of the identity of a corpse] save from [proof afforded by] the face together with the nose, even though there were [other] marks [of identity] on its body or its clothing. Evidence [of a man's death] may be given only after his soul gone forth, even though he was seen mortally wounded or crucified or being devoured by a wild beast. Evidence [of the identity of a corpse] may be given only during the first three days [after death]; but R. Judah b. Baba says: [Decay in corpses is] not alike in all men, in all places, and at all times" (m. Yeb. 16.3 [MD]). I have discussed this point in Holy Saturday Faith, 2–3.

20. See, for example, the surveys of Nickelsburg, Resurrection; and Wright, Resurrection, 32–206.

Bibliography

Achtemeier, Paul J. "Jesus and the Disciples as Miracle Workers in the Apocryphal New Testament." In *Aspects of Religious Propaganda in Judaism and Early Christianity*, edited by Elisabeth Schüssler Fiorenza, 149–86. Notre Dame: University Press, 1976.

Alexander, Philip. "Targum, Targumim." In *ABD* 6:320–31.

Allan, Nigel. "The Physician in Ancient Israel: His Status and Function." *Medical History* 45 (2001) 377–94.

American Psychiatric Association, *Diagnostic and Statistical Manual of Mental Disorders*. 4th ed. Washington, DC: American Psychiatric Association, 1994.

Amundsen, Darrel. *Medicine, Society, and Faith in the Ancient and Medieval Worlds*. Baltimore: Johns Hopkins University Press, 1996.

Anderson, Paul N. *The Fourth Gospel and the Quest for Jesus*. London: T. & T. Clark, 2006.

Aune, David E. "Magic in Early Christianity." In *ANRW* II.23.2.1:1510–16.

Avalos, Hector. *Health Care and the Rise of Christianity*. Peabody, MA: Hendrickson, 1999.

Bahrdt, Carl Friedrich. *Ausführungen des Plans und Zwecks Jesu. In Briefen and Wahrheit suchende Leser*. 11 vols. Berlin 1784–92.

———. *Briefe über die Bibel im Volkston: Eine Wochen Schrift*, Halle: Dost, 1872.

Basinger, David. "What Is a Miracle?" In *The Cambridge Companion to Miracles*, edited by Graham H. Twelftree, 19–35. Cambridge Companions to Religion. Cambridge: Cambridge University Press, 2011.

Bauckham, Richard J. *Jesus and the Eyewitnesses: The Gospels as Eyewitness Testimony*. Grand Rapids: Eerdmans, 2006.

Baumgarten, Joseph M. "The 4Q Zadokite Fragment on Skin Disease." *JJS* 41 (1990) 153–65.

Bazzana, Giovanni B. "Early Christian Missionaries as Physicians: Healing and its Cultural Value in the Greco-Roman Context." *NovT* 51 (2009) 232–51.

Beasley-Murray, George R. *John*. WBC 36. Dallas: Word, 1987.

Beilby, James K., and Paul R. Eddy, eds. *The Historical Jesus: Five Views*. London: SPCK, 2010.

Benson, Herbert, and Mark D. Epstein. "The Placebo Effect: A Neglected Asset in the Care of Patients." *Journal of the American Medical Association* 232 (1975) 1225–27.

Bieler, Ludwig. ΘΕΙΟΣ ΑΝΗΡ: *Das Bild des "göttlichen Menschen" in Spätantike und Frühchristentum*. 1935–36. Reprint, Darmstadt: Wissenschaftliche Buchgesellschaft, 1967.

Borg, Marcus J. *Conflict, Holiness and Politics in the Teachings of Jesus.* 2nd ed. Harrisburg, PA: Trinity, 1998.

———. *Jesus: A New Vision—Spirit, Culture, and the Life of Discipleship.* San Francisco: Harper & Row, 1987.

———. *Jesus: Uncovering the Life, Teachings, and Relevance of a Religious Revolutionary.* New York: HarperOne, 2006.

Bourguignon, Erika. *Possession.* San Francisco: Chandler & Sharp, 1976.

Bowie, Fiona. "Miracles in Traditional Religions." In *The Cambridge Companion to Miracles*, edited by Graham H. Twelftree, 167–83. Cambridge Companions to Religion. Cambridge: Cambridge University Press, 2011.

Bowker, John. *The Targums and Rabbinic Literature: An Introduction to Jewish Interpretations of Scripture.* Cambridge: Cambridge University Press, 1969.

Bradshaw, Paul F. *The Search for the Origins of Christian Worship: Sources and Methods for the Study of Early Liturgy.* 2nd ed. London: SPCK, 2002.

Brawley, Robert L. "The Pharisees in Luke-Acts: Luke's Address to Jews and his Irenic Purpose." PhD diss., Princeton Theological Seminary, 1978.

Broadhead, Edwin. "Echoes of an Exorcism in the Fourth Gospel?" *ZNW* 86 (1995) 111–19.

Brody, Howard. "Ritual, Medicine, and the Placebo Response." In *The Problem of Ritual Efficacy*, edited by William S. Sax, et al, 151–67. Oxford: Oxford University Press, 2010.

Brown, Colin. *Miracles and the Critical Mind.* Grand Rapids: Eerdmans, 1984.

Brown, Raymond E. *The Epistles of John: A New Translation with Introduction and Commentary.* AB 30. Garden City, NY: Doubleday, 1982.

Bultmann, Rudolf. *The Gospel of John: A Commentary.* Translated by George R. Beasley-Murray. Philadelphia: Westminster, 1971.

———. *The History of the Synoptic Tradition.* Translated by John Marsh. 2nd ed. Oxford: Blackwell, 1968.

———. "New Testament and Mythology." Translated by Reginald H. Fuller. In *Kerygma and Myth: A Theological Debate*, edited by Hans-Werner Bartsch, 1–16. London: SPCK, 1972.

Busse, Ulrich. *Die Wunder des Propheten Jesus: Die Rezeption, Komposition und Interpretation der Wundertradition im Evangelium des Lukas.* 2nd ed. Forschung zur Bibel. Stuttgart: Katholisches Bibelwerk, 1979.

Capper, Brian. "Essene Community Houses and Jesus' Early Community." In *Jesus and Archaeology*, edited by James H. Charlesworth, 472–502. Grand Rapids: Eerdmans, 2006.

Charlesworth, James H. "The Historical Jesus in the Fourth Gospel: A Paradigm Shift?" *Journal for the Study of the Historical Jesus* 8 (2010) 3–46.

———. *The Messiah: Developments in Earliest Judaism and Christianity.* Minneapolis: Fortress, 1992.

Chilton, Bruce D. *Jesus' Baptism and Jesus' Healing: His Personal Practice of Spirituality.* Harrisburg, PA: Trinity, 1998.

———. "Jesus ben David: Reflections on the *Davidssohnfrage.*" *JSNT* 14 (1982) 88–112.

———. *The Isaiah Targum: Introduction, Translation, Apparatus and Notes.* ArBib 11. Wilmington, DE: Glazier, 1987.

Chrysovergi, Maria. "Contrasting Views on Physicians in Tobit and Sirach." *JSP* 21 (2011) 46–54.

Collins, Adela Yarbro. *Mark: A Commentary*. Hermeneia. Minneapolis: Fortress, 2007.

Collins, John J. *The Apocalyptic Imagination: An Introduction to Jewish Apocalyptic Literature*. 3rd ed. Grand Rapids: Eerdmans, 2016.

———. *The Scepter and the Star: Messianism in the Light of the Dead Sea Scrolls*. 2nd ed. Grand Rapids: Eerdmans, 2010.

———. "The Works of the Messiah." *Dead Sea Discoveries* 1 (1994) 98–112.

Collins, John N. *Deacons and the Church: Making Connections between Old and New*. Harrisville, PA: Gracewing, 2002.

———. *Diakonia: Re-interpreting the Ancient Sources*. Oxford: Oxford University Press, 1990.

Cotter, Wendy J. *The Christ of the Miracle Stories: Portrait through Encounter*. Grand Rapids: Baker Academic, 2000.

———. *Miracles in Greco-Roman Antiquity: A Sourcebook for the Study of New Testament Miracles* Stories. Abingdon: Routledge, 1999.

Craffert, Pieter. *The Life of a Galilean Shaman: Jesus of Nazareth in Anthropological-Historical Perspective*. Matrix 3. Eugene, OR: Cascade Books, 2008.

Crossan, John Dominic. *The Birth of Christianity: Discovering What Happened in the Years Immediately after the Execution of* Jesus. San Francisco: HarperSanFrancisco, 1998.

———. *The Historical Jesus: The Life of a Mediterranean Jewish Peasant*. San Francisco: HarperSanFrancisco, 1991.

———. *Jesus: A Revolutionary Biography*. San Francisco: HarperSanFrancisco, 1994.

———. "Jesus and the Challenge of Collaborative Eschatology." In *The Historical Jesus: Five Views*, edited by James K. Beilby, and Paul R. Eddy, 105–32. London: SPCK, 2010.

Daunton-Fear, Andrew. *Healing in the Early Church: The Church' Ministry of Healing and Exorcism from the First to the Fifth Century*. Studies in Christian History and Thought. Eugene, OR: Wipf & Stock, 2009.

Davies, Philip. *1QM, and the War Scroll from Qumran: Its Structure and History*. Rome: Biblical Institute Press, 1977.

———. "War Rule." In *ABD* 6:875–76.

Davies, Stevan. *Jesus the Healer: Possession, Trance and the Origins of Christianity*. New York: Continuum, 1995.

Davies, W. D., and Dale C. Allison. *A Critical and Exegetical Commentary on the Gospel according to Saint Matthew*. International Critical Commentary. 3 vols. Edinburgh: T. & T. Clark, 1988–97.

Derrett, Duncan. "Contributions to the Study of the Gerasene Demoniac." *JSNT* 3 (1979) 2–17.

Dewey, Joanna. *Markan Public Debate: Literary Technique, Concentric Structure, and Theology in Mark 2:1–3:6*. Society of Biblical Literature Dissertation Series 48. Missoula, MT: Scholars, 1980.

Di Lella, Alexander A. "Wisdom of Ben-Sira." In *ABD* 6:931–45.

Dibelius, Martin. *From Tradition to Gospel*. Translated by Bertram Lee Woolf. New York: Scribner, 1965.

Dispenza, Joe. *You Are the Placebo: Making Your Mind Matter*. London: Hay House, 2014.

Duling, Dennis C. "Solomon, Exorcism, and the Son of David." *HTR* 68 (1975) 235–52.

————. "The Therapeutic Son of David: An Element in Matthew's Christological Apologetic." *NTS* 24 (1977) 392–410.

Dunn, James D. G. *Jesus and the Spirit: A Study of the Religious and Charismatic Experience of Jesus and the First Christians as Reflected in the New Testament.* NTL. London: SCM, 1975.

Duprez, André. *Jésus et les Dieux Guérisseurs: A Propos de Jean V.* Paris: Gabalda, 1970.

Ebeling, Gerhard. *Word and Faith.* Translated by James W. Leitch. London: SCM, 1963.

Edelstein, Ludwig, and Emma J. Edelstein. *Asclepios: Testimonies.* 2 vols. Baltimore: Johns Hopkins University Press, 1945.

Ehrman, Bart D. *Jesus before the Gospels: How the Earliest Christians Remembered, Changed, and Invented their Stories of the Savior.* New York: HarperOne, 2016.

————. *Lost Christianities: The Battles for Scripture and the Faiths We Never Knew.* Oxford: Oxford University Press, 2003.

Eisenberg, Leon. "Disease and Illness: Distinctions between Professional and Popular Ideas of Sickness." *Culture, Medicine and Psychiatry* 1 (1977) 7–23.

Esler, Philip F. "The Incident of the Withered Fig Tree in Mark 11: A New Source and Redactional Explanation." *JSNT* 28 (2005) 41–67.

Evans, Craig A. *Jesus and His Contemporaries: Comparative Studies.* AGJU 25. Leiden: Brill, 1995.

————. "Jesus and the Spirits: What Can We Learn from the New Testament World?" *Transformation* 27 (2010) 146–61.

Eve, Eric. *Behind the Gospels: Understanding the Oral Tradition.* London: SPCK, 2013.

————. *The Healer from Nazareth: Jesus' Miracles in Historical Context.* London: SPCK, 2009.

————. *The Jewish Context of Jesus' Miracles.* JSNTSup 231. Sheffield: Sheffield Academic, 2002.

————. "Spit in Your Eye: The Blind Man of Bethsaida and the Blind Man of Alexandria." *NTS* 54 (2008) 1–17.

Fagen, Ruth Satinover. "Phylacteries." In *ABD* 5:368–70.

Fanon, Franz. *The Wretched of the Earth.* Translated by Constance Farrington. New York: Ballantine, 1963.

Ferngren, Gary B. *Medicine and Health Care in Early Christianity.* Baltimore: Johns Hopkins University Press, 2009.

Fiddes, Paul S. *Participating in God: A Pastoral Doctrine of the Trinity.* Louisville: Westminster John Knox, 2000.

Fiensy, David A., and James R., eds. *Galilee in the Late Second Temple and Mishnaic Periods.* 2 vols. Minneapolis: Fortress, 2014.

Fitzmyer, Joseph A. *The Gospel according to Luke: A New Translation with Introduction and Commentary.* AB 28, 28A. 2 vols. Garden City, NY: Doubleday, 1981–85.

Flusser, David. "Healing through the Laying-on of Hands in a Dead Sea Scroll." *Israel Exploration Journal* 2 (1957) 107–8.

Foerster, Werner. "*daimōn, daimonion, ktl.*" In *TDNT* 2:1–20.

————. "*exestin, exousia, ktl.*" In *TDNT* 2:560–75.

Fortna, Robert T. *The Gospel of Signs: A Reconstruction of the Narrative Source Underlying the Fourth Gospel.* SNTSMS 11. Cambridge: Cambridge University Press, 1970.

Frank, Jerome D., and Julia B. Frank. *Persuasion and Healing: A Comparative Study of Psychotherapy.* 3rd ed. Baltimore: Johns Hopkins University Press, 1991.

Frost, Evelyn. *Christian Healing: A Consideration of the Place of Spiritual Healing in the Church To-day in the Light of the Doctrine and Practice of the Ante-Nicene Church.* 2nd ed. London: Mowbray, 1949.

Funk, Robert W., et al. *The Five Gospels: The Search for the Authentic Words of Jesus—New Translation and Commentary.* New York: Macmillan, 1993.

Garrett, Susan R. *The Demise of the Devil: Magic and the Demonic in Luke's Writings.* Minneapolis: Fortress, 1989.

Gerhardsson, Birger. *The Mighty Acts of Jesus according to Matthew.* Translated by Robert Dewsnap. Scripta Minora. Lund: Gleerup, 1979.

Gibson, Shimon. *The Final Days of Jesus: The Archaeological Evidence.* New York: Lion Hudson, 2009.

———. *Le Projet Béthesda (1994–2010): La Piscine Probatique de Jésus à Saladin Proche-Orient Chrétien.* Jérusalem: Sainte-Anne, Proche-Orient Chrétien, 2011. English translation: https://www.academia.edu/22894959.

Goodacre, Mark. *The Case Against Q: Studies in Markan Priority and the Synoptic Problem.* Harrisville, PA: Trinity, 2002.

Gowler, David. *Host, Guest, Enemy, and Friend: Portraits of the Pharisees in Luke and Acts.* 1991. Reprint, Eugene, OR: Wipf & Stock, 2008.

Guess, Harry A., et al, eds. *The Science of the Placebo: Toward an Interdisciplinary Research Agenda.* London: BMJ, 2002.

Guijarro, Santiago. "The Politics of Exorcism." In *The Social Setting of Jesus and the Gospels*, edited by Wolfgang Stegemann, et al, eds, 159–74. Minneapolis: Fortress, 2002.

Gunton, Colin E. *The Promise of Trinitarian Theology.* Edinburgh: T. & T. Clark, 1991.

Haber, Susan. "A Woman's Touch: Feminist Encounters with the Haemorrhaging Woman in Mark 5.24–34." *JSNT* 26 (2003) 171–92.

Hamilton, David R. *It's the Thought that Counts: Why Mind Over Matter Really Works.* London: Hay House, 2005.

Hanawalt, Emily Albu, and Carter Lindberg, eds. *Through the Eye of a Needle: Judeo-Christian Root of Social Welfare.* Kirksville, MO: Jefferson University Press, 1994.

Hardy, Alister. *The Spiritual Nature of Man: A Study of Contemporary Religious Experience.* Oxford: Clarendon, 1979.

Harnack, Adolf von. *The Mission and Expansion of Christianity in the First Three Centuries.* Translated and edited by James Moffatt. New York: Putnam', 1908.

Held, Heinz Joachim. "Matthew as Interpreter of the Miracle Stories." In *Tradition and Interpretation in Matthew*, edited by Günther Bornkamm, et al., 165–299. Translated by Percy Scott. NTL. Philadelphia: Westminster, 1963.

Henriksen, Jan-Olav, and Karl Olav Sandnes. *Jesus as Healer: A Gospel for the Body.* Grand Rapids: Eerdmans, 2016.

Heron, Alasdair I. C. *The Forgotten Trinity—Volume 3: A Selection of Papers Presented to the BCC Study Commission on Trinitarian Doctrine Today.* London: BCC/CCBI, 1991.

Hiers, Richard H. "'Binding' and 'Loosing': The Matthean Authorizations." *JBL* 104 (1985) 233–50.

Hollenbach, Paul W. "The Conversion of Jesus: From Jesus the Baptizer to Jesus the Healer." In *ANRW* II.25.1:196–219.

———. "Jesus, Demoniacs, and Public Authorities: A Socio-Historical Study." *JAAR* 99 (1981) 567–88.

———. "John the Baptist." In *ABD* 3:887–99.

Holman, Susan R. "Healing the Social Leper in Gregory of Nyssa's and Gregory of Nazianzus's '*peri philoptōchias*.'" *HTR* 92 (1999) 283–309.

Hooker, Morna D. *The Signs of a Prophet: The Prophetic Actions of Jesus*. London: SCM, 1997.

Horsley, Richard A., ed. *Hidden Transcripts and the Arts of Resistance: Applying the Work of James C. Scott to Jesus and Paul*. SemSt 48. Atlanta: Society of Biblical Literature, 2004.

———. *Jesus and Magic: Freeing the Gospel Stories from Modern Misconceptions*. Eugene, OR: Cascade Books, 2014.

———. *Jesus and the Politics of Roman Palestine*. Columbia: South Carolina Uni-versity Press, 2014.

———. *Jesus in Context: Power, People and Performance*. Minneapolis: Fortress, 2008.

———. *The Prophet Jesus and the Renewal of Israel: Moving beyond a Diversionary Debate*. Grand Rapids: Eerdmans, 2012.

———. *Revolt of the Scribes: Resistance and Apocalyptic Origins*. Minneapolis: Fortress, 2010.

Horsley, Richard A., and Neil Silberman. *The Message and the Kingdom: How Jesus and Paul Ignited a Revolution and Transformed the Ancient World*. 1997. Reprint, Minneapolis: Fortress, 2002.

Hull, John M. *Hellenistic Magic and the Synoptic Tradition*. Studies in Biblical Theology 2/28. London: SCM, 1974.

Hume, David. *Enquiries Concerning Human Understanding and Concerning the Principles of Morals*. Edited by L. A. Selby-Bigge, with texts and notes revised by Peter H. Nidditch. Oxford: Clarendon, 1975.

Hurtado, Larry W., and Paul L. Owen, eds. *'Who Is This Son of Man?' The Latest Scholarship on a Puzzling Expression of the Historical Jesus*. LNTS 390. London: T. & T. Clark, 2011.

Hutton, Robert. *Shamans: Siberian Spirituality and the Western Imagination*. New York: Continuum, 2001.

Instone-Brewer, David. "The Eighteen Benedictions and the *Minim* before 70 CE." *JTS* 54 (2003) 25–44.

Jensen, Robin Margaret. *Understanding Early Christian Art*. London: Routledge, 2000.

Jeremias, Joachim. *The Eucharistic Words of Jesus*. Translated by Norman Perrin. London: SCM, 1966.

———. *The Rediscovery of Bethesda, John 5:2*. New Testament Archaeology Monograph 1. Louisville: Southern Baptist Theological Seminary, 1966.

Johnson, Luke Timothy. *Religious Experience in Earliest Christianity: A Missing Dimension in New Testament Studies*. Minneapolis: Fortress: 1998.

Kee, Howard C. *Medicine, Miracle and Magic in New Testament Times*. SNTSMS 55. Cambridge: Cambridge University Press, 1986.

———. *Miracle in the Early Christian World*. New Haven: Yale University Press, 1983.

Keener, Craig. *Miracles: The Credibility of the New Testament Accounts*. 2 vols. Grand Rapids: Baker Academic, 2012.

Keller, Ernst, and Marie-Luise Keller. *Miracles in Dispute: A Continuing Debate*. Translated by Margaret Kohl. Philadelphia: Fortress, 1969.

Kelly, Edward F., et al. *Beyond Physicalism: Toward Reconciliation of Science and Spirituality*. Lanham, MD: Rowman & Littlefield, 2015.

Kelly, Edward F., et al. *Irreducible Mind: Toward a Psychology for the 21st Century.* Lanham, MD: Rowman & Littlefield, 2009.

Kelly, J. N. D. *Early Christian Creeds.* 3rd ed. London: Longman, 1972.

Kelsey, Morton. *Healing and Christianity: A Classic Study.* 3rd ed. Minneapolis: Augsburg, 1995.

Kertelge, Karl. *Die Wunder Jesu im Markusevangelium.* Studien zum Alten und Neuen Testament 33. Munich: Kösel, 1970.

Klawans, Jonathan. *Impurity and Sin in Ancient Judaism.* Oxford: Oxford University Press, 2000.

Kleinman, Arthur. *Patients and Healers in the Context of Culture: An Exploration of the Borderland between Anthropology, Medicine and Psychiatry.* Berkeley: University of California Press, 1980.

Koch, Dietrich-Alex. *Die Bedeutung der Wundererzählungen für die Christologie des Markusevangeliums.* Beihefte zur Zeitschrift für die neutestamentliche Wissenschaft 42. Berlin: de Gruyter, 1975.

Kolenkow, Anitra B. "Relationships between Miracle and Prophecy in the Greco-Roman World and Early Christianity." In *ANRW* II.23.2:1470–506.

Kvalbein, Hans. "The Wonders of the End-time Metaphorical Language in 4Q521 and the Interpretation of Matthew 11.5 par." *JSP* 18 (1998) 87–110.

Lampe, G. W. H. "Miracles in Early Christian Apologetic." In *Miracles: Cambridge Studies in Their Philosophy and History,* edited by C. F. D. Moule, 205–18. London: Mowbray, 1965.

Le Donne, Anthony. *Historical Jesus: What Can We Know and How Can We Know It?* Grand Rapids: Eerdmans, 2011.

———. *The Historiographical Jesus: Memory, Typology and the Son of David.* Waco, TX: Baylor University Press, 2009.

Lewis, Ioan M. *Ecstatic Religion: A Study of Shamanism and Spirit Possession.* 3rd ed. London: Routledge, 2002.

Lindbeck, George. *The Nature of Doctrine: Religion and Theology in a Postliberal Age.* Philadelphia: Westminster, 1984.

Lipton, Bruce H. *The Biology of Belief: Unleashing the Power of Consciousness, Matter and Miracles.* London: Hay House, 2004.

Lohmeyer, Ernst. *The Lord's Prayer.* Translated by John Bowden. New York: Harper & Row, 1965.

Lohse, Eduard. "*cheir, ktl.*" In *TDNT* 9:424–37.

———. "Hosanna." *NovT* 6 (1963) 113–19.

Lüdemann, Gerd. *Heretics: The Other Side of Early Christianity.* Translated by John Bowden. London: SCM, 1996.

MacMullen, Ramsay. *Christianizing the Roman Empire (A.D 100–400).* New Haven: Yale University Press, 1984.

MacMurray, John. *Persons in Relation.* 1961. Reprint, New York: Humanity Books, 1999.

Marcus, Joel. *Mark 1–8: A New Translation with Introduction and Commentary.* AB 27. New York: Doubleday, 2000.

———. *Mark 9–16: A New Translation with Introduction and Commentary.* AYB 27A. New Haven: Yale University Press, 2009.

Marshall, Christopher D. *Faith as a Theme in Mark's Narrative.* SNTSMS 64. Cambridge: Cambridge University Press, 1989.

Martin, Dale B. *The Corinthian Body*. New Haven: Yale University Press, 1995.

McCane, Byron R. *Roll Back the Stone: Death and Burial in the World of Jesus*. Harrisburg, PA: Trinity, 2003.

McCasland, Selby Vernon. "The Asklepios Cult in Palestine." *JBL* 58 (1939) 221–27.

———. "Religious Healing in First Century Palestine." In *Environmental Factors in Christian History*, edited by John T. NcNeill, et al., 18–34. New York: Kennikat, 1939.

McFadyen, Alistair I. *The Call to Personhood: A Christian Theory of the Individual in Social Relationships*. Cambridge: Cambridge University Press, 1990.

McGrath, Alister E. *The Genesis of Doctrine: A Study in the Foundation of Doctrinal Criticism*. Grand Rapids: Eerdmans, 1990.

Meadows, Edward P. "The 'Messianic' Implications of the Q Material." *JBL* 118 (1994) 253–77.

Meggitt, Justin. "The Historical Jesus and Healing: Jesus' Miracles in Psychosocial Context." In *Spiritual Healing: Scientific and Religious Perspectives*, edited by Fraser Watts, 17–43. Cambridge: Cambridge University Press, 2011.

Meier, John P. *A Marginal Jew: Rethinking the Historical Jesus*. ABRL. 5 vols. New York: Doubleday, 1987–2016.

Metzger, Bruce M. *A Textual Commentary on the Greek New Testament*. 3rd ed. London: United Bible Societies, 1975.

Miller, Robert J., ed. *The Apocalyptic Jesus: A Debate*. Santa Rosa, CA: Polebridge, 2001.

Moerman, Daniel. *Meaning, Medicine and the 'Placebo Effect.'* Cambridge: Cambridge University Press, 2002.

Moltmann, Jürgen. *The Trinity and the Kingdom of God*. Translated by Margaret Kohl. London: SCM, 1981.

Myers, Ched. *Binding the Strong Man: A Political Reading of Mark's Story of Jesus*. Maryknoll, NY: Orbis, 2003.

Naveh, Joseph. "A Medical Document or a Writing Exercise? The So-called 4Q Therapeia." *Israel Exploration Journal* 36 (1986) 52–55.

Nicklesburg, George W. E. *Resurrection, Immortality, and Eternal Life in Intertestamental Judaism*. Harvard Theological Studies. Cambridge: Harvard University Press, 1972.

Nolland, John. *The Gospel of Matthew: A Commentary on the Greek Text*. NIGTC. Grand Rapids: Eerdmans, 2005.

Nolland, John. *Luke*. WBC 35A, 35B, 35C. 3 vols. Dallas: Word, 1989–93.

O'Sullivan, Suzanne. *It's All in Your Head: True Stories of Imaginary Illness*. London: Vintage, 2016.

Oepke, Albrecht. "*iaomai, iasis, ktl.*" In *TDNT* 3:194–215.

Paulus, Heinrich E. G. *Das Leben Jesu als Grundlage einer reinen Geschichte des Urchristentums*. 2 vols. Heidelberg: Winter, 1928.

Perry, Michael. *Deliverance: Psychic Disturbances and Occult Involvement*. 2nd ed. London: SPCK, 1996.

Petuchowski, Jakob, and Brocke, Michael, eds. *The Lord's Prayer and Jewish Liturgy*. New York: Seabury, 1978.

Pilch, John J. "Altered States of Consciousness in the Synoptics." In *The Social Setting of Jesus and the Gospels*, edited by Wolfgang Stegemann, et al, 103–15. Minneapolis: Fortress, 2002.

————. *Healing in the New Testament: Insights from Medical and Mediterranean Anthropology*. Minneapolis: Fortress, 2000.

Piovanelli, Pierluigi. "Jesus' Charismatic Authority: On the Historical Applicability of a Sociological Model." *JAAR* 73 (2005) 395–427.

Poirier, John C., and Jeffrey Peterson, eds. *Marcan Priority Without Q: Explorations in the Farrer Hypothesis*. LNTS 455. London: Bloomsbury T. & T. Clark, 2015.

Polkinghorne, John. *The Trinity and an Entangled World: Relationality in Physical Science and Theology*. Grand Rapids: Eerdmans, 2010.

Porterfield, Amanda. *Healing in the History of Christianity*. Oxford: Oxford University Press, 2005.

Price, Robert M. *Deconstructing Jesus*. Amherst, NY: Prometheus, 2000.

————. *The Incredible Shrinking Son of Man*. Amherst, NY: Prometheus, 2003.

Priest, John. "A Note on the Messianic Banquet. In *The Messiah: Developments in Earliest Judaism and Christianity*, edited by James H. Charlesworth, 222–28. Minneapolis: Fortress, 1992.

Puech, Émile. "Une Apocalypse Messianique (4Q521)." *Revue de Qumran* 15 (1992) 475–519.

————. *Qumrân Grotte 4.XVIII. Textes Hébreux (Q521–4Q528, 4Q576–4Q579)*. Discoveries in the Judaean Desert 25. Oxford: Clarendon, 1998.

Reed, Jonathan. "Mortality, Morbidity, and Economics in Jesus' Galilee." In *Galilee in the Late Second Temple and Mishnaic Periods*, edited by David A. Fiensy and James R. Strange, 1:242–52. 2 vols. Minneapolis: Fortress, 2014.

Richards, John. *But Deliver Us from Evil: An Introduction to the Demonic Dimension in Pastoral Care*. New York: Seabury, 1974.

Risse, Guenter B. *Mending Bodies, Saving Souls: A History of Hospitals*. Oxford: Oxford University Press, 1999.

Rodriguez, Rafael. *Oral Tradition and the New Testament: A Guide for the Perplexed*. Guides for the Perplexed. London: Bloomsbury, 2013.

Russell, D. S. *The Method and Message of Jewish Apocalyptic*. OTL. Philadelphia: Westminster, 1964.

Sawyer, John F. A. *The Fifth Gospel: Isaiah in the History of Christianity*. Cambridge: Cambridge University Press, 1996.

Schenke, Ludger. *Die Wundererzählungen des Markusevangeliums*. Stuttgarter biblische Beiträge 5. Stuttgart: Katholisches Bibelwerk, 1974.

Schrage, Wolfgang. "*typhlos, typhlō.*" In *TDNT* 8:270–94.

Schwöbel, Christoph, and Colin E. Gunton, eds. *Persons, Divine and Human*. Edinburgh: T. & T. Clark, 1991.

Scott, Bernard Brandon. *Hear then the Parable: A Commentary on the Parables of Jesus*. Minneapolis: Fortress, 1989.

Scott, James C. *Domination and the Arts of Resistance*. New Haven: Yale University Press, 1990.

Shapiro, Arthur K., and Elaine Shapiro. *The Powerful Placebo: From Ancient Priest to Modern Physician*. Baltimore: Johns Hopkins University Press, 1997.

Sheldrake, Rupert. *The Science Delusion: Freeing the Spirit of Enquiry*. London: Coronet, 2012.

Skinner, Andrew C., et al, eds. *Bountiful Harvest: Essays in Honor of S. Kent Brown*. Provo, UT: Brigham Young University Press, 2012.

Smith, Morton. *Jesus the Magician*. San Francisco: Harper & Row, 1978.

Spiegel, David. "Placebos in Practice." *BMJ* 329 (2004) 927–28.

Spinoza, Baruch. *The Chief Works of Benedict de Spinoza*. Translated by R. H. M. Ewes. New York: Dover, 1955.

Stacey, David. *Prophetic Drama in the Old Testament*. London: Epworth, 1990.

Stark, Rodney. *The Rise of Christianity: How the Obscure, Marginal Jesus Movement Became the Dominant Religious Force in the Western World in a Few Centuries*. 1996. Reprint, New York: HarperCollins, 1997.

Steele, E. Springs. "Jesus' Table-Fellowship with Pharisees: An Editorial Analysis of Luke 7.36–50, 11.37–54, and 14.1–24." PhD diss., University of Notre Dame, 1981.

Stegemann, Wolfgang, et al, eds. *The Social Setting of Jesus and the Gospels*. Minneapolis: Fortress, 2002.

Strathearn, Gaye. "4Q521 and What it Might Mean for Q 3–7." In *Bountiful Harvest: Essays in Honor of S. Kent Brown*, edited by Andrew C Skinner, et al, 395–424. Chicago: University of Chicago Press, 2012.

Strauss, David F. *Das Leben Jesu, kritisch bearbeitet*. 4th ed. 3 vols. Tübingen, 1839–40.

————. *The Life of Jesus Critically Examined*. Translated by George Eliot. Lives of Jesus Series. Philadelphia: Fortress, 1972.

Strecker, Christian. "Jesus and the Demoniacs." In *The Social Setting of Jesus and the Gospels*, edited by Wolfgang Stegemann et al., 117–33. Minneapolis: Fortress, 2002.

Taylor, Joan E. *John the Baptist within Second Temple Judaism: A Historical Study*. New ed. London: SPCK, 1997.

Taylor, Vincent. *The Formation of the Gospel Tradition*. London: MacMillan, 1935.

Telford, William R. *The Barren Temple and the Withered Tree: A Redaction-Critical Analysis of the Cursing of the Fig-Tree Pericope in Mark's Gospel and its Relation to the Cleansing of the Temple Tradition*. JSNTSup 1. Sheffield: JSOT Press, 1980.

Theissen, Gerd. *The First Followers of Jesus: A Sociological Analysis of Earliest Christianity*. Translated by John Bowden. London: SCM, 1978.

————. *The Gospels in Context: Social and Political History in the Synoptic Tradition*. Translated by Linda A. Maloney. Minneapolis: Fortress, 1992.

————. *Miracle Stories of the Early Christian Tradition*. Translated by Francis McDonagh. Edited by John Riches. Edinburgh: T. & T. Clark, 1983.

————. *Social Reality and the Early Christians: Theology, Ethics, and the World of the New Testament*. Translated by Margaret Kohl. Edinburgh: T. & T. Clark, 1992.

Theissen, Gerd, and Annette Merz. *The Historical Jesus: A Comprehensive Guide*. Translated by John Bowden. Minneapolis: Fortress, 1998.

Trunk, Dieter. *Der messianische Heiler: Eine redaktions- und religionsgeschichtliche Studie zu den Exorzismen im Matthausevanglium*. Herders Biblische Studien 3. Freiburg: Herder, 1994.

Tuckett, Christopher. "Messianic Secret." In *ABD* 4:797–800.

Twelftree, Graham H., ed. *The Cambridge Companion to Miracles*. Cambridge Companions to Religion. Cambridge: Cambridge University Press, 2011.

————. *In the Name of Jesus: Exorcism among Early Christians*. Grand Rapids: Baker Academic, 2007.

————. *Jesus the Exorcist: A Contribution to the Study of the Historical Jesus*. WUNT 2/54. Tübingen: Mohr/Siebeck, 1993.

————. "The Miraculous in the New Testament: Current Research and Issues." *Currents in Biblical Research* 12 (2014) 321–52.

———. *Paul and the Miraculous: A Historical Reconstruction.* Grand Rapids: Baker Academic, 2013.

Van der Loos, Hendrik. *The Miracles of Jesus.* NovTSup 9. Leiden: Brill, 1965.

Van Voorst, Robert E. *Jesus Outside the New Testament: An Introduction to the Ancient Evidence.* Grand Rapids: Eerdmans, 2000.

Vermes, Geza. "Essenes–Therapeutai–Qumran." *Durham University Journal* 52 (1960) 97–115.

———. "Hanina ben Dosa: A Controversial Galilean Saint from the First Century of the Christian Era (Part 1)." *JJS* 23 (1972) 28–50.

———. "Hanina ben Dosa: A Controversial Galilean Saint from the First Century of the Christian Era (Part 2)." *JJS* 24 (1973) 51–64.

———. *Jesus the Jew: A Historian's Reading of the Gospels.* Philadelphia: Fortress, 1973.

Vögtle, Anton. "The Lord's Prayer: A Prayer for Jews and Christians?" In *The Lord's Prayer and Jewish Liturgy,* edited by Jakob Petuchowski, and Michael Brocke, 93–117. London: Burns & Oates, 1978.

von Wahlde, Urban C. "Archaeology and John's Gospel." In *Jesus and Archaeology,* edited by James H. Charlesworth, 523–86. Grand Rapids: Eerdmans, 2006.

Vonhoff, Heinz. *People Who Care: An Illustrated History of Human Compassion.* Philadelphia: Fortress, 1971.

Wallis, Ian G. "Before Big Bang: Echoes of Jesus in the Faith of His Followers." *Theology* 106 (2003) 12–19.

———. *The Faith of Jesus Christ in Early Christian Traditions.* SNTSMS 84. Cambridge: Cambridge University Press, 1995.

———. *Holy Saturday Faith: Rediscovering the Legacy of Jesus.* London: SPCK, 2000.

———. "Jesus the Believer—A Fresh Approach." *Modern Believing* 36 (1995) 10–17.

———. "New Directions in Jesus Studies." *Theology* 117 (2014) 349–56.

———. "Relating Mark's 'Stilling of the Storm' Pericope (Mark 4.35–41) to Discipleship Today: An Experiment in Resurrection Faith." *Theology* 111 (2008) 346–51.

———. "'Your Faith Has Saved You': A Redaction-Critical Analysis of the Synoptic Logion." MLitt diss., Cambridge University, 1984.

Warfield, Benjamin B. *Counterfeit Miracles.* 1918. Reprint, Edinburgh: Banner of Truth, 1972.

Webb, Robert L. *John the Baptizer and Prophet: A Socio-historical Study.* JSNTSup 62. Sheffield: JSOT Press, 1991.

Weeden, Theodore J. "The Heresy that Necessitated Mark's Gospel." *ZNW* 59 (1968) 145–58.

———. *Mark: Traditions in Conflict.* Philadelphia: Fortress, 1971.

Wells, George A. *The Jesus Myth.* Chicago: Open Court, 1999.

———. *The Jesus of the Early Christians: A Study in Christian Origins.* London: Pemberton, 1971.

———. *Who Was Jesus? A Critique of the New Testament Record.* Chicago: Open Court, 1989.

Whitaker, E. C. *Documents of the Baptismal Liturgy.* Rev ed. Revised and expanded by Maxwell E. Johnson. Collegeville, MN: Liturgical, 2003.

Wiles, Maurice F. "Miracles in the Early Church." In *Miracles: Cambridge Studies in their Philosophy and History,* edited by C. F. D. Moule, 221–34. London: Mowbray, 1965.

Wilkinson, John. *Health and Healing: Studies in New Testament Principles and Practices.* Edinburgh: Handel, 1980.

———. *Jerusalem as Jesus Knew It: Archaeology as Evidence.* London: Thames & Hudson, 1978.

Wink, Walter. *John the Baptist in the Gospel Tradition.* SNTSMS 7. 1968. Reprint, Eugene, OR: Wipf & Stock, 2000.

———. *Unmasking the Powers: The Invisible Forces That Determine Human Existence.* Philadelphia: Fortress, 1986.

Witmer, Amanda. *Jesus, The Galilean Exorcist: His Exorcisms in Social and Political Context.* LNTS 459. London: T. & T. Clark, 2012.

Witt, Reginald E. *Isis in the Ancient World.* Baltimore: Johns Hopkins University Press, 1971.

Wolff, Hans Walter. *Anthropology of the Old Testament.* Translated by Margaret Kohl. Philadelphia: Fortress, 1974.

Wrede, William. *The Messianic Secret.* Translated by trans J. C. G. Greig. Cambridge: James Clarke, 1971.

Wright, N. T. *Jesus and the Victory of God.* Christian Origins and the Question of God 2. Minneapolis: Fortress, 1996.

———. *The Resurrection of the Son of God.* Christian Origins and the Question of God 3. Minneapolis: Fortress, 2003.

Yeung, Maureen W. *Faith in Jesus and Paul: A Comparison with Special Reference to 'Faith that Can Remove Mountains' and 'Your Faith Has Saved/Healed You.'* WUNT 2/147. Tübingen: Mohr/Siebeck, 2002.

Young, Allan. "The Anthropologies of Illness and Sickness." *Annual Review of Anthropology* 11 (1982) 257–85.

Young, Frances. *The Making of the Creeds.* London: SCM, 1991.

Ziesler, John A. "Luke and the Pharisees." *NTS* 25 (1978–79) 146–57.

Zizioulas, John D. *Being as Communion.* Contemporary Greek Theologians 4. Crestwood, NY : St. Vladimir's Seminary Press, 1985.

———. *Communion and Otherness: Further Studies in Personhood and the Church.* Edited by Paul McPartlan. Edinburgh: T. & T. Clark, 2006.

Name/Subject Index

Ancient Sources Index

DEUTEROCANONICAL BOOKS

NEW TESTAMENT

RABBINIC & RELATED TEXTS